Otto III

‡‡‡

Otto III

‡‡‡

GERD ALTHOFF

translated by Phyllis G. Jestice

‡‡‡

THE PENNSYLVANIA STATE UNIVERSITY PRESS

UNIVERSITY PARK, PENNSYLVANIA

This English translation of *Otto III*
was made possible through the kind support of
GOETHE INSTITUT INTER NATIONES

Library of Congress Cataloging-in-Publication Data

Althoff, Gerd.
[Otto III. English]
Otto III / Gerd Althoff ; translated by Phyllis G. Jestice.
p.   cm.
Includes bibliographical references and index.
ISBN 0-271-02232-9 (alk. paper)
1. Otto III, Holy Roman Emperor, 980–1002.
2. Germany—History—Saxon House, 919–1024.
3. Holy Roman Empire—Kings and rulers—Biography.
4. Holy Roman Empire—History—843–1273.
I. Title.

DD140.4 .A4813   2003
943'.022'092—dc21
2003009373

First published in Germany by Wissenschaftliche Buchgesellschaft
as part of the series *"Gestalten des Mittelalters und der Renaissance"*
edited by Peter Herde.
© 1996 Wissenschaftliche Buchgesellschaft, Darmstadt

English translation
© 2003 THE PENNSYLVANIA STATE UNIVERSITY
Published by The Pennsylvania State University Press,
University Park, PA 16802-1003

Contents   ‡ ‡ ‡

OTTO III, KING of the Germans 983–1002 and emperor 996–1002, is among the most flamboyant and controversial of the German emperors. He was born in 980, the only son of Emperor Otto II and the Byzantine princess Theophanu. Otto II continued his own father's policy of perpetuating Ottonian rule by having a council of magnates assembled at Verona on 27 May 983 elect the young Otto king. The three-year-old child was then sent to Aachen, where he was crowned king of the Germans on Christmas Day, 983. As it happened, this coronation took place several weeks after Otto II's death in Italy. For the first time in German history a minor was sole ruler.

For most of Otto's short life, a series of informal regents governed his empire. At first, Duke Henry II the Quarrelsome of Bavaria claimed guardianship over the child, since he was the new king's closest male relative. But Henry soon tried to supplant his charge, claiming kingship in his own name. When this plot had been thwarted, Otto III's mother, Theophanu, assumed guardianship and operated as regent from behind the scenes. After Theophanu died in 991, Otto III's grandmother Adelheid directed affairs until the young ruler came of age, probably sometime in late 994.

Most of what we know about Otto's adult life comes from accounts of the three expeditions he made to Rome: to be crowned as emperor, to support the pope he had created (his cousin, Gregory V), and finally . . . Well, this is the point at which certainties end. The question of Otto III's intentions on his expeditions to Rome forms the heart of a long controversy about the policy and goals of this emperor. Was Otto trying to re-create the ancient Roman Empire, a *renovatio imperii Romanorum*, something that flew in the face of all traditions of German rulership? Was he an unrealistic dreamer, whose hopeless idealism harmed Germany without helping Italy? Or was he a practical politician with a grand scheme to enhance and transform the power of Germany, the strongest state in Western Europe at the time? Whatever his plans or dreams, Otto III's story must remain the tale of largely unrealized potential. He died on 24 January 1002 at the age of only twenty-one.

The early modern era rediscovered Otto III. From the sixteenth to the twenty-first century a long series of German historians, artists, dramatists, novelists, and poets have interpreted Otto's story, largely in light of their own political agendas and aspirations. In the process, Otto, along with his fellow German emperors, has come to symbolize all that is best and worst of Germany itself. Thus the history of Otto III's portrayal is significant not just for a small pool of medieval historians but for a much broader understanding of German identity.

Gert Althoff's awareness of this problem within the historiographical tradition is central to his new approach to studying Otto III. At first glance this work is a biography, but it actually interweaves three other studies within this rich text. First and foremost, this is a study of medieval kingship, the principles upon which it was based and the practices with which it was carried out. Otto III is an excellent case study within that broader phenomenon. But it is only possible to do justice to this important subject by questioning and testing earlier suppositions about this ruler. At a secondary level, therefore, the work is an intellectual history of nineteenth- and twentieth-century Germany. And, not least, Althoff provides a manual for medieval historians, especially stressing important lessons about subjectivity and the need to understand the sources of the era on their own terms.

I would like to thank Dr. Elaine Beretz for her invaluable help with the translation of this work. I am also grateful to Inter Nationes for subsidizing this translation. Most of all, my thanks go to Gerd Althoff for allowing me to make this translation and for the inspiration I have found in his work as a whole.

Preface to the German Edition ‡ ‡ ‡

HOW MUCH DO individuals influence historical development? That is, to what extent is it possible for the individual to shape and change events in different eras? This fundamental question of historical research has been explored many times. The historiographical genre of biography, venerable but ever fresh, certainly owes its popularity mostly to this question. It appears particularly difficult to answer for the Middle Ages, however. Scholars have justly doubted whether it is possible to write a biography, in the modern sense, about a person from this era. In medieval sources, the individuality of a person all but disappears behind the topos representing his or her office or position. The actions of people are too explicitly dictated by the roles they played in the God-ordained order. Thus people of the Middle Ages only rarely have personal profiles. Consequently, it is not change or development that is characteristic of the time, but preservation of the existing order. Emperor Otto III certainly is among the few medieval people whose personality has been attested by scholars. Nevertheless, it is a preeminent concern of this book to consider the social, political, and mental framework within which Otto III's actions were conducted or from which they diverged. To join together biography and structural history, rather than perceive them in opposition to each other, is nothing new. But it remains a thoroughly justifiable enterprise, to which I attempt to do justice in the following work.

I have received counsel, criticism, and encouragement from three medievalists whose own work has had a decisive impact on our current picture of Otto III: Helmut Beumann, Knut Görich, and Hagen Keller. I thank them very much for their willingness to read rough drafts of the manuscript and to help me think through the problems. I am also grateful for the climate of unrestricted and intensive discussion that I have enjoyed with the colleagues and fellows of the Gießen graduate college's seminar "Medieval and Modern Nationalisms." I did not, to be sure, test out this book itself there, but rather its main questions about the "rules of the game" for interaction in medieval public life. The help that I received in preparing this book went far beyond the usual bounds. Special thanks are due to the energy and precision with which Claudia Beinhoff, M.A., Alheydis Plassmann, M.A., Stefanie Hamm, Sven Jessen, Elke Klaus, Nico Kuhlmann, Friederike Scheinpflug,

Olaf Schneider, Ulrike Wagner, and Tobias Weller in Gießen and Bonn undertook the necessary work and shored up many of my weaknesses. Those errors that remain are naturally my own.

Gerd Althoff
Bonn, July 1995

Preface to the English Edition ‡ ‡ ‡

THIS BOOK WAS originally written for a German-speaking audience. In consequence it would be wise to draw the attention of English-speaking readers to some peculiar circumstances. Otto III—the figure around whom this book revolves—was an emperor in the Saxon line. The Saxon rulers have continuously played a central role in the national consciousness of the Germans because they were regarded as the founders of the German Empire and bestowed upon this empire its alleged power, magnitude, and worldwide authority. Thus, for a long time, they have occupied a prominent place in the historical consciousness of the Germans and German scholarship. Concerning Otto III, however, the national sentiment split: while some praised him as a young genius with audacious conceptions, others criticized him for entertaining boyish fantasies, thereby carelessly squandering the great heritage of his prominent grandfather. All of these judgments clearly displayed the firm bond linking any historical evaluation to contemporary categories. This seemed reason enough to portray the whole spectrum of evaluations in an introductory chapter—and thereby warn of the danger of anachronisms. This chapter is written especially for German readers, who are familiar with the nuances of their national history. Nevertheless, I believe that the chapter will be enlightening also to non-Germans—as documentation of the national quest for meaning by means of history, and its manifest problems.

Another peculiarity of this book can also be explained by pointing to the history of German scholarship. In light of Otto III's high-flying plans and concepts, which modern historians have sometimes constructed from few fragments of surviving sources, I have made it my particular mission to keep sight of and illuminate the sources on whose basis such accounts have been formed. I thus quite often point out how meager is the textual support for certain statements and consequently how bold are the hypotheses that have been constructed on the basis of such a fragile foundation. A number of scholars in Germany have read the book as an articulation of a methodological standpoint against that of Johannes Fried, *Der Weg in die Geschichte* (Berlin, 1994), since I had previously criticized this author's approach to sources. Even though I had already finished writing *Otto III* when I first became acquainted with this particular work by Fried, such an impression is by no means wrong:

it is indeed possible to discuss the fundamental questions regarding treatment of so-called sources by considering the accounts that have passed down concerning Otto III and the use to which they have been put.

One of these fundamental questions has heavily influenced my account: How can the behavior and the politics of this emperor be evaluated in light of the rules and requirements that by custom were incumbent upon any sovereign? To what degree was his behavior shaped by the patterns of tradition? When, where, and to what extent can individual deviations and a distinct personality be discerned? Citing examples, I have repeatedly pointed out that Otto III's behavior conformed with the rules that existed and were obeyed in the nobles' society in the tenth century, even though they were not fixed in writing. This led one German critic to accuse me of supposedly purposely writing a "biography without a subject." No, I have not. I have only avoided constructing a subject where the sources have not seemed to provide enough grounds for doing so. However, especially in the case of Otto III, enough areas remain in which an individual signature, even some playing with the conventions of his time, can be discerned. It is this part of his personality as a ruler—contemporaries felt uncomfortable about it—that can still fascinate us today, independent of diverse national images of history.

Gerd Althoff
Münster, February 2002

INTRODUCTION

The Modern Assessment of Otto III

No age can avoid situating itself in relation to the past—something the Germans have experienced in the twentieth century more persistently and painfully than any other nation. This fundamental point about historical understanding is especially necessary at the beginning of a book about a medieval emperor. This is because the Middle Ages, especially the "German imperial age," has for a long time and persistently conditioned the Germans' historical vision of their position and their mission in Europe.[1] The legacy of the medieval emperors to the Germans in this view amounts to a special right to take a leading role in shaping Europe. This presumed inheritance presents itself to contemporaries in the most widely varying situations as both a legacy and a mandate. In this way it motivated radically different German undertakings in the nineteenth and twentieth centuries. Most notably, calling upon this heritage justifies both defensive and offensive wars. It is therefore imperative that we should examine the content of this historical consciousness before adopting any of it. Questioning our assumptions about the past has gained new urgency in recent years, especially following the reunification of the two Germanies. What is more, Emperor Otto III is one of the central historical figures upon whom historians of the modern era have projected the triumphs and trials of their own time. This introduction is thus obligated to survey how scholars have traditionally assessed Otto: What have they emphasized, and where have they disagreed? On what foundations were past judgments based? Such an undertaking facilitates and sharpens awareness of our own underlying assumptions about this medieval emperor.

It took a long time for judgments about Otto III to become objective—essentially until our own time. Modern historians have experienced first hand limitations inherent in many assessments of a national past that were themselves overly influenced by a subjectivity their own era imposed. In that way we have lost a little of the naïveté implicit in earlier anachronistic judgments. We are also confronted with the problem that the older assessments of Otto III themselves lacked agreement. The scholarly literature divides roughly between Otto's resolute detractors, the larger group, and his admirers, a smaller but still important group. It is almost a cliché in that scholarly discussion that assessment of Otto has ranged along the entire spectrum from enmity to admiration. More significantly, each period's pressing political problems, hopes, or fears have influenced or determined how historians of that period judged medieval emperors. The most persistent influences include the fight between the Great German and Little German visions for forming a German national state in the nineteenth century, efforts to surmount failure in World War I in the twentieth century, and finally the Third Reich's appropriation of medieval history. These influences cannot be dealt with individually here. But they should be kept in mind, since they all helped to create the image of Otto III.

His detractors measured him by the yardstick of duty to the nation and were unanimous in their judgment. Otto had lightly gambled away a great inheritance, had gone chasing after whims and fancies. He surrounded himself with intellectuals and foreigners, and listened to the wrong people. There is a long list of famous proponents of this view. Wilhelm von Giesebrecht established this tradition in his much-read *Geschichte der deutschen Kaiserzeit* (History of the German imperial age):

[I]t was a particular misfortune for the German people that, as soon as this gifted prince grew to self-awareness, he considered himself a Greek and a Roman rather than a German, that he despised Saxon crudeness and looked toward the more developed but moribund culture of Byzantium as his ideal. All of his plans therefore loosed him from the national ground from which the work of his fathers had grown. . . . His thoughts did not even pause at the monarchy of Charlemagne; soaring away in fantastical flights over wide reaches of time, he stopped only at the world empire of the old emperors of Rome and at the great fragment of their rule that had survived as the Byzantine Empire. "Restoration of the Roman Empire in the west": soon all the emperor's objectives concentrated on this one idea as their highest pinnacle.

The criticism that Otto III lacked national consciousness combined with the reproach that he was an unrealistic dreamer to form the core of Giesebrecht's analysis:

Otto III's fantasies were just as magnificent as they were unclear. The sen-
ate of old Rome with its wisdom, the triumphs and victory pomp of a Trajan
or Marcus Aurelius, the court of Constantinople with its half-antique, half-
oriental splendor—those were the magic circles in which the thoughts of the
fanatical youth ran, and from which he hardly found an escape even in the
midst of his penitential practices.

Giesebrecht saw Gerbert of Aurillac as spiritual director of this fantasy, whose influence on the emperor Giesebrecht regarded as the source of all evils: "We see in him only the power of a bright, brilliant spirit and of a rich experience, won through his many changes in fortune; but with magical power he ensnared the heart of the young emperor and was not the least cause of his ruin."[2]

Albert Hauck, in his *Kirchengeschichte Deutschlands* (Ecclesiastical history of Germany), gives an appraisal not much different, although lacking the emphasis on the national duties Otto failed to fulfill. Hauck provides a psychological interpretation of one of the emperor's fundamental defects:

He lacked harmony of mind . . . the best gift that can be given to a man. . . .
Nobody was more susceptible to the impression of the unusual than he: in
whatever form it entered his awareness he seized it. So the most varied
things pulled him with equal force: the inexhaustible many-sided education
of Gerbert, the world-renouncing earnestness of the hermit Nilus, the senti-
mental piety of the Czech Adalbert. But he was not strong enough to control
the impressions that flooded over him. They disturbed and ruled him; he
never succeeded in raising himself above them. This is the error of youth;
who can deny it? But the fate of this gifted youth was that he became
emperor before he was a man. He swung back and forth between widely
opposing poles: between joy in a gold-embroidered robe and contentment
with a coarse hair shirt. At one time ambition stirred him to found an
empire such as the world had never seen, and at another time he found
melancholy contentment in the thought of renouncing his rule to become a
saint. One day he surrounded himself with the splendor of the Byzantine
court. The next day he sat at the feet of some ascetic who proclaimed to him
the old but always equally gripping truth: all is vain. It seems a bizarre fancy
and yet is characteristic of the emperor who had the visions of the apoca-
lypse embroidered in gold on his coronation mantle. So his soul wandered
here and there, between this world and the next.[3]

These judgments established the leitmotivs adopted by later historians, especially in general works, and with some variation they were applied to Otto III's entire reign. In this way they created the historical consciousness of the Germans and shaped it in a particular way. Ferdinand Gregorovius in his *Geschichte der Stadt Rom* (History of Rome) thus took a marginal position for the nineteenth century, when he argued that Otto III was a "victim" because of typical German traits:

Otto III is perhaps the most illustrious historical victim of the German enthusiasm for the beautiful southern world of Italy, where an idealistic impulse continually drew them. Other peoples in ancient and modern times have looked to foreign lands with political longing and ambition. Our only conquest was Italy, the land of history, beauty, and poetry, which has repeatedly summoned us. The deep impulse of their religious feeling made the Germans into protectors of the Roman church and chained them to Rome with the bonds of necessity. The desire to know forced them to the treasuries of antiquity, and it will make Italy and Rome eternally precious to us. The political implications created the idea of empire, which Germany bore. The Germans weakened their own nationality for the sake of these universal ideals—the church and the empire—which promised to order and preserve peaceful relations of peoples to one another.[4]

In the first half of the twentieth century Giesebrecht's judgment was accepted in its basic substance without question. The first significant break came when Percy E. Schramm in 1929 in his *Kaiser, Rom und Renovatio* (Emperor, Rome, and renewal) considered Otto III's plan to renew the Roman Empire within a framework of intellectual history.[5] Through this new perspective, Otto's fantastic enthusiasms were transformed into a carefully planned policy of *renovatio*. Schramm claimed that this made sense of such diverse policies as the rule of Rome and relations with the neighboring kingdoms to the east. In addition, it integrated both Carolingian and Ottonian traditions.[6] The new theory faced an uphill battle at first against accepted appraisals and prejudices in the historiography. One can see this, for example, in Karl Hampe's discussion in *Hochmittelalter* (The High Middle Ages), which first appeared in 1932. Hampe attempted to completely reappraise Otto by taking into account Schramm's findings:

Otto's overall behavior cannot be judged from the standpoint of modern realist politics, nor can it be measured with a nationalist yardstick. By either standard, certainly, the effects of this short reign would have to be judged as wholly negative, at least for Germany. Instead, one should assess him only on the basis of the universal and supraworldly perceptions accepted in his own time. Indeed, his "Roman renewal policy" has only recently been evaluated with more fitting understanding by situating it within the ideology of Rome as a significant theme in the history of ideas. Historical evaluations have been marred again and again by a cardinal error. Scholars paid too little attention to the fact that in the final analysis the emperor was working from a transcendent worldview. Even leadership over earthly things based itself on the highest mediation of the ecclesiastical salvific institution. Further, the imperial office had a leading role only because the imperfection of the world, still inadequately permeated by the true Christian spirit, meant that the Church needed the strong arm of a protector. It was necessary to continually build up and hold together the available foundations of power by all appropriate means, which for the empire now rested primarily on the superior strength of Germany. Otto III erred in neglecting to do so, and one must thus find him at fault in all assessments of the tragedy in his consequent failures and premature death. The Western Empire had completely abandoned the taut bureaucratic apparatus of the Byzantine Eastern Empire, and a central administration based on Rome could not be created in a hurry. If one further ignores that fact, then every principle of power upon which the imperial office ultimately rested would be undermined. And if one then considered the achievement of religious goals as the increasingly exclusive province of imperial rule, one would bypass the often-emphasized dualistic division of power. But then one would have to dismiss what was after all the emperor's most important secular duty, the protection and preservation of the peace. This was exercised essentially on the papacy's behalf, since the Church itself lacked the capacity to assert its exalted status once the underpinnings of its power collapsed.[7]

Here Otto III is raked over the coals for failing to live up to presumed principles of imperial rule in the tenth century—principles established according to a twentieth-century understanding of what rule ought to entail. At the same time, a clear warning is expressed: it is wrong to insert views drawn from the history of ideas into the field of policy and power. And that charge was leveled specifically against Schramm. Karl Hampe was so provoked at Schramm's attempt to fundamentally reassess Otto III that, even before Schramm's book appeared, Hampe stated the grounds for his disagreement in a lengthy article published in *Historische Zeitschrift*.[8] In light of this, it seems remarkable that Schramm dedicated his work to Hampe in honor of his sixtieth birthday.

A little later Hampe was assisted in his challenge to Schramm's theories by Albert Brackmann, who in 1932 analyzed the "Roman renewal idea and its significance for the imperial policy of the German imperial age." Brackmann, too, undertook to critically examine what significance phenomena in the history of ideas, such as the idea of Roman renewal, had for the "practical political life of the Middle Ages." Like Hampe and unlike Schramm, he believed that this significance was negligible. He did not delve into the political rhetoric of the period, but concentrated on Otto III's "great political actions." In these he saw the "resumption of old Carolingian-Ottonian plans in a changed form." He built up his interpretation of the "facts" by arguing his views far beyond the evidence of contemporary sources. Thus he attempted a positive assessment of Otto III's work without the help of Schramm's edifice of "Roman renewal thought" as Otto III's main motivation:

"Renovatio imperii Romanorum" in the ancient sense concerned him [Otto III] as little as it did Charlemagne and Otto the Great. The guiding principles of his policy sprang from the old Carolingian-Ottonian tradition that the Christian ruler was obligated to be "defender of the Church" and champion for the kingdom of God on earth. Compared to these principles during the time of Otto the Great, the only thing that changed for Otto III was that his relationship to the papacy looked back toward Charlemagne's policy and the program of 796. Thus, when he rejected the Donation of Constantine and its legal claims, he sought to check the curia's aspiration to power as it had developed since the Pseudo-Isidorian decretals. The shift also necessarily involved a greater adaptation to the political thought of the Romans, but only as a means toward better safeguarding Rome. Despite this, Rome remained for him, as for his predecessors, primarily a place where the apostles had acted and suffered. When he and his circle occasionally praised "golden Rome" and the old emperors, in the final analysis such comparisons served him and his friends only to glorify the city of the apostles and the Imperium christianum.[9]

In this way, Otto III was freed from the stigma of being "un-German" and excessively idealistic and placed squarely within the traditions of Charlemagne and Otto the Great.

About a decade later, Robert Holtzmann returned to the well-worn paths of Giesebrecht's assessment in his *Geschichte der sächsischen Kaiserzeit* (History of the Saxon imperial age), published in 1941. In this work, Holtzmann undertook a renewed and complete analysis of Otto III that departed significantly from the views of both Schramm and Brackmann:

For the historian the question remains: what significance did the short, idea-laden rule of the "wonder of the world" have for the history of our land? In the past decades intensive research has clarified many points related to this question. Not only do we know the specifics better than before, but we also see far more clearly into the emperor's aspirations and his goals for renewing the Roman Empire. And one should admit without question that the constructive ideas at work here attest to vitality and internal consistency. But these ideas have little in common with the states created by Charlemagne and Otto the Great. These had their roots in Germany, while Otto III's focus was on Rome. Here, however, he built on a foundation of air. In reality the empire at that time could only be based upon German power. Conditions in Rome and Italy were much too uncertain to allow them to serve as a suitable foundation. As a matter of fact, Otto III, too, had to call again and again upon German armies. That lasted for a couple of years. Then Otto himself experienced the extent to which the Germans, from sound instinct, rejected this kind of imperial policy, which made them tools of a foreign concern and succeeded to their detriment. Truly the Roman Empire of Otto III presented an evil appearance in the German homeland! There a friend and adherent of the emperor like Margrave Ekkard of Meissen could have himself elected as duke in Thuringia without opposition and make the duke of Bohemia into his vassal. There the head of the German church, Willigis of Mainz, could defy the commands of emperor and pope and disperse the synod of a papal legate. There, Poland and Hungary had won the establishment of their ecclesiastical independence, while nothing was accomplished to bring the Danes, Abodrites, and Liutizi back under subjection. There ecclesiastical and secular princes could conspire against the head of the empire and cast an imperial levy to the winds. There, strife and acts of violence spread alarmingly in some regions where no strong duke or margrave held sway. There was a development dangerous to the empire in Hennegau, too, about which I will speak below. Otto the Great's state was coming apart at the seams when Otto III died. If this emperor had lived longer, his empire would have disintegrated;

he would have lost the Germans without winning the Italians. A complete change in imperial policy was necessary to avert such an evil.[10]

Judgments of Otto III as harsh as Holtzmann's became rare after the end of World War II, although certainly there were still some. Just recently, Carlrichard Brühl, in his general assessment of Otto III, gave the following summary:

An assessment of Otto III's personality is a difficult undertaking, since he died before the age of twenty-two. There can be no doubt of his charisma and emerging luminous talent, which earned him the laudatory nickname "Mirabilia mundi." But he died at a moment of political delicacy, "in the first great crisis of his policy, which was at the same time an inner crisis for himself," as Schramm pertinently remarks. Schramm continues: "how he would have found his way out of this is an unanswerable question, and thus the assessment of Otto III must always hang in the balance." To this he adds the thought: "What would the judgment be if an equally coincidental illness had snatched away Otto the Great between the rebellion of the dukes and the victory at Lechfeld?" One must undoubtedly agree with all this, and it would certainly be a mistake to make a political assessment of Otto dependent on the coincidental state of affairs at the moment of his death. Despite this, one cannot suppress grave reservations. By this I do not refer specifically to the Roman rebellion, which Otto would certainly have been able to quell as he had Arduin's revolt in the region of Vercelli in 997. What appears dubious to me are, first, how rapidly Otto III's governmental system in Italy collapsed after his death, so that the young emperor's body could scarcely be brought back to East Francia, and, second, the Byzantine marriage. The ardently longed-for porphyrogenita, for the first time granted by Byzantium to an emperor of the west, landed at Bari at the moment of Otto's death. A son of this union would have been three-quarters Greek and only one-eighth Saxon! Would such a successor have been accepted as king north of the Alps, when even the Salian Henry V appeared to be a foreigner to the Saxons? So I believe that the early death of Otto III, tragic as it was as a personal ruin for the emperor, saved the empire from a sacrifice that would have been hard and in the long term completely useless.[11]

However, one can certainly not consider this judgment the dominant view of the postwar era.

In 1954 the *Jahrbücher Ottos III.* (Yearbooks of Otto III) by Mathilde Uhlirz entered the fray firmly on the side of Schramm's work. True, this work almost completely ignored the idea of Roman renewal, but in many other respects it drew a positive picture of Otto III. Uhlirz provided a detailed assessment that, besides the "Political Fundamentals," also dealt with "Education," "Character," and "Interest in Art and Science." In this way Uhlirz gave a positive spin to many of the old reproaches leveled against Otto. But in the process she too exhibited a tendency toward idealistic transfigurations. To give an example:

On the one side he strove for intimacy with God, freed from all earthly desires. On the other side he was held by the duties of his high office, to which he was also bound in a religious sense, as protector of Christianity and the Church, with a thousand bonds, and certainly also by the beautiful world, which recommended itself to his youth in alluring images. How could anyone perceive this opposition as obsessive and unstable, and thus call the emperor a weakling, a dreamer? These oppositions were instead deeply grounded in the special character of his age, pervading the evolving piety of the lands of the west. They did not preoccupy Otto alone, but also his friends, Margrave Hugo of Tuscany and many other important men. This opposition within the spirit of his age without doubt combined with the emperor's gruesome treatment of Crescentius and the antipope Johannes Philagathos, when influenced by his cousin Pope Gregory V, to cast the emperor into a deep inner conflict. This robbed him of his earlier certainty and made him more susceptible than he otherwise might have been to the influence of fervent ascetics like Nilus and Romuald of Camaldoli. They elevated into an unrelenting spiritual anguish the self-reproaches of the youth, which were deeply felt and likely his heritage from his so widely different parents. This prematurely consumed the strength of his body exactly at the time that his political efforts were making the greatest demands on him.[12]

Here it is worth noting that a particularly important task of this book is to measure this sort of psychosomatic interpretation of Otto III, as assured as it is, against the yardstick of the sources.

Following the publication of Uhlirz's book, scholars accepted something like a combination of Schramm's and Uhlirz's views, even though the two had completely different points of emphasis. In any case, the result was a fundamental change in assessments of Otto III. In part, the bitter reproaches of the nineteenth and early twentieth centuries were supplanted by unreserved admiration of Otto III's brilliance in policies and in life. However, the readiness to explain Otto III's policies by means of his "essence," his personal character and personality, remained unchanged. In 1970 Josef Fleckenstein expressed this view most pithily in Gebhardt's *Handbuch der deutschen Geschichte* (Handbook of German history):

Clearly the fundamental characteristics of the rule of the young, brilliant Otto III appear at least in rudimentary form as early as during the first expedition to Rome. They must have been deeply rooted in him. The young shoots then quickly unfurled themselves, the ideas became more precise. This was a process in which several helpers and friends of the young king (who by the way had a genius for friendship just like his hero Charlemagne) played an important role. It was characteristic of Otto, like Charlemagne, to always keep an eye out for talent, in order to bring the most outstanding men he encountered to his court. Otto, too, then also joined in friendship with those among them whom he recognized as soul mates.

Following Schramm's lead, the policy of Roman renewal was also assessed positively without any reservation:

The aspiring and talented young emperor, eagerly seeking models, characteristically nourished in himself an ideal based on the most important impressions from his first years of rule. He deepened and broadened it in exchanges with his friends, in order to make it the standard gauge of his rule. He brought it to life in the old formula "renovatio imperii Romanorum," which, as its use shows, is much more exciting in content than the words alone suggest, however.

Fleckenstein's final conclusion also accentuates the positive, and the author allows himself an intimation of the old critique simply by using the little expression "all too":

Although his ideal of renovatio was all too keenly envisioned, he could not transform it into reality. Because of the brevity of his reign, he also found no other opportunity to perhaps align it with the possibilities of his time. But he had still preserved the foundations upon which Henry II, a true admirer of Otto III, would rebuild with more moderate goals. Yet there still remained the embers of his great will, which, rising above reality in order to

elevate it to his ideal, preserved Ottonian culture and its high art. Otto III
contributed to their enrichment like few other rulers. Like historiography,
art mirrors the image of the young, brilliant emperor, whom contemporaries
admiringly called "wonder of the world."[13]

The most recent scholarship tends to avoid the "high tone" customary
when portraying Otto III's age and ideas ever since Schramm and Uhlirz.
Helmut Beumann expressed the scholarly conclusions now generally
accepted in this way:

The "renewal of the Roman Empire" remained a vision. . . . The weakest
point of the bold plan was the key role given to the city of the apostles. Here
more than elsewhere theory departed from reality. Seemingly this was less
the case with eastern policy. The powerful and expanding state of Poland,
whose ruler had himself expanded missionary work as his own cause, pre-
sented no alternative to the Gniezno policy, until Henry II adopted a policy
of confrontation that abandoned "apostolic" legitimation. True, the sub-
lime imperial level upon which Otto III had operated in Gniezno skated on
thin ice. We must, though, avoid a conclusive judgment. We only have a
rough sketch before us, whose artist passed away prematurely. In summing
up, however, we must not overlook what remained. Otto's successors . . .
further developed the imperial church system. Henry III systematically
raised German bishops to the Roman see. The Roman imperial title held its
own. Although Poland and Hungary finally freed themselves from the
empire, at the same time Europe's Latin state complex was expanded with
two important new members. This was a step of great consequence on the
path to forming Europe as a family of nations.[14]

Moreover, modern historians are acutely conscious of the problem
implicit in all attempts to judge the emperor's individual characteristics.[15] I
must delineate this problem emphatically, without dealing with it here in
any more detail. The problem is this: at first glance, the sources would seem
to allow an insight rare for the central Middle Ages into Otto III's personality, his individuality, and his "essence." But that is only at first glance. We
must test how much the many apparently individualistic details about Otto
III appearing in the sources—from his esteem of friendship to his ascetic,
world-rejecting inclinations—arise from modern misunderstandings, which
have not properly considered the context and intended purpose of various

accounts.[16] It is certainly not easy to reach Otto III's "essence"—this is seen particularly in the history of the ways scholars have assessed Otto, which I have roughly sketched above.

Since even historians have not been able to avoid contention and debate in their discussion of Otto III, it is no wonder that this emperor has also been an alluring object for writers of fiction. Since the sixteenth century countless plays have had Otto III as title character—not surprising in view of his short life and the dramatic events of his short reign.[17] Hardly any of this literary effusion was of lasting value. A few examples might, however, illustrate how poets, dramatists, and novelists have transplanted the judgments of historians into their own genres. The effect of this "historical fiction" upon the German historical consciousness, as the number of editions of these works testifies, may have been even greater than that of the much-read works of the historians discussed above. I cite here part of Platen's poem "Klagelied Kaiser Ottos III." (Eulogy for Emperor Otto III), from the year 1833. Here we already encounter, condensed into literary form, the devaluing of the emperor to satisfy a nationalist agenda. The editor of this poem agrees, pointing out that "his [Otto III's] mind vacillates. On one side it focuses on high-flown plans—which amount to the refoundation of the Roman Empire with Rome at its center, without Otto's knowing how to make these fantastic dreams into reality. On the other it focuses on world-denying asceticism like that which had attracted a wide circle around the turn of the first millennium, when people supposed the world would end."[18] This is Platen's assessment:

> Oh Earth, receive this Pilgrim,
> The Burdened One by life
> Who at this Southern border
> Completes his worldly plight.
> For I have reached the limit
> Where body parts with soul.
> And all my twenty springtimes
> Flee fast and come annul.
> Still full of dreams unfinished,
> Deserted, sorrow bound,
> I drop the reins that governed
> This kingdom, firm and sound.
> Let others grip the bridle
> With gentler hold and rein

From seven hills of Rome
Till Northern vast terrain.

Disgrace conveys my body,
Divested of all fame,
Into the Heav'nly Kingdom—
My soul suffers shame.
In vain I plead for mercy
For breaking of the ban.
Against my case have spoken
Crescentius and Johann.

How futile are the gifts of fortune
With what regret I now perceive;
How childishly did I wear the crown
In days of early youth received.
That what I deemed the whole cosmos
Has shrunk down to an element.
Oh World, you are so inconsequent;
You, Rome, so insignificant!

Oh Rome, where all my blossoms
Have withered into dust,
To guard the royal coffin
Does not befit your cast!
You have destroyed my honor,
Have broken every limb:
In Aachen with great Charlemagne—
There I will lie by him.

Immortal palms secure
His standards evermore.
In full imperial glory
I saw him there entombed.
What tempted me to open
His coffin and upset
The guarding wreath of laurel
On his imperial bed?

My friends, forget your mourning!
Collect your swords and shields

And make my final journey
Ornate with weapons, smooth!
Throw roses on my coffin
That I have earned so young,
And place my idle body
By this dynamic man![19]

Similar in tenor is Ricarda Huch's 1934 assessment in the multivolume work *Römisches Reich Deutscher Nation* (Roman Empire of the German nation). This occupies the cusp between poetry and historical writing, a genre of historical literature that in those years inspired much literary production.[20] She measured Otto III especially against his predecessor Otto I. While she devalued the younger ruler, she still remains true to earlier evaluations:

It was Otto I's fate to be a brilliant ruler who had to leave his empire to inadequate successors. His son and grandson were buds from the paternal tree, not stems that grew from the earth with their own roots. . . . The Germans bitterly felt the change in their king's policy. The great-grandson of Duke Henry of Saxony, the grandson of the great Otto—neither of whom even understood Latin, who preferred living at Quedlinburg and hunted in the forests of the Harz—was a stranger in the north. To the Romans, though, he remained almost more foreign than his grandfather. The one was mighty in deeds, successful, a ruler who knew the right time to command, to punish, to forgive. Otto III wanted to rule the world and be a saint at the same time. Otto I was loved and honored, but also feared. . . . Otto III let himself be admonished by Bishop Adalbert of Prague (who had abandoned his diocese because he suffered from the brutality and obstructiveness of the Bohemians). Adalbert warned not to overvalue the imperial office but to bear in mind that he was dust. Otto III also knelt weeping before the hermits who had a reputation for sanctity in Italy at that time. He alternately indulged in unrestrained claims of rule and unstable contrition. "On your account," he proclaimed to the rebellious Romans, "I have left my homeland and my supporters. My love for you led me to spurn my Saxony and all Germans, my own blood. On your account I have brought the disfavor and hatred of all upon myself, since I regard you above all. And in return for all that you have repudiated your father, have gruesomely murdered my servants, and me, whom you cannot indeed shut out, you have shut out!" The Romans did indeed submit to a ruler who showed

them his strength. But they despised a pious dreamer and barbarian, who
wished to fetter them to him with tearful words.[21]

The positive reassessment of the emperor in the twentieth century also
found a literary echo. It is probably not coincidental that two historical
romances about the life of Otto III appeared in Germany shortly after the end
of World War II. Gertrud Bäumer, who besides her literary activity was active
in politics and had been removed from her offices by the National Socialists,
entitled her account of Otto III *Der Jüngling in Sternenmantel: Größe und*
Tragik Ottos III. (The youth in the starry mantle: The greatness and tragedy
of Otto III).[22] This work ran through four editions in two years, with over
16,000 copies sold. It is written completely on the basis of extant sources and
historical studies. But the freedom of the literary form makes it perfectly
clear that the old and new assessments of Otto III both stood sponsor here.
For example, here is a scene in which Otto III, Margrave Ekkehard of Meissen, and Gerbert of Aurillac argued about a new imperial seal used for the
first time in 998:

The new seal, however, bothered the proud margrave. Why were none of the
field insignia of the German army seen on it? They had carried the Holy
Lance and the banner of Saint Michael when they conquered Rome. And
now the emperor sealed his orders with the standard and the shield of
Rome? The emperor restrained his impatience. It offended his imperial self-
esteem that the margrave asked such questions. But the conqueror of Rome,
to whom Empress Theophanu had once entrusted the entire eastern march,
possessed such a high reputation and so much natural authority over the
young emperor that he certainly could not ignore his question. Gerbert took
the answer from him: but the image of Emperor Charles! The German claim
to the imperial throne could not be made more clearly. The Holy Lance and
the archangel mean more than the image of Emperor Charles, responded
Ekkard. Emperor Charles cannot grant us victory. The emperor thought of
his conversations with Abbess Mathilda, whom he had now made patricius
of Germany. She would probably agree with Ekkard. But then she was not
empress. And this magnificent and giddy feeling of his emperorship flowed
through him like a rushing spring from a secret chasm. He was directly con-
scious of his role as cultor dei, *by election as well as by commission, to*
unite the earthly empire and the kingdom of God, in a way that did not
require approval, nor could it be experienced by others. Such an experience

had not been granted them. He was the Only. He could not—indeed he might not—follow any other counsel; he had to follow his own intuition. He stood up abruptly, as if for a departure.[23]

In the same period, Henry Benrath attempted to encapsulate Otto III's personality still more subjectively and emphatically. He spoke of the "spiritual-emotional vision of a ruler's life," which "creatively embodied the most splendid thoughts of the early Middle Ages."[24] The result was, in any event, a vision that probably had less to do with Otto III than with the author's own imagination.

Royal Rule and the Idea of the State at the End of the Tenth Century
A biographical study like this one easily succumbs to the temptation of assuming the reasons behind historical events, implicitly if necessary, on the basis of historical facts. It is absolutely essential to reflect on the political, and in this case especially the governmental, circumstances, precisely when one inquires into the contingencies on which a medieval ruler had to act and that he had to organize. To put it more simply: What was the basis upon which Otto III had to build his power? What rules and customs for royal activity and political interaction formed the context in which he exercised power?

When modern research has concerned itself with the "foundations" of Ottonian kingship, scholars have rightly emphasized the pre-state. This denotes an archaic quality of exercising rule in this era, which in terms of state structures fell far below the level of the earlier Carolingian age.[25] It is easy to enumerate deficiencies, if one measures Ottonian ruling practices against a yardstick of later constitutional governments. There was next to no administration, hardly any institutions, and a scarcely visible dependence on the written word in any area of public life. In place of these, the modern observer notes a wealth of ceremonial and ritual acts and activities, which served to display rule. One sees complicated networks of personal alliance upon which rule was established at a personal level. These networks, however, had to compete against alliances based on kinship or friendship. The observer hears that it was necessary to do nothing without advice (*consilium*), and identifies widely varying groups of advisors, whose position was based on special closeness (*familiaritas*) to the ruler. It is, however, impossible to discover national structures in these alliances, to demarcate fields of competence, hierarchies, or jurisdictions. Notwithstanding, one finds that the state structures created during the dissolution of the more-developed Carolingian Empire endured, and that contemporaries accepted these ruling practices as adequate, even if the development certainly did not take place without conflict. Apparently the actors of the tenth century behaved in accordance with a thoroughly manifest rationality, even though it is alien to us.

An entire system of rules, customs, and usages evolved that lay at the base both of royal activities and of public communication and interaction, even if it was not fixed in writing anywhere. Awareness of this structure of rules seems highly important for understanding not only the tenth century but much of the Middle Ages. It would therefore be a grave error to undervalue its binding force just because it was not committed to writing. It was a system of rules within whose boundaries Otto III, as well as other rulers and political figures, had to act.

What were the constitutive elements of this system of rules? Let us begin by considering the structure of alliances around the king that helped him rule. Every king of the Middle Ages gathered a circle of confidants around himself. They had access to him, advised him, and carried out all suitable business. The position of members in this circle, although not precisely delineated, was so high mainly because there was no general right of direct access to the ruler. In this way the circle acted on one hand as a filter, and on the other hand conveyed petitions and business to the king. In his choice of this close entourage the ruler had a certain discretionary latitude but certainly not an unlimited one. Even more, he had to consider firmly established rights. These rights came from either ecclesiastical or secular status. Toward the end of the tenth century the dominant position of an entire series of noble families was so well established in all regions of the Ottonian empire that the members of these families could lay claim to closeness with the ruler. This involved special consideration in decisions and in the allocation of ecclesiastical and secular preferment. Similarly, the role of the Church in royal service was so well established that not only archbishops and bishops but also abbots of imperial monasteries had a right to a share of the ruler's company and of the business conducted there. It is not known how these certainly divergent interests and claims were portioned out in specific circumstances. But the concept of honor is, without a doubt, key to understanding how their cooperation functioned. Each ruler had to take the *honor* of each person in this circle into account. By this is meant the sum of all earned and acquired possessions, offices, abilities, and the rank that they conferred. Each ruler had to value each person proportionate to this *honor*, in

other words give preferential treatment, listen, give gifts. For the acknowl-
edgment of honor, a wealth of material and even more importantly immate-
rial distinctions were at his disposal. The spectrum ranged from presents to
offices, to honorary positions like that of sword-bearer, honorable place-
ment, greeting, conversation, and many others.

Such events were staged at the numerous court days, when the magnates
appeared before the ruler, and where the policies of the Ottonian age were
crafted. According to contemporary accounts, this included consultation on
all matters, conducted for the most part publicly between the ruler and his
magnates. Rulers asserted countless times that they did something according to the *consilium* of their *fideles*, or with their *consensus*. But still, it is
difficult for the modern observer to understand this proceeding. Doubtless
there were no strict notions of what had to be submitted for advisement; in
the same way there was no clear concept of who was entitled to take part in
deliberations. The circle of participants at many court days appears accidental. There were neither principles of a minimum number of advisors nor of
persons who had to be there. It would be just as anachronistic to imagine
these consultations as an open discussion about the best solution. Rather,
such councils observed strict processes of confidential discussion beforehand, so that the public consultation only took place after it was clear that
all accepted a desired decision. This sort of consultation assured that everyone could save face; it had the character of a staged production.[26]

The formal rules of medieval consultation, already very difficult to understand, become even more complicated when one asks about the goal of all
this consultation. To answer this question is to address the scope of activity
for medieval kings. To express it another way: for what areas of human corpo-
rate life did a ruler feel himself answerable? To what extent did he attempt to
put specific policies into effect, using the means allowed him by the age? This
sort of deliberation fulfilled central functions that facilitated the medieval
ruler's specific duties. He was primarily responsible for peace (*pax*) and justice
(*iustitia*). After these duties, only the responsibility to protect the Church as
well as the poor, the weak, and the defenseless assumes equal importance.
Medieval sources incessantly stress these duties of kingship. Many times
these obligations motivated the kings themselves to action. But besides these
duties, which modern scholars take very seriously, they postulate a wealth of
other areas that supposedly preoccupied medieval "policy makers." So for the
tenth century it is traditional for historians to speak of Italian policies, eastern policies, western policies, and monastic policies. It is also customary to

portray rulers and magnates as acting as if political plans had first been developed and then been put into effect in these areas and others. Such portrayals carry the implicit assumption that the rulers took counsel and agreed with their magnates on such plans, which then became guiding principles of a policy applied for a certain period of time or even long-term.

By contrast, the sources of the tenth and other centuries refer to such reasoned policies only very seldom, if at all. This rather forcefully raises the question: do we not deal in anachronisms if we categorize medieval royal rule according to the model of modern government with its plans and policies, especially since we are unable to trace where and how such alleged policies arose? Indeed, one would be right to doubt whether this supposed intense planning is in any way at all in harmony with the conceptual framework and mentality of the central Middle Ages. Plans and policies may have been quite alien in a society whose understanding of politics centered with such certainty on the idea that a God-ordained order must either be guarded or reestablished. Such an understanding also set its stamp on the duties and powers of medieval kings, as the significance of peace and justice among the ruler's duties attests. But performing such duties did not so much require some sort of future-oriented planning as the employment of the customary usages by which people had always performed these duties. These customs offered guidelines for right behavior.[27]

In sketching the norms and rules at the base of ruling activity in the tenth century, I wish to emphasize two points. The first is that the rules are deeply anchored in worldviews and mentalities of their age and that those are not readily accessible to our understanding. Nevertheless, every failure to pay attention to these rules at the very least presents the danger of anachronistically false explanation. This is because much of what appears accessible and familiar to our understanding of politics only seems so at the first glance. With a closer look, however, the unsatisfactory state of research in this precise area becomes very evident. The issue of how the medieval state functioned is currently plagued by unresolved questions. In addition to this inescapable problem, it should not be forgotten that this book applies implicitly the basic picture of the tenth century other scholars have devised. Points of that basic picture bear mentioning here as an outline for discussion.

Throughout the Middle Ages, including the tenth century, medieval royal rule was peripatetic.[28] This theme is of special importance when evaluating Otto III, since he supposedly planned to make Rome his permanent residence. Putting such plans into practice would have involved a fundamental change in accepted methods of rule.[29] The medieval king along with his court traveled on established routes through his kingdom for two main reasons: the means were lacking to provide the necessities for a settled ruler, and rule was only effective where the king was physically present. It was not possible to transport enough food to a certain location and keep it palatable for a group of people as large as the royal court, so the court traveled from place to place to consume the resources on the spot. Their route led, in Otto III's time as in others, from palace to palace, since the attached royal estates were able to provide provisions. In the Ottonian era the most important complexes of royal estates lay in the Harz region (the heartland of Ottonian kingship), on the middle Rhine with the palaces of Frankfurt and Ingelheim, and on the lower Rhine. This constellation of sites created a triangle typical for the Ottonian period, within which the king normally moved. The location of the royal estates also fixed Otto III's itinerary north of the Alps.

It was not only the needs of provisioning that made it necessary for the medieval king to travel. In the mentality of the age, the king "honored" his people by coming to them. Further, since the necessary institutions did not exist, royal rule was only effective where the king was present. In this way, changes in itinerary, evident when Otto III turned greater attention to the south German duchies, indicate a change in the ruler's relationship with the magnates of these regions.[30] Otto's short reign prevents us from drawing easy conclusions about any major changes intended. But by the time of Henry II there was an unmistakable change: the royal court went more often and purposefully to the imperial churches.[31] The consequences of this shift were consistent with other developments of the tenth century. The king now was provisioned by that very institution, the imperial church, upon which he more and more based his rule.

This connection and collaboration between king and Church grew in intensity in the course of the tenth century. German scholarship has long termed this the "Ottonian-Salian Imperial Church System" (*ottonisch-salischen Reichskirchensystem*), and in recent years it has been critically and contentiously discussed.[32] Whether it was a system or not, nobody questions the fact that, since the Ottonian period, the king ruled with the help of the Church even more than had ever been the case in the Carolingian era. What is doubtful is whether the Church let itself be "instrumentalized" as a compliant tool or whether it remained in a position to adopt independent positions, even against the crown. In fact there are enough instances of the second possibility to preclude simplistic classification of the imperial church as a tool in the hands of the kings. But what are the particular characteristics of the relation between king and Church during the Ottonian period? In the first place, there is the "real" side of the relationship: the Ottonian kings granted possessions and privileges to the imperial churches, bishoprics, and monasteries in such abundance that this phenomenon cannot be explained simply as pious support of the churches. Its fundamental motivation was as a way in which the rulers freed themselves from the need to form their own central government. The privileges granted included rights to hold markets, coin money, and collect tolls. Through these grants, the principal royal rights were delegated to churchmen, and in part also to the secular nobility. Beginning in the late tenth century, counties as they became available were no longer given to noble families, but were turned over to churches. Scholars have regarded this concerted and conscious advocacy as the crown's answer to the growing unreliability of the secular nobles, clear in their noticeably decreased willingness to exert themselves in royal service.

What made this "system" function, however, was its personal side. The kings needed the authority to promote reliable bishops from the ranks of institutions they favored, those institutions that displayed steady willingness to serve the state. This requirement for success was met to a large extent through the royal right, dating from late in Otto the Great's reign, to raise chaplains from court chapels to bishoprics.[33] According to canon law, election of a bishop was the right of the cathedral clergy, but was now carried out with the king's consent. The kings used this right of consent to such effect that their recommendation de facto decided the election. Otto III was not the least of those who used this power. In this way he elevated personal confidants from his chapel into popes, archbishops, and bishops. For the kings, promoting chaplains had a distinct advantage. These men, during their time serving the chapel, had entered into a relationship of personal trust with the ruler. They addressed him as *senior*, in the same way as vassals did their lords. This personal bond strengthened considerably after promotion to the episcopate, since this gift by the ruler made a countergift necessary. That countergift was service to the state. The times in which reformers could brand such practices as simoniacal were still far in the future. Overall, the bishops of the Ottonian era played a considerable role in stabilizing royal rule. But this does not mean that they were complacent tools.

It is important to keep two things in mind when evaluating the political behavior of Ottonian imperial bishops: 1. The vast majority of them came from the ranks of the nobility, against whom they were then obligated to support the king. A very high percentage of the Ottonian bishops were younger sons of the secular ruling class. They had followed a typical career path: entry into a cathedral school and a cathedral chapter, entry into the court chapel, and, after serving and proving themselves there, promotion to a bishopric. Thus there is an important question of what ties these bishops maintained to the noble kinship groups to which they belonged, and how they behaved when there were conflicts in loyalty. 2. According to the understanding of the time, the bishop "married" his church. But in this way he committed himself to a high degree to that church's interests and claims. This bred conflicts as well, usually when there was an attempted change in the ranking or the boundaries of a bishopric.[34] In such circumstances, bishops rarely hesitated to oppose the kings who harmed the interests of their churches.

The relationship between crown and Church had been regularized into a "system." By contrast, the relationship between the ruler and the secular nobility is less clearly evident and therefore less frequently studied. Clearly the Ottonian rulers in principle accepted the heritability of fiefs and thus in effect supported the basis of noble ruling structures. In practice, the personal property of the nobles, allods and thus free from all duties to the ruler, remained completely distinct from their fiefs, even though sometimes as a special privilege a fief could be changed into an allod.[35]

The relationship of Ottonian kings with their nobility is different from that between the nobility and both their Carolingian predecessors and their Salian successors. Notably, in conflicts between kings and nobles people bothered less with royal law courts. Instead, the kings as well as private individuals conducted feuds, in which mediators worked to find an amicable settlement. In the process of forging such compromise-filled solutions, nobles were often able to win forgiveness and resume their earlier position, at least "on probation," after they performed ritual acts of satisfaction.[36] In much the same way, kings of the Ottonian period accepted in principle the sworn association, the *coniuratio*, in which nobles joined to pursue political goals. This marks a clear change from Charlemagne, who had tried to forbid all such *coniurationes*.[37] This form of sworn alliance among the nobility apparently saved the young Otto III his throne, while at the end of his reign it was used against him.[38] Contemporaries never directly remarked on the way the noble ruling structure evolved during the tenth century. But the sources do at least give indirect evidence that the position of the nobles strengthened in relation to the crown, or perhaps was established for the first time. This development, therefore, forms part of the environment in which Otto III had to operate.

Central Questions and the Problem of Sources

The beginning of this introduction, roughly outlining earlier opinions about the life and mental world of Otto III, exposed how earlier historians drew on the assumptions of their own times to form mistaken judgments. Still, a complete overview of Otto III and his rule would not be possible without their studies to prepare the way. Indeed, examining these earlier works teaches awareness of the danger of anachronistic judgment, a danger a historian can never completely avoid. Taking on the perspective of a time in the past, seeing the world with the eyes of contemporaries, is never fully possible. It is even questionable whether this is desirable. But we must understand the thought world and circumstances of contemporaries if we are to assess their affairs, and not simply employ our own categories of evaluation. Otherwise we blame them for omissions or praise them for actions while completely disregarding what may have been decisive circumstances. In this regard praise as well as blame says more about us than it does about the people we judge. Paying careful attention to contemporary circumstances to avoid (as far as possible) anachronistic conclusions has decisive consequences, but not always pleasant ones. Sometimes it is only possible to declare earlier judgments false or to problematize them, without being able to put a new assessment in their place. If every age must reexamine its past, this cannot occur simply as an ongoing progress and with increasing knowledge. Apparent certainties and problematic certitudes must also be repudiated, even if no new certainty takes their place. Unfortunately, but certainly not coincidentally, this is the case for important points in the career of Otto III. Still, it seems more suitable to acknowledge the difficulty of understanding the fragments transmitted to us than to erect entire systems of explanation upon uncertain ground. Accepting these premises makes it necessary to establish the principal questions on which to base a new portrayal of Otto III, questions that would use the interests and methods of modern medieval studies as a foundation. Two currents in modern historiography stand out. We are currently learning to understand the essence of medieval kingship in new ways, and we also have an increasing sensitivity toward medieval texts that goes far beyond the traditional methods of historical source criticism (even though its value should not be underrated). Both areas offer new possibilities for assessing Otto III, but also raise new difficulties. Since in many respects they form the foundation for the following detailed discussions, a few general remarks are necessary beforehand.

Historians of the Middle Ages had long described kingship essentially as the exercise of power, which came to encompass more and more spheres of life with improvements in efficiency and the foundations of power.[39] Without a doubt, power was exercised in the Middle Ages, but contemporaries describe the "essence" of royal rule differently. They speak of the duty to maintain peace, to work for justice, to protect the poor and defenseless, "to bestow, to give, to reward."[40] If we dismiss this sort of ideal description of the king's duties as the unrealistic babbling of clerics, at the very least we neglect the evidence of the sources. The sources do not speak of optimizing the exercise of power, and in fact the necessary institutions and the means of control to do that simply did not exist. Researchers ignored this for a long time. They instead created the notion that the foundations of rulership in Germany weakened in the course of the Middle Ages, when their base of power increasingly slipped away or was wrested from them. Today, it is still common to assess the prestige of medieval rulers to a large extent on the basis of how much and how successfully they opposed this supposed encroachment on their power. Conversely, guilt is assigned to those considered responsible for this loss of power: the German princes, who acted from personal aims and lust for power, and the popes, who schemed to withdraw the Church's support from the emperors.[41] This focus on exercise of power relates to another peculiarity in the description of medieval kingship, which must be analyzed carefully. The kings and emperors allegedly made plans in the most widely ranging fields of politics, be it policies in regard to Italy, eastern Europe, cities, the Church, monasteries, or many other areas. All of these plans and underlying conceptions supposedly shared the goal of increasing, supporting, or winning back royal power. Such theories derive from modern worldviews, in which the state and its leadership systematically aim to penetrate all life within the state and apply the same to international relations, whether by peaceful or less peaceful means. Such assumptions must be proven for the Middle Ages, especially the earlier part of the era. By no means can they be taken for granted.

Recent research into broader political structures has revealed how much medieval kingship depended on representational behaviors.[42] The sources speak of the festive procession of ecclesiastical high feasts, of public donations to widows, orphans, and the poor, of harshness toward evildoers and generous friendship toward loyal followers. They speak of lengthy hunting expeditions and pious visits to churches and monasteries "for the sake of prayer." They also speak of consultations on all appropriate questions, and relate that the king heeded the counsel of his faithful followers. The sources do not, however, mention planning to increase power or such plans being turned into reality. Nor do they show how interests in the various political arenas worked toward particular larger goals. With only a little exaggeration one can say that the medieval kings apparently exercised power essentially through ritual acts. For such acts were certainly no "empty" stage plays. Instead, they made public how the ruler and his circle understood his purpose, rights, and duties, his dignity and his honor. They also made clear what role others—such as ecclesiastical and secular magnates—played in this ruling system. Thus ritual acts had a stabilizing function, confirming the king's power within his circle and exhibiting the bonds of society to those outside. These acts were specific to the exercise of power. Nobody who wanted to keep influence could avoid them. As strange as this may sound to us, these symbolic acts, as described in the sources, were apparently so effective that to a large extent they made other means of exercising power superfluous.

Policies to intensify rule are foreign to such a political understanding. When scholars have reconstructed such policies, they have always followed the same line, postulating plans (or motivations) that underlie the events our sources describe. And such conclusions are problematic. They are based on the idea that there was an intensity of rational planning in the exercise of medieval kingship, even if important preconditions—literacy and the institutions to carry plans out—were lacking.[43] Consequently we must look again and more closely at the parameters within which politics in the tenth century operated. This is a goal of this book. We speak of an archaic society. It acted according to norms fixed by custom, which is by no means to say that these were not binding. Implicit to all political actions were without a doubt well-defined views about what should be done and permitted. There was a precise knowledge of the proper forms for communication and interactions.[44] This knowledge is no longer available to us today. We know that kingship took concrete form in an unbroken but irregular succession of court days. There the king took counsel with those present on all pertinent issues. But we know nothing more precise. More specific descriptions do not exist, either about the duty of attending such assemblies or about the form of counsel given and the establishment of an "agenda." Modern scholarship took a long time to pay attention to these issues. Instead, scholars have automatically and apparently without reflection assumed that everything was essentially the same as it is today. That was not the case, however. To give an example: the simple question of how a person brought a suit before the king presents medievalists with difficulties. It is anachronistic to think that a petitioner could have simply addressed the ruler, or presented him with the facts of the case, or placed a petition on an agenda. One can suppose nothing of the sort. The sources report too much anger when people discovered that they were blocked from this kind of access to the king. On the other hand, there is evidence that poor or even powerful people prostrated themselves before the king and then were heard. But we can discern the circumstances in which such a technique was proper and likely to succeed only if we take into account the "rules of the game" for such modes of interaction. These rules, of course, were never written down in some sort of medieval "Miss Manners."[45]

The following chapters, arranged chronologically, will pay special attention to the reports and tales in the sources that give information about the concrete functioning of kingship. This sort of report can only be understood, though, in the context of a general comparison with the manners, rules of action, and boundaries within which all parties conducted public business in the Middle Ages. Only in that way is it possible to decide whether some behavior agreed with the rules, injured them, or changed them. This complex of questions is important for judging Otto III, a supposedly radical "innovator." In the normal course of things the customs of an archaic society do indeed leave a certain elbowroom, but they allow little space for fundamental changes. The act of forming policy according to sophisticated plans and preconceived ideas was unknown at that time. Postulating it therefore draws from modern views, which were completely foreign to the tenth century.

To some extent the same is true in analyzing the ruler's choice of a circle of advisors, something that assumes great significance in the historiography of Otto III. In the view of historians, he supposedly made this choice on the basis of personal impressions and preferences. Doing so changed the customs that had prevailed up to that point. Here again it is improbable that such changes in rank and the potential to exert influence would have taken place without opposition. Therefore we must explore whether Otto III's conduct as ruler was in this regard really so very different from the conduct of his father and grandfather. Thus, the goal of this study is a source-oriented description of the parameters of kingship using Otto III as example. In light of earlier research, it is necessary to pay special attention to what changes were implemented in the categories of ideas, plans, and advisors, and what allowance was made for encouraging creativity and putting it into practice.

Carrying out such objectives naturally depends on the state of the sources. In essence, sources for the reign of Otto III are quite unusual, in both positive and negative regards. On the positive side, sources at our disposal are of both a quantity and a quality that otherwise do not exist for this period. But on the negative side, these sources conceal serious problems. For the most part they represent the history of Otto III in an extremely subjective way, largely with no particular interest in fairness to the emperor and his policies. Taken as a whole, these sources characteristically report Otto III's deeds from widely varying outside perspectives. An account from what might be termed the inner perspective—be it ever so panegyrical—is completely lacking. We do not have an established tradition upon which to base a portrait, or with which we can assess the value of other, more heterogeneous sources by comparison.

The most important historical sources from the German lands are the chronicle of Thietmar of Merseburg and the Quedlinburg Annals.[46] Thietmar is certainly a well-informed source of information for Otto III's reign. However, his main preoccupation for that particular period revolved around the vicissitudes of his bishopric of Merseburg—in other words in loud denunciation of the bishopric's dissolution in 981 and in recording the efforts to restore it, a struggle that only succeeded in 1004. This issue determines Thietmar's perspective and especially his judgments. The consequences of this perspective are compounded when one uses an entire series of Thietmar's assessments. The Quedlinburg Annals, by contrast, were written entirely from the perspective of the Ottonian family convent and its royal abbesses. In many places one has the impression that the personal views of the abbesses, the aunt or sister of Otto III, are embedded here. Certainly the views of the female members of the ruling house are not necessarily identical to the emperor's. This is shown particularly well in the sides taken during the so-called Gandersheim controversy. Still, in all, the Quedlinburg Annals are doubtless the source with the truest claim to be "Ottonian" historiography.

This historiography is supplemented by hagiographical texts dedicated to the lives of saints who had contact with Otto III. These include the *vitae* of Adalbert of Prague and of the Five Brothers, both from the pen of the missionary bishop and Saxon nobleman Bruno of Querfurt. We also have the *vita* of Bishop Bernward of Hildesheim, as well as those of the Italian hermits Romuald and Nilus.[47] All of these works are at pains to underscore the influence their heroes had on the emperor and the relationship of intimate closeness that they enjoyed. And the authors write within the tradition of hagiography, with its rich supply of topoi. We certainly know that the use of a topos in the historiography and hagiography of the Middle Ages does not prove the presentation and claims unrealistic. At the same time, the use of customary topoi certainly does not prove historical accuracy. To a large extent, those who interpret them must acknowledge that such reports are impossible to evaluate. Many claims about Otto III's personal qualities are affected by this problem, since these claims were mostly based on the hagiographical sources. Further, this group of sources includes such detailed statements about the saints' intimacy with the emperor or about Otto's world-fleeing ascetic inclinations that they can only be understood within the larger context of hagiographical description.[48]

For many areas of Otto III's reign the letter collection of Gerbert of Aurillac is a source unparalleled for this period.[49] The letters offer highly welcome insights into the otherwise absolutely confidential exchange of information. They further provide assessments and evaluations not available in other sources. At the same time, this uniqueness creates a fundamental difficulty in evaluation. Lacking materials for comparison, we have difficulties understanding the diction, the polemics, and the allusions in many of the letters. Certainly Gerbert's style is characterized by a thoroughly ambitious and mannered rhetoric, but we cannot tell if these are "empty" phrases or historically significant statements with rhetorical polish added. This, by the way, is true not only of Gerbert's rhetoric. This has led some to see pure irony in Otto III's declaration that he wanted to put off his Saxon *rusticitas* (boorishness) with the help of Gerbert's instruction. Others have taken the statement at face value and diagnosed Otto's lack of feeling for the Germans as if it were an ailment (which they then still classified as typical of the German character).[50] This particular difficulty in interpretation shows the larger problem in all its clarity: as yet, no one has succeeded in reducing Gerbert's rhetoric to its factual core. And this is not only true of Gerbert's letter collection. We are confronted with similar problems in the diplomatic style of the royal and imperial charters, especially when Leo of Vercelli, the chancellor Heribert, or Gerbert himself is named as author.[51]

This heterogeneity of the sources for the history of Otto III has been raised here only briefly with their specific problems. Their varied nature makes it necessary to show clearly which judgments are based upon which sources. Accordingly, in the chapters that follow, the source of statements will receive special attention. Wherever possible, the reports of the sources will be situated within their larger context.

✝ Chapter 1 ✝

A CHILD ON THE THRONE

Henry the Quarrelsome and the Disturbances over the Succession

Otto's reign certainly began inauspiciously. When the three-year-old was consecrated king at Aachen on Christmas Day, 983, Emperor Otto II, his father, had already been dead for three weeks. But nobody in Aachen knew that yet. The news of the senior Otto's death arrived shortly after the coronation ceremonies and "brought the festivity to an end."[1] The situation was now critical in many respects. One issue was fundamental—the kingship of minors placed the medieval ruling bond under an almost intolerable strain. Contemporaries knew they should fear fulfillment of the Bible's lament "Woe to the land whose king is a child and whose princes feast in the morning."[2] But the actual situation for Otto III involved an even more disturbing circumstance: the last years of his father's reign had been unfortunate also.

In July 982 the German army had suffered a devastating defeat at the hands of the Saracens at Crotone in southern Italy. More great nobles, both secular and spiritual, had fallen on the battlefield at Crotone than at any time since the Magyar invasions at the beginning of the century. In fact, the emperor himself only escaped to a ship under conditions filled with adventure.[3] One year later the Slavs east of the Elbe staged an uprising. They destroyed the bishoprics of Brandenburg and Havelberg, and thus at a single blow wrecked the hitherto successful Ottonian missionary policy.[4] The true importance of these reversals for the makers of political decisions is very difficult to assess. Only Thietmar of Merseburg discusses the matter, reporting that "all our princes came sorrowfully together after receiving the evil tidings [from Italy] and unanimously demanded to see him [Otto II] again."[5] This report by a later chronicler suggests that the magnates wanted to influence policies after Crotone. But we cannot say what these nobles hoped to accomplish. All we know is that they met with the emperor at a great assembly in Verona. Certainly scholars have assumed that Emperor Otto II hurried to Mainz to prepare for this assembly and while there discussed the possible consequences of the predicament in which he found himself. Available evidence cannot support this assumption, however.[6] According to the sources, the assembly of Verona set about appointing new dukes for Bavaria and Swabia, but its main business was to elect Otto III as coruler with his father. The proceedings were unusual: this was the only royal election ever held south of the Alps. The sources give no reason for this departure from custom. Conceivably, time was running short for arranging matters in south Italy. Possibly, too, the choice of venue aimed to enhance the importance of a part of the Ottonian empire that Otto I had won only after 951: Italy.

Whatever the reason for the election, immediately thereafter the new three-year-old king, who until that time had lived in Italy with his parents, departed for the north. His goal was Aachen, the Ottonians' traditional coronation site, where he would receive royal consecration. The report that not only Archbishop Willigis of Mainz but Archbishop Johannes of Ravenna performed the ceremony is striking in this context.[7] This report, too, suggests a concerted effort to include representatives from the Italian part of the empire in ceremonial acts, and in that way a tendency to integrate the various regions under imperial control. These, however, remained only isolated occurrences.

The death of Otto II created a precarious situation. In Italy there were rebellions against Ottonian officials. Matters soon became even more complicated in the empire north of the Alps. There, Duke Henry the Quarrelsome of Bavaria, a first cousin of Otto II, again emerged as a political force. His relationship to the imperial house was already greatly strained.[8] As a member of the Bavarian branch of the Ottonians, Henry had been involved in several armed rebellions against Emperor Otto II in the years after 974. At first he had been pardoned. After a second rebellion, though, Henry lost his duchy and was imprisoned in the custody of Bishop Folcmar of Utrecht. This imprisonment, which had already lasted an unusually long time by tenth-century standards, ended abruptly with the death of the emperor who had ordered it. In the same way that treaties of this time were only valid *inter vivos* and lapsed with the death of the treaty signatories, so too had Henry the Quarrelsome been not a "state prisoner" but the personal prisoner of the emperor. Naturally, he received his freedom again when Otto II died.[9] There is hardly a better example of how underdeveloped "transpersonal state representations" still were in this period.[10]

In point of fact, Henry was not simply released. He immediately claimed a role in political events. He did so by demanding that Otto III, at that time staying in Cologne in the care of Archbishop Warin, be handed over to him. Apparently this was in accord with the law of propinquity as it was understood at that time.[11] Apparently there was no opposition to this move, because Henry could claim his rights as Otto's nearest male relative. Moreover, the *dominae imperiales,* the young king's grandmother, mother, and aunt, were still in Italy and by all appearances were in no hurry to return.[12] According to the sources, almost everyone believed that Henry was only seeking the guardianship of the young king. Henry's behavior and actions, however, soon taught them otherwise.[13]

As a matter of fact, Henry took action in a very characteristic way. Henry immediately made an agreement with King Lothar of France through emissaries and hurriedly arranged a meeting in Breisach, to conclude a friendship alliance with Lothar there. To assure Carolingian support, Henry supposedly even planned to turn the disputed province of Lotharingia over to the French king.[14] A letter authored by Gerbert in the name of Adalbero of Rheims to Bishop Notger of Liège is essential for assessing Henry's actions. In this letter Gerbert warns Notger against King Lothar, who was on his way to Breisach, and against Henry the Quarrelsome, whom he designates as an enemy of the state. The letter can be dated to the end of January 984 and thus shows that by this time the Quarrelsome's activities had already gone beyond mere guardianship and were considered dangerous.[15] However, we also learn through several reports and references among Gerbert's collected letters that the West Frankish king Lothar announced his own right to assume Otto's guardianship. Indeed, Lothar could also call upon the law of propinquity, because he was related to Otto III in the same degree as was Henry the Quarrelsome.[16] This claim perhaps even explains why Henry made a surprising change in direction. Henry did not turn up at the agreed-upon meeting in Breisach, despite his oath to do so. King Lothar consequently used the conflict over the German throne as a pretext to attack Lotharingia. This was part of a long tradition of West Frankish/French efforts to recover the region. Because of resistance by the Lotharingian nobles, this effort had no lasting success.[17]

Henry the Quarrelsome apparently made no arrangements at all to keep this meeting with the French king. The Saxon chronicler Thietmar gives a full and detailed report that Henry traveled directly from Cologne, where he had taken possession of the young Otto, to Saxony by way of Corvey.[18] It is

Figure 1. Henry the Quarrelsome, duke of Bavaria, 955–76 and 985–95.
(photo: Bildarchiv Foto Marburg)

not possible to say what motives lay behind this apparently abrupt change of mind. One thing is clear, however: in Saxony Henry the Quarrelsome did not hide his true aims under the mask of guardianship for long. Instead, his actions there quite openly aimed at usurping the throne. It is impossible to say whether he intended to set himself in Otto III's place or to establish some sort of joint rule.[19] Before he had even reached Saxony, however, something occurred that significantly worsened Henry's prospects. In Corvey, two Saxon counts, Dietrich and Siegbert, came to him barefooted and begged his pardon. In other words, they underwent a ritual of submission, for which there was a well-established tradition.[20] Henry, however, refused them his forgiveness, after which these counts "sought with all their strength to entice their relatives and friends from the duke's service."[21] We know neither the reason for the discord between Henry and the counts nor Henry's reason for refusing to forgive them. Still, we can assert from numerous similar incidents: clemency is always near to the scepter.[22]

Kings of the tenth century never missed an opportunity to provide clear visible proof of their *clementia,* public events at which opponents prostrated themselves before the ruler and begged for forgiveness. On the contrary. Public submission was a ritual commonly used in conflict resolution. As a rule, all the particulars were settled beforehand, and the ceremony thus had the character of a staged production, through which public conflict was concluded.[23] Henry the Quarrelsome had not heeded these rules of the game. Possibly he did not want to accept a *fait accompli* by the counts without reaching a previous agreement; perhaps he felt too deep a bitterness to forgive them. In either case, though, Henry the Quarrelsome's refusal injured him in Saxony as the dismayed counts' understandable reaction shows. From then on they worked against Henry in every way possible. Not surprisingly, a little later they are also numbered among those opponents of Henry who began to form themselves into a party in support of Otto III.[24] As in the case of the Breisach meeting, Henry's conduct is incomprehensible. A politically experienced man must have known the consequences of refusing a *deditio,* of not accepting a proffered submission. In this way he had demonstrated his unwillingness or incapacity for practicing *clementia,* one of the most important kingly virtues. Unfortunately, we almost never have evidence to explain what motivated Henry's behavior.

In Saxony, Henry's position was at first so strong that he could seek out the most important places in the region and use ecclesiastical festivals to present himself as would-be king: he celebrated Palm Sunday in Magdeburg and Easter

in Quedlinburg, following royal custom. Already in Magdeburg he began negotiations with the attendant princes, with the goal of convincing them to recognize his kingship. The majority of the magnates, however, countered this
demand with the pretense that they needed first to obtain the consent of their
current king—the young Otto.²⁵ The form this permission might have taken is
unclear. Would it have been through the child himself or his guardian? Apparently the nobles involved were playing for time and working against Henry the
Quarrelsome's plans, as Henry himself immediately recognized. His public
indignatio, his displeasure at the way some Saxons were hanging back, motivated these nobles to withdraw from Magdeburg and to discuss in secret meetings possible measures against Henry.

Up to this point, Henry the Quarrelsome's supporters still dominated the
public scene. At the Easter festivities in Quedlinburg they publicly greeted
Henry as king and honored him through ecclesiastical *laudes,* the formal
songs of praise addressed to a ruler. Many of those present at Quedlinburg paid
him homage, and "swore their support to him as king and lord."²⁶ In this
regard Thietmar particularly singles out Dukes Mieszko of Poland and
Boleslav of Bohemia, as well as the Abodrite prince Mistui. Mistui's presence
at Quedlinburg is especially surprising because only the year before he had
attacked and destroyed Hamburg during the Slav rebellion.²⁷ That a long list of
bishops was ready to support Henry's candidacy also demonstrates the domi-
nance of Henry's supporters at this time. Among them was Archbishop Giselher of Magdeburg, whose activities during this Easter week are unknown.²⁸

We are better informed about the reaction of Henry the Quarrelsome's
opponents. After leaving Quedlinburg they met at Asselburg, and agreed to
resist Henry's attempt to seize the kingship by forming a compact, a *coniuratio.* It is important to note that this form of compact by oath was a common way in which the Saxon nobility dealt with political issues from the
tenth century on.²⁹ The nobles involved met in *urbes* or *civitates,* that is in
fortified places, and effected their political agreement with an oath obliging
those swearing to act toward a common goal. This *coniuratio* thus offered a
particularly effective political coalition against enemies—including the
Ottonian or Salian kings. Thietmar names the most prominent participants
in the Asselburg meeting: Duke Bernhard of Saxony, Margrave Dietrich from
the northern march, Ekkehard (the later margrave of Meissen), Counts Bio
and Esiko of Merseburg, Bernward (the later bishop of Hildesheim, whom
Thietmar designated at Asselburg as "count and cleric"), along with a whole
series of further Saxon counts. The *milites* of Saint Martin (the vassals of the

archdiocese of Mainz) were also present. Aside from these men, no representatives of spiritual institutions are named.³⁰ Henry the Quarrelsome immediately recognized the danger of this sworn association. As soon as he learned
of the *coniuratio,* he moved with a strong military force from Quedlinburg to
Werla, either to disperse his opponents or to reach a peaceful agreement with
them. The conduct Thietmar reports is typical of the age: brewing conflicts
evoked a characteristic mix of threatening military gesture and offers to
negotiate. It was typical to confront an opponent with strong military force
and to threaten him with armed might; at the same time, however, a leader
would send a negotiator to attempt a peaceful settlement of the conflict.
Bishop Folcmar of Utrecht undertook this task for Henry. However, he could
not convince Henry's enemies to submit; he only won their agreement to
meet in the future for a peace conference at Seesen.³¹

As had happened when he negotiated with the West Frankish king, Henry
the Quarrelsome did not consider himself bound by such arrangements made
on his behalf; he immediately set out for Bavaria instead. There all the bishops and some of the counts accepted him very quickly. Then he continued
his journey toward Franconia. His behavior is probably best interpreted as a
conscious policy not to resist opposition by individuals and groups of enemies, but rather to win as many supporters as possible as quickly as possible.
His aim was to force his opponents into a position of weakness.³² His Saxon
opponents used Henry's failure to appear to their own advantage: they
attacked and destroyed Alaburg, in the process freeing Otto III's sister Adelheid, who was living there. Then they returned joyfully to their homes with
the princess and a large amount of booty.³³

After Henry's failures in Saxony and successes in Bavaria, much now
depended on the decision of the Franconian magnates. Prominent among
the Franconian princes who entered into negotiations with Henry at
Bürstadt near Worms, Thietmar names Archbishop Willigis of Mainz and
the Swabian duke Conrad, a Franconian, as preeminent representatives of
these Franconians. The outcome of the talks was unambiguous enough to
spell bad news for Henry: the Franconian magnates were not prepared under
any circumstances to discount Otto III's claim to the throne. This decision
now gave Henry the Quarrelsome a larger view of power divisions within
the realm. He had the choice either to pursue his claims to the kingship
with military force or to give them up. According to Thietmar, Henry
shrank from armed strife. While he was still in Bürstadt, Henry supposedly
promised to restore the royal child to his mother at an assembly in

Thuringian Rohr on 29 June, and in that way demonstrate that he renounced his claims to the succession.[34]

Significantly, a typical strategy of the time, negotiations conducted through mediators, might have delayed indefinitely impending military escalation. Henry the Quarrelsome apparently made a realistic appraisal of his position and prospects, and thus seems always to have regarded a peaceful end to the conflict as a realistic possibility. Not surprisingly, therefore, this peaceful compromise was not entirely to his disadvantage. He certainly did not attain his ultimate goal, the succession to the throne. Still, further negotiations and agreements sufficed to assure his restoration as duke of Bavaria. After the Bürstadt assembly and his agreements with the Franconians, Henry traveled to Thuringia by way of Bohemia. There he transacted similar agreements with his Saxon opponents. These agreements allowed him to remain unmolested in Saxony until the Rohr assembly. From there Henry journeyed on to Merseburg (where his wife, Gisela, had been living up until then), conferred with his vassals, and prepared himself for the negotiations in Rohr.[35]

The *dominae imperiales* also came to Rohr: Otto III's mother, Theophanu, his grandmother Adelheid, and his aunt, Abbess Mathilda of Quedlinburg. All three had been in Italy when Otto II died, and by all appearances had waited there for the outcome of events north of the Alps. But that also means that early on they had either avoided active support of Otto III or seen no opportunity for intervening in the disturbances. When they returned to the north, nearly half a year after Otto II's death, King Conrad of Burgundy accompanied them. Conrad, Henry the Quarrelsome's father-in-law and Empress Adelheid's brother, was certainly the obvious mediator in the difficult negotiations that awaited them.

It is characteristic of medieval narrative sources that we know next to nothing about the specifics of the presumed negotiations, about offers of compromise and about the circle of people who played a part. It is also crucial to remember this when analyzing medieval sources. The sources inevitably focus their attention in a completely different direction. When the great nobles of the entire empire came together at Rohr, "to the astonishment of all who were present and saw it, a star of brilliant light shown down upon the partisan struggle from the midst of heaven, in unheard-of fashion in the middle of the day, as if it wanted to grant God's help to the captive king—a wonderful sign, memorable to posterity. Having seen this, the unjust party quickly reacted with horror, and the aforementioned Henry, deprived by law of his usurped title and kingdom, was compelled to turn over the king to his grandmother, mother, and aunt. Granted mercy at the intervention of his father-in-law, King Conrad, and the princes, he returned sorrowfully to his own homeland."[36] It is evident in this description from the Quedlinburg Annals that one of the author's main interests was typological. The author is eager to connect this journey of the *dominae imperiales* and King Conrad to Otto III to the journey of the Three Kings. A striking meteorological event during the meeting at Rohr perhaps motivated this comparison.

By contrast, Thietmar's report offers more details about the political problems involved in this amicable settlement. According to him, the child was merely turned over to his mother and grandmother, and peace was concluded, with the rest of the arrangements prorogued to a future assembly at Bürstadt. But at Bürstadt, too, there was no final agreement. A great dispute arose instead between Henry the Quarrelsome and Henry the Younger, made duke of Bavaria when the Quarrelsome lost his office.[37] Clearly there was still no consensus on Henry the Quarrelsome's future position. Apparently Henry the Quarrelsome had agreed to renounce his kingly ambitions in return for restoration to his earlier office and honors. But no source so much as mentions this condition. The best way to detect it with reasonable certainty is from the reaction of the current duke. Henry the Younger stood to lose his duchy if such a settlement was reached. Still, opposition availed Henry the Younger, duke of Bavaria, nothing. Forced to yield to preserve the peace treaty as a whole, he was compensated with the duchy of Carinthia, which the duke of Bavaria could claim again only after Henry the Younger's death.[38]

Even though we know nothing about the specific negotiations or the mediators who carried out the confidential negotiations, we are well informed about the results of their activity. This is because the peace agreement and its terms were "published" in several ritual and ceremonial acts. It is possible to understand these scenes as a typical means of public communication in the Middle Ages. The essential points of the peace agreement, arranged confidentially, were promulgated in a public presentation. This assumed an unequivocally staged character. Every step and act was arranged in advance—the players display the new situation through specific behaviors and in that way obligate themselves to act in accordance with their own public conduct.[39] The Quedlinburg Annals give this account of the proceedings, the first part of which took place in Frankfurt:

When the royal child Otto III came to Frankfurt, he [Henry] also came and humbled himself according to custom, to evade the punishment due for his unjust elevation. Humble in demeanor and action, hands clasped, he did not blush to swear his faith under the eyes of the assembled people and in the presence of the imperial ladies who cared for the kingdom, the child's grandmother, mother, and aunt. To them he yielded the royal child whom he had taken captive when he was orphaned and whose kingdom he had torn away by force. In true faith he promised furthermore to serve him, asking nothing but his life and begging only for mercy. But the ladies, as we said, through whose care the kingdom and the king's youth were guided, received him [Henry] with renewed honor, greatly rejoicing at the humble demeanor of such a high man—for that is the custom of the pious, not only not to requite good with evil, but indeed to render good in return for evil. When he was pardoned and raised again to the ducal dignity, they were not only among his friends but also among his closest friends in dutiful love, as the law of kinship urged.[40]

The significance of this scene only becomes clear to the modern reader when it is compared to other descriptions of ritual and symbolic acts. It is notable that in the sources most acts of homage by vassals to lords involved the imposition of hands, the vassal swearing faith with his hands placed within the hands of his lord.[41] But it is evident that the Quedlinburg account describes other elements having nothing to do with homage. The "humble in demeanor and action" and above all the plea for life and mercy belong in this category. But these elements form a central part of the act of submission, the ritual of *deditio*, as it was performed at this time.[42] The essential gesture of *deditio*, the prostration, however, is missing from the ritual at Frankfurt. The way Henry the Quarrelsome's public act of recognizing Otto III was staged at Frankfurt thus suggests a combination, specially tailored for this case, of the act of homage with that of submission. Those who had arranged it had, in effect, made the act of submission milder, by sparing Henry the Quarrelsome the prostration. They did, however, expand the act of homage in turn by demanding a public display of the significant tokens of humility and the plea for life and mercy. This publicly displayed Henry's need to beg for forgiveness from the child-king whom he "had taken captive when he was orphaned and whose kingdom he had torn away by force."[43]

Henry's public acknowledgement of the new political reality was not limited to this single act. Otto III, by now six years old, celebrated the next Easter at Quedlinburg with a large number of magnates in attendance. Among them were Dukes Boleslav of Bohemia and Mieszko of Poland, who there formally acknowledged Otto III and who were sent home again with rich gifts. In a single sentence, however, Thietmar recounts an event that was a second and even more public demonstration of this new state of affairs: "The king celebrated the next Easter in Quedlinburg, where four dukes served him: Henry [the Quarrelsome] as steward, Conrad [of Swabia] as chamberlain, Henry [the Younger of Carinthia] as cupbearer, Bernard [of Saxony] as marshal."[44] It is probably no coincidence that the time was Easter and the place chosen for this demonstration was Quedlinburg. It was there in 984 that Henry the Quarrelsome had celebrated Easter as king; now he served the young king.

Conflicts over the throne came to an end with this festivity. The ruling class had as a whole accepted a new regime under Otto III. Otto's mother, Theophanu, would be regent, with the special assistance of Archbishop Willigis of Mainz and Hildebold of Worms, the head of the court chapel, but also with the dukes.[45]

In conclusion, this crisis of authority during the dispute over the throne is a particularly good case study in both the specifics and the essential characteristics of medieval politics. First it teaches the legal consciousness in a so-called "personal-alliance state." The imprisoned enemy of a ruler, at the moment of the ruler's death, again becomes a full member of the ruling elite. As a member of the royal family he announces—again in accordance with prevailing legal concepts—his claim to the succession. Interestingly, more secular nobles than members of the episcopate had problems accepting him. Apparently those who found it most difficult to accept Henry were those who had already paid homage to the royal child. Not least, Henry's political maneuvering to assume the kingship for himself did not transgress the legal sensibilities of the time. This also shows the mechanisms for compromise, through which Henry the Quarrelsome was able at the very least to regain the position he had held before his imprisonment.

This conflict also demonstrates many general techniques of medieval conflict resolution and reconciliation. People in situations like this did not simply strike out uncontrollably at each other, but employed a completely rational blend of threats and attempts at negotiation. This mixture of methods put a brake on every military escalation in the dispute over the throne, and both sides acted on the conviction that the process of negotiation was the more promising. This conviction also motivated Henry the Quarrelsome when he was compelled to renounce his ambitions for the crown. It throws a remarkable light on this man's political reasonableness, something the nickname scholars have given him has perhaps permanently discredited.[46] A third and most notable point evident in the course of this crisis over the throne is the peculiar character of public conduct in the Middle Ages. Scholars have largely ignored this issue. Rituals, demonstrative acts and symbolic deeds, were all theatrical devices to publicize claims, objectives, or new circumstances. That such devices multiply significantly in times of conflict justifies us in seeing them as a basic means of medieval communication. Since the negotiation and reasoning behind decisions remained private, the parties involved used gesture and ritual to publish these decisions. From this single short period, examples include the (clever) public submission of the Saxon counts to Henry the Quarrelsome, Henry's imposition of hands in Frankfurt, and his service at the table of the royal child in Quedlinburg. All of these acts required intense confidential negotiations before they were effected. To judge from their mature techniques of amicable conflict resolution, the ruling elite of the tenth century were by all appearances in a good position to carry out such negotiations.[47]

The Regency of the Empresses

Recently, scholars have more thoroughly examined the political and personal profile of the Ottonian ruling women. This resulted in part from celebration of the thousandth anniversary of Empress Theophanu's death, which encouraged scholarship.[48] But the truth of the matter is that the regency of Empresses Theophanu and Adelheid for the underage Otto III has always been of special interest. Contemporaries viewed positively the actions both empresses took for the young king, and modern scholars still accept that assessment. Despite "the weakness of her sex," Thietmar of Merseburg writes of Theophanu, "she guarded her son's rule with masculine watchfulness in steady friendship toward the law-abiding, in terrifying superiority toward the rebellious."[49] Without doubt this judgment is an unassailable fact. The long period of regency, from 985 to 994, in fact remained largely free of conflicts and crises. Its very peacefulness speaks positively for the quality of the regents. Still, and significantly, Thietmar was not impartial. His sympathies were conditioned to a large extent by whether somebody had been involved with the dissolution of his own bishopric of Merseburg or its refoundation. Theophanu was involved in the latter.

The positive tenor of contemporary reports, however, has resulted in a tendency to assume grand political motivations behind the actions of the regents. As a consequence, Theophanu's eastern, Italian, and western policies are accorded a creativity scarcely seen even in the adult males who ruled in their own names during the tenth and eleventh centuries. The source of Theophanu's presumed talent for sophisticated political thought is usually attributed to her Byzantine background and the knowledge she had acquired there of international policies.[50] Many factors argue against that conclusion. Above all, it is suspicious when the governmental policies of medieval rulers are attributed to ideas more in accord with the way modern people understand politics than their own time.[51]

Moreover, this scholarly tradition is burdened with a fundamental problem: it assumes an articulated ideology behind events. It is most rare to see behind a political event to the ideas of the participants, what these ideas in fact were, and even whether those ideas shaped the outcome of the event. The danger of misunderstanding is particularly great when there are few facts upon which to base an analysis. This is especially the case for the period of the regency. Before seeking to understand underlying motivations, therefore, it is necessary to begin with an account of what really happened in this period, the decade between 984 and 994. Only then can one appropriately ask what clues the sources provide for any reasonably articulated policy on the part of the regents.

To explore the practical administrative policy of the regency it is important to keep in mind that all evidence for the issuing of charters, typical activity for Otto III's chancery, dates only from October 984.[52] It is possible to discuss conscious administrative policy only from that time on. The court chaplains from the chapel of Otto II were kept on, and the chancellor Bishop Hildebold of Worms and the arch-chaplain Willigis of Mainz oversaw their activities. Both bishops appear so frequently in charters alongside the regent Theophanu in the years following 984 that their influence on the regency is not in doubt.[53] Royal charters from the regency record activities that allow instructive insight into structures of power and ways to exert influence at court. They also reveal that most magnates were intensely involved in the governance of the empire.[54] Clearly, the empresses' regency depended more on consensus by the great nobles than was customary for kingship in the Middle Ages. It is very difficult to separate influence and power within this circle of advisors, since the sources give only rare evidence concerning the specifics of decision making or indeed of dissenting positions.

All available evidence is necessary to determine, as far as is realistic, how the regency functioned. Part of this is an examination of underlying assumptions. For example, the *vita* of Bernward recounts in detail the rules of the game for operating in the circle around the young king. This is central to its account of the events involved in the so-called Gandersheim controversy.[55] In 987 Otto III's sister Sophia, according to the account, refused consecration as a nun by Bishop Osdag of Hildesheim, who had proper authority over the convent of Gandersheim. She approached Willigis, the archbishop of Mainz, who promised to bestow the nun's veil on her "without considering how much he thus injured ancient canon law." According to the Hildesheim account, Willigis's presumptuous behavior exceeded all bounds: he did not, as was usual, request permission to enter the diocese of Hildesheim, but commanded his Hildesheim "brother" and "fellow bishop" to come to Gandersheim for the investiture of the Gandersheim nuns. When Willigis was privately and cautiously rebuked for this, he responded, "stirred up with warning look," that Gandersheim belonged to his diocese. The Hildesheim bishop was not intimidated by this reprimand. He instead continued the argument on the very day set aside for the consecration of the nuns. The royal child, Otto III, and his mother, Theophanu, as well as several bishops and princes were present for the argument. The disagreement came to no resolution; instead, the bishop of Hildesheim had his episcopal throne set up by the altar, in order to defend his rights as diocesan bishop. And he succeeded. The people of Hildesheim agreed with his position: "almost all favored him, because the archbishop's animosity displeased them, even though through fear of him they did not show it openly."[56]

The tale permits insight into the dynamics of power at Theophanu's court. At least according to the Hildesheim viewpoint, the empress was in no position to hinder the arrogant and uncanonical behavior of the Mainz archbishop. His power within the regency in this way is clearly revealed. The bishop of Hildesheim was not intimidated. He defended his rights through the physical act of placing the episcopal throne beside the altar, through which he forcefully demonstrated his claim to carry out the liturgical ceremony. Such an alarming escalation of the dispute, which in other circumstances would have resulted in armed conflict, fortunately was avoided at Gandersheim. From the Hildesheim perspective, the behavior of the Mainz archbishop was responsible for this: "He who previously had promised all scarcely obtained the right to celebrate mass at the high altar that day and then only with Theophanu and the bishops pressuring and he himself requesting it in a nearly unbelievable fashion. The two bishops agreed to veil the lady Sophia together, while Lord Osdag alone invested the other nuns."[57] In a subordinate clause, the Hildesheim account mentions a detail of the event significant for evaluating influences at court: the archbishop's request, made "in nearly unbelievable fashion," gained him the support of Theophanu and the other bishops. Just as a king could not refuse the petition of a prostrate suppliant, so too did magnates have the option of making a request that put the whole of their influence in the balance but that the ruler must weigh in their favor. What appears a passing reference in the source in this way offers a realistic impression of power relations and interactions within the court. Other cases of royal minorities, in regencies such as this one, offer other examples of how high-handedly and arrogantly bishops behaved. Hatto of Mainz, Anno of Cologne, or Adalbert of Hamburg-Bremen are famous examples of this behavior.[58] Frequently such conduct gave rise to serious conflicts. Certainly it attests to Theophanu's aptitude, that she could avoid an escalation of the conflict—and not only in this case. Her regency is best imagined as an effort to navigate between the claims and presumptions of different interests and interest groups, charting a course that left only narrow parameters within which she could assert her own creative will.

Scholars' positive judgment of Theophanu's political actions are based on a number of areas, of which her so-called western policy is best examined first.[59] As already mentioned, Otto II had already been engaged in armed disputes over Lotharingia. A surprise attack against Aachen prompted Otto's campaign through northern France and his subsequent siege of Paris.[60] In addition, Henry the Quarrelsome, as part of his scheming after Otto II's death, had established contact with the West Frankish king Lothar. Scholars have pinpointed the principles Theophanu followed in her western policy: a constant watchfulness accompanied by constant readiness to attack. By these means she is supposed to have prevented the threatened loss of Lotharingia. Older research here postulated an early form of "watch on the Rhine," although in this period the Rhine certainly did not mark the border. Evidence for this assessment in the sources is sparse. First it is significant that important East Frankish sources such as Thietmar of Merseburg or the Quedlinburg Annals did not mention the threat to Lotharingia at all. Nor did Richer of Rheims, the contemporary West Frankish historian, so much as speak about Theophanu and her policies. Our knowledge of certain incidents rests entirely on Gerbert's letters, written on behalf of various people intensively involved in the inner conflicts of the west.[61] In part, these letters only hint in passing at the disputes. And yet, it is clear that again and again Theophanu's demands led to, or influenced, the need for peacemaking through mediation. This was not at all surprising, since Theophanu, because of her kinship to the disputing parties as well as her

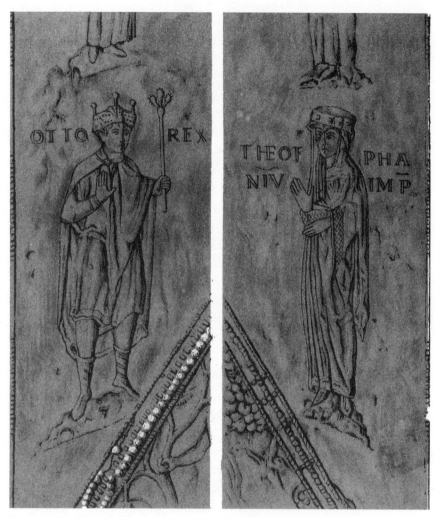

Figure 2. Otto III with his mother, Empress Theophanu. From the Codex Aureus of Echternach. (photo: AKG Berlin)

position, was the most suitable mediator. Techniques for peaceful resolution of conflicts through mediators, as attested on all sides for conflicts in the upper class at this time, until now have prompted little scholarly interest. As a result, they have never been analyzed as background for Theophanu's participation in West Frankish–Lotharingian conflicts. Nevertheless, they form the core of the empress's engagement in a "western policy."

Political activity by the women of the West and East Frankish ruling houses is attested as early as the year 985. Two of Gerbert's letters, to Duchess Beatrice of Upper Lotharingia and to Bishop Notger of Liège, refer twice to a *colloquium dominarum,* a "meeting of the ladies" in Metz. This gathering apparently had a peacemaking function.[62] Gerbert wrote both of these letters on behalf of Archbishop Adalbero of Rheims. The meeting may have actually taken place, because Gerbert congratulates Beatrice in a later letter on a success: "peace established among the princes, the state well ordered, and through you turned to better things."[63] Still, the congratulations are not necessarily connected to a meeting of the ladies. Unfortunately, little is known of the agenda of the colloquium or its participants. Peace with Henry the Quarrelsome might have been its central purpose, but perhaps also stabilization of Lotharingian relations. Besides Duchess Beatrice of Lotharingia (Hugh Capet's sister), the participants may have included the following ladies: Empress Theophanu, Abbess Mathilda of Quedlinburg, Queen Emma (wife of King Lothar and daughter of Empress Adelheid), Queen Mathilda of Burgundy, Adelheid (Hugh Capet's wife), Gisela (wife of Henry the Quarrelsome and daughter of King Conrad of Burgundy), and also Gerberga (sister of Henry the Quarrelsome and abbess of Gandersheim).[64] Thus a great majority of ladies of royal blood were possibly in attendance. However, there is no concrete information that they were actually there. It is more significant, however, that ladies of the royal houses played a special role in mediation and peacemaking. On this point Gerbert's letters leave no doubt.

This observation also is reinforced by further evidence. A letter from Queen Emma, written in 986 to her mother, Empress Adelheid, asks for her mediation with Empress Theophanu. After the death of her husband, Lothar, Emma was banished and also accused of improper relations with Bishop Adalbero of Laon. In this thoroughly unpleasant situation, during which Emma was expelled from her son's court and apparently took refuge in Rheims, she hoped to improve her situation through the intervention of Adelheid and Theophanu.[65] The epistolary distress call was apparently heeded. Adelheid set out for Theophanu's court after receiving the letter— although it is only a surmise that the letter prompted the journey.

In 987 the princesses again attempted to bring peace among enemy factions. Again Duchess Beatrice took the leading role. At her initiative Empress Adelheid, Duke Conrad of Swabia, King Louis, Queen Emma, and Duke Hugh Capet supposedly met to discuss peace.[66] At first, Empress Theophanu was not asked to this meeting, which gives pause for thought, although Archbishop Everger of Cologne might have represented her.[67] The mediation of royal and imperial women is detected a fourth time in July 988, when the newly elected king Hugh Capet wrote to Empress Theophanu that his rival Carl of Lower Lotharingia had failed to accept the mediation proposals that the empress had made in their dispute, while Hugh himself had been ready to fulfill all her conditions.[68] To establish friendship with Theophanu in perpetuity, Hugh continued, he wanted to send his "companion and sharer in the kingship" Adelheid, that is, his wife, to a meeting with Theophanu at Stenay on 22 August. He promised that everything the two ladies agreed upon there would be permanently binding both for him and for Theophanu's son Otto III, "without deceit or fraud." Apparently the meeting did not take place. Still, Hugh's plan shows yet again the apparently key role of female rulers and female relatives in bringing about peace through negotiation. The activities discussed here are by no means isolated. Instead, the role of intermediary in conflicts for the women of royal and princely houses seems customary. They were prominent intermediaries between the parties in a conflict, and their recommendations for conflict resolution rested on their authority as mediators.[69]

Theophanu and her court, according to all appearances, engaged forcefully in the process of peacefully ending the conflicts in the west and in Lotharingia, using all means available at the time. However, many of the initiatives for mediation on both sides appear unsuccessful, although we cannot say why. On the whole, it would be wise to tone down high praise for the significance of Theophanu's western policy. Not every visit of the court to the western part of the empire was necessarily a reaction against West Frankish desire for conquest.[70]

During the regency, the situation in the east was even more complicated than in the west. In the east, the Liutizi rebellion of 983 had been a massive setback for Ottonian missionary policy, and the penetration of German rule to the territory east of the Elbe had also come to nothing.[71] It is true that Saxon military musters led by bishops and margraves had been able to prevent a still worse state of affairs. Still, the unstable situation on the border demanded the full attention of the regency—not least for conducting retaliatory attacks.[72] In addition to the non-Christian Slavic tribes, however, the Christian dukes of Poland and Bohemia, Mieszko and Boleslav, also played a considerable role in the concatenation of forces on the eastern border. In 984 they had unmistakably supported Henry the Quarrelsome.[73] Mieszko and Boleslav were also locked in rivalry with each other, so that friendship with one would likely precipitate enmity with the other. The Saxons and Otto III made a coalition with Mieszko of Poland first, who gave them military support for campaigns against the Elbe Slavs in 985 and 986. Otto III, then six years old, personally took part in the campaign of 986. Mieszko of Poland supported him with a strong force and interestingly paid him homage on this campaign. The sources also expressly state that Mieszko used this as an occasion to give Otto III a camel.[74] Several campaigns, both with and without the king's participation, took place during Otto III's minority. They appear generally successful. For example, in September 991 a Saxon army accompanied by the king besieged and took Brandenburg.[75] The goal of these immense military campaigns is not clearly apparent. Perhaps it was revenge for the defeat of 983. A strategy of reconquest or indeed improvement of the former defensive positions is not in evidence.

Perhaps it is completely anachronistic to regard the battles on the eastern border as part of a concerted policy for conquest and subjugation of territory. That these battles took place in accordance with different rules and conditions than modern observers expect is much clearer in two events from this period that the sources fully report. The story of the Saxon Kizo, which Thietmar of Merseburg considered worthy of detailed narration, is particularly illuminating.[76] Kizo, a "famous knight" [*miles*], perhaps a kinsman of the famous Margrave Gero, felt that Margrave Dietrich had treated him unjustly. Because Kizo saw no other possibility of gaining his rights, he defected to the Elbe Slavs. His behavior was similar to that of another famous rebel of the tenth century, the Billung Wichmann the Younger.[77] The Liutizi tested Kizo's dependability and then put him in charge of the fortress of Brandenburg so that he would have enough opportunities to do harm to the Saxons. Some time later Kizo reconciled with the Germans, at which time he surrendered himself and the fortress to Otto III. This in turn incited the Liutizi to a violent attack. By now Kizo, with the help of the Saxons, could successfully defend the fortress. However, he later lost it again because of the disloyalty of one of his own *milites,* a man with the Slavic name Boliliut. Kizo was killed in the attempt to regain Brandenburg. Thietmar of Merseburg does not represent Kizo's conduct as traitorous. On the contrary, he expressly praises this Saxon's courage and warlike feats—as, by the way, Widukind of Corvey had already done in the case of Wichmann Billung.[78] To change sides when one has been treated unfairly or offended by his own side is not usually considered honorable. In this case, though, the non-Christian Elbe Slavs did not seem surprised by Kizo's behavior either. They apparently gave troops to such "turncoats" gladly because they were impressed by their warlike abilities. The lesson of this tale is that relations on the eastern border were not at all like those between warring states that are concerned with the reconquest of land and that have a central command to coordinate all activities. Saxon margraves and bishops active even without the king and without his mandate were apparently motivated by a longing for revenge and a greed for booty or tribute.

We are also indebted to Thietmar for two stories that reveal the complexity of relations and the complications of alliances.[79] Conflict broke out between Mieszko of Poland and Boleslav of Bohemia in 990. Both sought allies. Mieszko found help from Empress Theophanu; Boleslav made an alliance with the Liutizi. The empress sent Archbishop Giselher and several Saxon margraves from Magdeburg with "four weak troops" against Boleslav. When they met Boleslav, one of the duke's advisors counseled against battle because the Saxons were well armed. This allowed the duke of Bohemia to immediately make peace with the Saxon contingent. But this was not all. The Saxon leaders sent their troops home while they themselves went on with Boleslav to intercede for him with Mieszko, in other words, to negotiate a peace. Having reached the Oder, Boleslav sent an intermediary to Mieszko with the news that the Saxons (Mieszko's allies) were now in Boleslav's power. If they surrendered the conquered land, Boleslav would let them go free; otherwise he would kill them. Mieszko refused the demand; under no circumstances was he willing to suffer harm on their account. Still, Boleslav did not carry out his threat. Quite the contrary. He released the Saxon magnates at dawn, ordering them to hurry, because his allies the Liutizi would certainly use the opportunity to capture them. With the argument that "it would be neither honorable nor smart for us to make good friends into open enemies," he succeeded in keeping the Liutizi from immediately pursuing the Saxons, so they were able to reach Magdeburg unmolested. This detailed account, too, teaches that we should not imagine the fronts too inflexibly. Besides this, it betrays a notable independence of action by the Saxon leaders, who could on their own authority make peace and dismiss their troops. Thietmar ends the tale with the statement: "the empress rejoiced at the report of their luck." Quite clearly, the regency took no offense at the behavior of the Saxon magnates either.

In this period of battles and coalitions, though, there is one event that the available sources make particularly difficult to interpret and place in context: Duke Mieszko of Poland's gift of the *civitas* of Schinesghe (Gniezno) to the papacy.[80] Analysis of this act has sparked much controversy. Various scholars have made widely bifurcated arguments about this gift: that it worked against imperial interests, or that it was negotiated by one of the regents.[81] The sources, however, give no evidence that any power within the empire took part in this donation. This issue will arise again in the context of Otto III's policies in favor of eastern independence, plans that reached a high point in the foundation of the archbishopric of Gniezno. Otto's new eastern policy could be connected with Mieszko's donation, but the state of the sources renders this unclear.[82] Despite this lack of evidence, recent scholarship has credited Theophanu with an eastern policy that consciously promoted this ecclesiastical independence of Poland, supposedly on the basis of her advocacy for the monastery of Memleben, characterized specifically as a "sally-port" to the east.[83] According to this interpretation, which again applies analogies from Byzantine missionary policy, Theophanu by favoring a missionary monastery presumably consciously countered the claims of the archdiocese of Magdeburg to supremacy over the missionized regions. First of all, such theories are mostly without basis in the sources. There is no concrete evidence that Memleben served a missionary purpose, not to mention any evidence that it was designed to take over a missionary function usually carried out by the bishoprics and the archbishopric. There is also no evidence that Theophanu initiated any changes in mission policy. The only hint in the sources that Memleben played any missionary role comes from the nomination of Bishop Unger of Poznán as abbot of this monastery.[84] This, by the way, was after Theophanu's death, when Unger made an exchange with Empress Adelheid. However significant Unger of Poznán's appointment as abbot of Memleben may be, it simply does not suffice for reconstructing an eastern policy supposedly planned by Theophanu.

What scholars have understood as Theophanu's Italian policy, on closer examination, comes down simply to one journey she made to Italy. Without doubt, this had a straightforward purpose: to visit her husband's grave on the anniversary of his death, 7 December, and to pray there for his soul. Theophanu met in Rome with Bishop Adalbert of Prague, who was making a pilgrimage to Jerusalem. She convinced him with generous gifts to contribute his prayers for Otto II's soul.[85] That Otto III did not accompany his mother on this trip to Rome probably explains why Theophanu issued several legal documents in her own name during her journey. This was completely unprecedented. North of the Alps the legal fiction was always preserved that the underage king issued legal transactions himself—the regent's hand in affairs was attested in the charters solely in the form of requests for a particular action. It is logical in this regard to assume that Theophanu's conduct was based on Byzantine precedents.[86] What makes this especially evident is that the three surviving documents issued in Italy give Theophanu's name and title in a masculine form: *Theophanius gratia divina imperator augustus*—if this is indeed something more than a copyist's error.[87]

Theophanu's governmental activities in Italy are known to us from yet another source. In Pavia she attempted a reform of the royal central administration, the *camera regis*. She did so by subordinating the *ministeria* there to her special confidant Johannes Philagathos, whom she also made archbishop of Piacenza.[88] Johannes Philagathos, according to the anonymous author of the *Honorantie civitatis Papie*, was the source of all evils and decline to his city: "When that devil came . . ."[89] Whether or not we should take this accusation at face value, we can still see in it traces of the regent's efforts to transfer leadership of the treasury to a royal confidant. It is impossible to say precisely how effective the archbishop of Piacenza and two helpers were in assuming office and what motivated Theophanu to appoint them. Even a short time later a letter from Bishop Liudolf of Augsburg to Empress Adelheid makes evident that the innovations had had little success: the loyal officers appointed by Theophanu were forced to flee.[90]

Johannes Philagathos, who had been promoted by Theophanu, showed striking self-assurance. When he signed a royal charter as chancellor on 18 April 991, he gave himself the following titulature: "Johannes by the grace of God archbishop and protonotary of the holy Roman Church, first of the counselors and chancellor of King Otto."[91] His control of the royal treasury apparently did not demand daily management, since his duties seemed not to interfere with his accompanying the empress on her return journey to Saxony and turning over the office to two helpers, whom the author of the *Honorantie* describes as "servants."[92] Notable with regard to Theophanu's interference in Pavia is the fact that Empress Adelheid resided there while Theophanu was regent. There is further evidence that Adelheid had been performing administrative functions in Pavia and had presided over the law court. Theophanu's intervention in Pavia, therefore, might also be related to the known rivalry between the two imperial ladies.[93] In any case, when Theophanu came to Italy, Adelheid had already left for a visit to Burgundy.

Theophanu died on 15 June 991 in Nijmegen, before her son Otto came of age. She was buried in the Cologne monastery of Saint Pantaleon, that is, in the church of the saint whose relics she had personally brought with her from Constantinople to the west, and who was quite likely her personal patron.[94] Otto's grandmother Adelheid took Theophanu's place as regent, apparently without difficulty and with the support of the other *domina imperialis*, Abbess Mathilda of Quedlinburg. The "most august of all augustuses," as

Odilo of Cluny called Adelheid in his epitaph,[95] continued the regency without discernible problems, but also without visible changes in policy. The new regency assumed a new shape in but one respect. Archbishop Giselher of Magdeburg seemed to move into a close relationship to the court in the years 991 to 994, as is clear from gifts and the appearance of his name as intercessor on documents.[96] A new policy is equally evident in 992 when Otto III, the imperial ladies, Archbishop Giselher, and many other bishops festively consecrated the cathedral of Halberstadt.[97] In the course of the festivity, the underage Otto laid a golden staff upon the altar of Saint Stephen, symbolically expressing his guarantee of Halberstadt's stability and possessions.[98] Implicit in this was a promise not to try to reestablish the bishopric of Merseburg, which would have been detrimental to Halberstadt. When Otto came of age, he did not honor this promise—perhaps following the wishes of his mother, Theophanu.[99] That Adelheid and Theophanu differed in policy on the vexed question of the dissolution or refoundation of Merseburg is apparent here. It speaks well for the circumspection and skill of both regents that this difference did not generate more serious conflicts—at least none revealed by the surviving sources.

The interpretation of the regency of Empresses Theophanu and Adelheid presented here assumes something of a reductionist character. The accepted scholarly judgment was tested against the sources. The conclusion is that the sources do not support many of the far-ranging plans and conscious policies attributed to Theophanu. To assume them is therefore highly problematic. The methodological principles discussed in the introduction are worth recalling. They are especially justified in analyzing eras with few surviving sources. The fewer the accounts that form a basis for reconstruction, the more arbitrary are inferences of plans and ideas that cause events. Despite this, the positive judgment scholars have made of the regency still stands. Much was probably not as carefully planned as once supposed. The regents did not initiate other events at all. Still, the fact that they succeeded in ruling throughout the long period of the regency without great crises and conflicts is uncontested and uncontestable. And that is surely accomplishment enough, when one considers how rarely such a statement can be made of rulers in this era.

Chapter 2

THE BEGINNING OF
INDEPENDENT RULE

The First Independent Decisions

t may at first seem surprising, in light of so much new research on the regency and guardianship, that we do not know when the regency ended, when Otto III came of military age, or was inducted into knighthood. The sources say nothing of a specific event; it is solely by inference that scholars have suggested a formal "coming of age" supposedly took place at a royal assembly in Sohlingen in the fall of 994.[1] Historians have skimmed over the fact that on 6 July 994 Otto III had already issued a charter whose contents show that at that time he already considered himself of age.[2] On that occasion he gave his sister Sophia the estate of Eschwege—as the document expressly states, because of the request of their mother, Theophanu, on the day of her death (15 June 991).[3] The interval of several years between the expression of these last wishes and their fulfillment could mean that only in 994 was Otto III in a position to carry out the request in a legally binding fashion. But such an interpretation is not compelling. Otto had in fact officially issued a large number of gifts—including for his sister Sophia—in the years when he certainly was still underage.[4] It is not really clear why he should have waited for so long, until his majority, to grant the gift of Eschwege. The context of the document indicates (as the editor of Otto III's charters has already commented) that Theophanu's request was quite general—that Otto should safeguard the *sustentatio* (maintenance) of his sister, robbed as she was of both father and mother. And he therefore simply recalled this request when he made the gift to his sister.

The difficulties in interpretation just discussed make clear how little is known about the beginning of Otto III's personal rule. Any fanfare with which the king might have freed himself from the regents' long-term guardianship and during which he declared himself of age left few traces.

Indeed, only Thietmar of Merseburg reports that after Theophanu's death Empress Adelheid supposedly sought out the young king "to comfort him, and she remained with him, in his mother's place, until he, led by the insolent counsel of youth, dismissed her, to her grief."[5] It is difficult to assess the veracity of this statement, especially since we have a letter from Otto III to his grandmother, composed by Gerbert in 996, that relates Otto's imperial coronation.[6] There is no trace of ill feeling or indeed of discord between the two in this letter. Even if such a rift occurred, however, Otto's banishment of his grandmother, as Thietmar reports it, cannot have fallen at the beginning of Otto III's personal rule. As early as the end of 994 Otto III was evidently in extensive personal contact with Adelheid—and with other female relatives, his sister Sophia and aunt Mathilda. In Sohlingen Sophia intervened in favor of the cleric Burkhard, the later bishop of Worms, and she herself received a further gift there.[7] In late November Otto's Aunt Mathilda, the abbess of Quedlinburg, received a market privilege in Bruchsal at the intervention of Empress Adelheid.[8] And at Erstein, where Otto celebrated Christmas with his sister and grandmother, the king made several gifts richly endowing the monastery of Selz, Empress Adelheid's own foundation.[9]

Between granting these two gifts during November Otto traveled with perceptible haste to Alemannia to deal with another "family affair." This concerned the inheritance of Hathwig, widow of the duke of Alemannia, who had died widowed and childless in August of 994. It is no wonder that the nearest relatives soon met at Hohentwiel—including, most notably in addition to Otto III, Henry the Quarrelsome, Hathwig's brother. The specifics of how the inheritance was divided are unknown. We only learn that Otto III upheld his "hereditary right" over the family monastery of Waldkirch, originally founded by Duke Burkhardt II and his wife, Reginlind, and granted it the same legal position as the imperial monasteries of Reichenau and Corvey.[10] The king's inheritance makes it evident that such monastic foundations were regarded as the private possession of the founder's family and were freely bequeathed. Otto III fundamentally changed Waldkirch's legal position after he inherited it. He did so by subjecting the monastery to "royal right," in other words making it an imperial monastery. In general, the activities of the fourteen-year-old Otto III in 994 for which there is evidence show little striking or new that points to an abrupt change in policy when he took over personal rule. On the contrary, the *dominae imperiales* among his relatives spent much of the year near the king, and Otto readily supported their interests.

The ladies of the imperial family no longer accompanied the king on his travels in 995. However, in the autumn of that year they were once again gathered at Quedlinburg for the consecration of Otto's sister Adelheid as a canoness.[11] Here, too, gifts and interventions show clearly that the amity between Otto and his kinswomen was undisturbed. A chance survival informs us about Empress Adelheid's self-perception and sphere of activity in precisely this period. A letter from Adelheid to a Würzburg cleric preserved in the Tegernsee letter collection records that she ordered preparation of food and lodging for herself and her entourage for a specific day on her journey from Augsburg to Saxony.[12] More revealing still is Adelheid's choice of titulature at the beginning of the letter. She is grandly referred to in this way: "At the command of almighty God's clemency, Adelheid ruler and augusta at the forefront of the temporal rule of the Christian people" (*Inperitante Dei omnipotentis clementia Adelheida regnatrix augusta regimini christianę plebis temporaliter prelata*). Researchers agree that this letter dates from the period of Otto III's personal rule. It therefore suggests that the shift from regency to personal rule was not too abrupt. Even after the majority of her grandson, the grandmother retained a high perception of her position as ruler. Indeed, all reports show that Otto III's kinswomen were close to him in this period, accompanied him on his travels, and influenced him, carrying out all of these activities with great flexibility. This is clear in the cases of the already elderly Empress Adelheid and of Abbess Mathilda of Quedlinburg, who was entrusted with ecclesiastical business. This is not even to mention Otto's sister, the young canoness.

In the year 995 the young king must also have been occupied with the long-term conflict over the archbishopric of Rheims, although we cannot know the details of his involvement with any certainty.[13] The account of Richer of Rheims, whom historians regard as unreliable, is our only source of information for the conflict. Richer reports that the Roman abbot Leo was sent to the north as papal legate at the beginning of the year. His orders were to call together a synod of both East and West Frankish bishops, who were supposed to settle the struggle over the archdiocese of Rheims raging between Gerbert and Arnulf, rival claimants to the archbishopric. Interestingly, no evidence supports the assumption that the Rheims problem was a "French" concern. In fact, the legate first appeared at the court of Otto III rather than the French court, probably meeting with Otto at the Easter festival in Aachen.[14] King and legate apparently agreed to call a synod for 2 June at the border monastery of Mouzon. The Capetian kings Hugh and Robert, as well as Otto III, were to come, each with his bishops. Richer then tells a scarcely credible tale about an exposed plot of Bishop Adalbero of Laon and Count Odo of Chartres. With Otto III's help they allegedly plotted to seize the French kings at this meeting, with plans to put Otto III in their place. According to Richer, the plot was betrayed, after which the Capetians refused to appear at the arranged place and also forbade their bishops to attend.[15] As a consequence, the synod was all too poorly attended.

We do not know whether Otto III was present at Mouzon, and are equally unable to determine the truth of this story, only recently characterized as "cock-and-bull." Still, the question of the story's factual core—whether Otto III was deeply involved in the conflicts and partisan divisions of the Rheims archbishopric—cannot be swept under the table so simply. After all, both Gerbert and Otto III regarded the Rheims cleric Richer's *History* so highly that they obtained the autograph of the work for their book collection. From there, through the agency of Henry II, it reached Bamberg.[16] Such esteem suggests that they did not regard Richer's accounts as "cock-and-bull stories." In any case, Abbot Leo tried unsuccessfully to settle the conflict in Rheims by negotiating only with the West Frankish kings and bishops. After that, a synod met at Ingelheim on 5 February 996. The outcome is unknown. The choice of venue, however, shows a further involvement by Otto III and his bishops in trying to resolve Rheims's difficulties. At the same time, Otto, using the bishop of Strassburg as his emissary, demanded from Gerbert a written justification of his claim. Gerbert dutifully provided this document.[17] That, however, is the only direct evidence of the young king's personal intervention in the controversy, which was resolved later in 996 at Rome with Otto in attendance. The picture is most unsatisfying. The state of the evidence in the extant sources allows only the conclusion that at the very beginning of his reign Otto III was confronted with the Rheims problems. There is no more detail concerning how the young king personally set out to influence events.

Several activities in the fall of 994, in addition to the assembly at Sohlingen, point to the beginning of the king's personal rule. Margrave Hugo of Tuscany arrived from Italy, and Otto III gave him land in Ingelheim so that Hugo could build a place to stay when he attended royal assemblies.[18] In October of the same year Abbot Hatto of Fulda journeyed to Rome at Otto's orders. This is likely part of the young king's plan to travel himself to Rome, seeking imperial coronation. Further activity at this time focused on another issue, one essential for the dynasty. Already in September 995 Archbishop Johannes Philagathos of Piacenza and Bishop Bernward of Würzburg were en route to Constantinople to negotiate for a bride for Otto III.[19] Significantly, the circle around the king took up the important issue of his marriage immediately after he came of age, and they looked first to the Byzantine Empire. Otto's earliest personal decisions around the time of the Sohlingen assembly reveal what would be his characteristic approach to political appointments: Otto appointed Heribert as chancellor of the Italian branch of the chancellery. Heribert would later become Otto's confidant and archbishop of Cologne. He had already served as one of the young king's tutors.[20] This choice was unusual. Until then, an Italian had always held the position. After Heribert, one of Otto III's counselors, entered royal service, his influence would make itself felt in many areas.[21]

Before he traveled to Rome, Otto needed to attend to business in Saxony, which he accomplished in the summer of 995. He held an assembly in Quedlinburg and launched a destructive raid against the northern Elbe Slavs, with the support of Bohemian and Polish troops.[22] These actions played themselves out entirely within traditional perimeters, and only a single charter reveals any further engagement in eastern policy from this period. This source does not permit any clear insight into the aims and intention behind the action described. It is, however, unusual. After returning from Saxony and while staying in Frankfurt, Otto redefined the diocesan boundaries of Meissen.[23] Otto's initiative expanded the bishopric of Meissen significantly, in addition to multiplying its revenue from tithes. The contents of the charter are most unusual and of clear advantage to Meissen. It is not surprising, therefore, that scholars have widely suspected this document to be a forgery. Thorough diplomatic and paleographical examinations, however, have authenticated it.[24] But the border changes Otto III undertook, according to his own assertion "in the manner of his imperial and royal predecessors," clearly impinged upon regions central to the political struggles of the time. Otto granted Meissen parts of the bishopric of Prague that belonged to Bohemia. He also gave Meissen regions of Silesia that Duke Mieszko had given to the apostolic see. Technically those regions were answerable to Rome, however nominal this overlordship might have been in reality. Otto did all this, if one can trust the charter, only a few months after he had eradicated the Slavníks, the main rivals of the Premyslids for rule over Bohemia. Finally, this charter gave Meissen still more territory, which until then had belonged to the archdiocese of Magdeburg.

Viewed in light of the extremely sensible balance of power formed in this period between the empire, Bohemia, and Poland, with its shifting conditions

and military disputes, this document's attempt to completely realign ecclesiastical jurisdictions appears to a certain extent utopian. Doubtless, Poland
and Bohemia, as well as Magdeburg and Rome, opposed such changes in order
to preserve their own vital interests. That these alterations were made in a
fashion unacceptable in canon law, that is, if the king carried them out without synods and the consent of the bishops involved, adds another difficulty.
Still, on the basis of this document alone, there have been many attempts,
most very controversial, to reconstruct the young Otto's supposed early eastern policy. Historians have suggested that the changes outlined in the gift to
Meissen were significant and central to a larger plan for the eastern border.
Scholars have even claimed to know who convinced Otto to take such an
action, although, oddly, no such person is named in the document itself, even
though documents normally included the names of those who intervened to
win gifts and favors.[25] If the document was part of a broad policy, however, the
ruler must have soon reconsidered the matter. There is no evidence that the
redistribution was actually carried out as described. Nor is there any trace of
opposition to it. All of this makes the account of Meissen's expansion
extremely problematic. This circumstance forces historians to admit that a
convincing explanation of this isolated piece of evidence has been lacking
until now. If it was the core of the ruler's new eastern policy, this grant to
Meissen would in any case have completely ignored old interests and well-
developed power relations. But more evidence than this one charter is necessary to accuse the young Otto of such a weak grasp on reality. The royal
charter for Meissen confirms what was said in the introduction. It is better to
admit ignorance on specific issues than to manufacture apparent certainties
that create more problems than they resolve.

Two months after issuing this royal document Otto III undertook his first
expedition to Italy. While he was still in Regensburg, though, events tran-
spired in which it is extremely difficult to evaluate Otto III's personal characteristics and motivations. In 994 Otto III had imposed his chaplain
Gebhard as bishop of Regensburg, thus to all appearances overriding the
interests of the duke of Bavaria, Henry the Quarrelsome.[26] This Gebhard fell
into conflict with Ramwold, abbot of the Regensburg monastery of Saint
Emmeram. While the king was visiting Regensburg, Bishop Gebhard now
tried to prevent a meeting between the abbot and the king—according to the
account written at Saint Emmeram's—so his intrigues would remain undis-
covered and unpunished.[27] It was the confidant and chancellor Heribert who,
despite Gebhard's machinations, arranged a meeting between king and

abbot. The king made a visit to the monastery, as was customary. There the abbot and monks prostrated themselves by way of greeting. This prompted Otto III to grant the abbot an interview. They had a long conversation tête-à-tête, in the course of which the abbot was able to show that all the accusations made against him were false. Once he was convinced of the truth, Otto III confessed his sins to Abbot Ramwold. Our account explicitly states that Otto returned weeping to his entourage. Immediately he summoned the bishop of Regensburg and made a judgment in favor of the abbot and the monastery.[28]

This account is clearly partisan and devoted to the praise of Saint Emmeram and his monastery. What can it tell us about how the rules of interaction between the king and his subjects played out in the tenth century? First: there was apparently no unrestricted access to the ruler. To bring a petition before the king, a person needed the mediation of someone in the king's trust. This need for a go-between was the basis of the power and influence of his "associates," who had the power to grant or withhold access to the ruler. Further: this incident shows the visible form that a request could take. In this case it was through wordless prostration, which the king received graciously by drawing the abbot aside to speak about the problem. It is not easy to evaluate what was going on here. Was this an especially expressive and successful chess move by the monks that caught the ruler by surprise, impressed him, and won him over to an unplanned conversation? Or are the specifics described only the ritual forms that preceded an already-planned meeting and hearing? We cannot answer this question on the basis of the Saint Emmeram account alone. However, numerous comparable ritual acts are described in sources of the time. They suggest strongly that what we see at Saint Emmeram's was a staged public act. The monastery as well as the ruler ritually demonstrated their readiness for petition and discussion.[29] It is harder, though, to explain the confession and tears with which Otto closed the scene. The demonstrative elements of these interactions are clearly visible, although the rationale behind the actions remains unclear. Through his confession the king recognized the integrity and indeed the religious authority of the abbot; through his tears Otto may well have demonstrated ritually his regret for his hitherto negative attitude toward the abbot and monastery and his wish to change it. This proposed interpretation cannot be determined conclusively on the strength of one story; but there is a river of ritual tears in comparable situations to support such a view.[30] Whether or not these events actually played out in this way, one must understand the rules for the game of interaction with the king in the tenth century in order to interpret the history. Without this perspective, one can never understand the forms interactions took. This knowledge also prevents us from using the story to establish the young ruler's religious sensibilities. For the question of Otto III's personal religiosity, his overt actions are not useful evidence.[31]

The First Italian Expedition

Like his behavior in the city, the king's departure from Regensburg for Italy was a public ritual: he rode from the city to the accompaniment of psalms, and had the Holy Lance carried before him.[32] In Verona, too, we again hear that Otto acted in a way that drew from the arsenal of royal governmental practice with its expressly ritual overtones. In accordance with tradition, the Italian magnates were waiting for the king at Verona after he crossed the Brenner Pass. Otto marked the occasion by creating a bond of spiritual kinship with the doge of Venice: Otto stood as sponsor in the confirmation of the doge's son.[33] This was a significant sign of alliance: the confirmand in such a case even took the name of his sponsor. The political implications of this alliance were readily visible even while the ruler was still in Verona. At an assembly (placitum) over which Otto presided, a controversy between Venice and the bishop of Belluno was decided in favor of Venice.[34] By taking on the sponsorship, Otto III confirmed the traditional good relationship between the Ottonians and the doges of Venice. In other words, he was following the traditional lines of Ottonian Italian policy. In the next stages of his journey to Rome, at first everything also unfolded in customary patterns. In Pavia the Italian magnates paid Otto homage, renewing the oaths of fidelity they had sworn in Verona in 983. From Pavia the journey then continued by ship down the Po to Ravenna.

During this period, however, a Roman embassy reached Otto III, to negotiate with him about a successor to the deceased Pope John XV. Before he left Ravenna, Otto settled the question by naming his chancellor and cousin Bruno as successor to the chair of Saint Peter. In doing so, Otto broke away from the typical practice of papal elections, which allowed only for the emperor's consent, not his right to impose a candidate.[35] Archbishop Willigis of Mainz and Bishop Hildebold of Worms afterward escorted the king's candidate, Bruno, to Rome, where he, elevated to the office of pope, adopted the name Gregory V. Historians have considered Otto's interference in Roman affairs audacious and have commented that he seemingly treated the chair of

Saint Peter as if it were an imperial bishopric. The way Otto seized the initiative is certainly remarkable, as is the election of a non-Roman to the papacy. However, we know too little about the party divisions in Rome and the course of events to give a more certain interpretation of Otto III's actions. All that we know for certain is that the urban prefect Crescentius, apparently outmaneuvered by Otto's actions, caused a great stir shortly afterward.

In addition to these activities, the royal court met in Ravenna and condemned a Count Rudolf along with two associates to blinding. This was punishment for oppressing the bishopric and the *pauperes* of Rimini. This judgment is also unusual, indeed unique, against a nobleman in the tenth century.[36] Quite clearly the young king had set out to make his rule fully effective in Italy. On 20 May Otto III himself then made a public appearance in Rome. He was admitted with festive ritual by the senate and nobles of the city, and on the very next day, the feast of the Ascension, he was crowned emperor by his new pope. At Otto III's request, Gerbert of Aurillac drafted a report about these events, addressed to Empress Adelheid. This letter contains no hint of any distance between grandmother and grandson; what is clearer is that Otto offers thanks, in the triumph of the imperial coronation, for Adelheid's "maternal affection, care, and duty" (*maternum affectum, studia, pietatem*).[37] The coronation festivities lasted many days and included a synod in Rome, over which pope and emperor presided jointly.[38] The gathering dealt with a large number of ecclesiastical problems. These included not only Italian issues but also the controversy over possession of the archbishopric of Rheims and the problem of Bishop Adalbert of Prague, who had abandoned his diocese several years before. The Rheims and Prague problems assumed great importance in the career of Otto III, because at this council the emperor became better acquainted with two people who would exercise great influence over him in the future. For this reason, the life histories of both men previous to the synod are discussed in the next section of this chapter. In addition to these major problems, the synod dealt with other difficult themes. A series of confirmations and immunities for Italian bishoprics and monasteries manifested the synod's concern with the question of alienating Church property and with ways to counter this development. These efforts were continued to a greater degree during Otto III's second Italian expedition, among other means in the famous Capitulare Ticinense.[39]

Witnesses from the periphery of this synod, who report an extensive collaboration between emperor and pope, are equally important. The emperor and the pope did not merely share presidency of the synod. Over and above this public collaboration, Pope Gregory intervened in favor of the ecclesiastical recipients of royal charters; for his part, Otto III subscribed to a papal document issued for the nunnery of Vilich. In addition, the pope commissioned the monks of Monte Amiata to pray, not only for the souls of his papal predecessors and successors as well as for himself, but also for the stability of the empire.[40] These reports of collaboration between pope and emperor are important because, supposedly, this unity of purpose and action had already been abruptly destroyed at the coronation synod. This is according to the conclusions of Mathilde Uhlirz, which are generally accepted. Otto III supposedly refused to restore to the pope eight contested counties in the exarchate of Ravenna and the Pentapolis. Moreover, he allegedly refused to recognize the Donation of Constantine and the Ottonianum of 962. This angered Gregory V, or so it is argued, who had adopted the interests of the Roman curia immediately after he took office. According to Uhlirz, the emperor withdrew from Rome with relative haste and, although he remained a long time in central and northern Italy, returned to Germany without seeing Gregory V again.[41] This view of events finds slim support in the sources; its internal logic is weak. It is based solely on one sentence in a letter sent by Gerbert to Pope Gregory V at Otto III's command. There, the emperor writes that "natural necessity" calls him, and he must thus leave Italy for the sake of his health, a turn of events that he claims saddens him greatly. For protection and comfort of the pope he is leaving Margrave Hugo of Tuscany and Count Conrad of Spoleto; the latter would also, as imperial legate, take charge of the contested eight counties (octo comitatus, qui sub lite sunt) and assure that the pope would receive the taxes owing to him.[42] Only Otto's complete donation to the Holy See in 1001, in which eight counties were turned over, and the emperor's argument in this latter document, evidences a serious disagreement or even a rift in the relationship between pope and emperor.[43] Naturally the formulation "sub lite" indicates a conflict about eight counties. However, it is a stretch to theorize from this to a break in the relationship between emperor and pope. Such assumptions anticipate relations during the Investiture Contest that surely cannot have prevailed between Gregory V and Otto III. Gregory V must have been certain that his position in Rome was untenable without imperial support. An immediate defection to the curial position, one in opposition to Otto III, is therefore most unlikely.

Moreover, the close working relationship between the pope and the emperor during that time is clear from the way they handled the Roman urban prefect Crescentius. Crescentius's attempts to dominate the popes were certainly very well known to the court. Otto III sentenced Crescentius to exile, but then pardoned him at Gregory V's intercession and recommendation.[44] Clemency in the treatment of Crescentius no doubt was intended to put him in the debt of both the emperor and Gregory V, and thus to obligate him to good behavior. Even though this hope was later disappointed, such joint action toward Crescentius is clear evidence of a good rapport between Otto and Gregory. The notion that Pope Gregory V, barely consecrated, adopted the principles of curial politics against his imperial cousin thus merits little credence.[45] How much he depended on the emperor's goodwill and support is also demonstrated in dramatic fashion after Otto III's departure from Italy. The imperial officials Hugo of Tuscany and Conrad of Spoleto, already mentioned, were not strong enough to keep Crescentius from driving Gregory V out of Rome.[46] Gregory's flight from the city occurred in late September/early October 996, in other words only a few months after Otto had pardoned the prefect. Despite military efforts, Pope Gregory V was not able to return to Rome until 998, when he had the assistance of Otto III's army. We will see the consequences of Crescentius's behavior later.[47] In the fourteen months of his exile from Rome, Gregory V stayed mostly in northern Italy, several times sending ambassadors to demand help from the emperor. Meanwhile, in February Crescentius succeeded in installing an antipope in Rome in the person of Archbishop Johannes Philagathos of Piacenza, the earlier confidant of Theophanu. Still, he does not appear to have extended his authority beyond the Eternal City itself—if he even wanted to do so. As a result Pope Gregory V, unmolested and publicly acknowledged by all in Italy, could hold a synod at Pavia in February 997 that not only excommunicated Crescentius but also dealt with the urgent problems of Rheims.

But another theme of this synod is still more surprising. Unexpectedly and apparently out of the blue Pope Gregory V with his ten northern Italian bishops brought up the question of legality in the dissolution of the bishopric of Merseburg. Emperor Otto II had suppressed the diocese in 981; at that time the bishop of Merseburg, Giselher, had been elevated to the archbishopric of Magdeburg, a move he himself had urged.[48] In a letter to Archbishop Willigis of Mainz, Gregory V asserted that the *bishop* (not *archbishop*) Giselher had abandoned his see in contempt of canon law and had occupied another by force. The pope ordered that Giselher should appear in Rome at Christmas to atone for his behavior. If he refused, he would be suspended from his priestly office.[49] This formulation clearly indicates that Giselher had been condemned before he was even heard. Researchers have been inclined to consider this unheralded attack on a serving prince of the Church as an outrage. According to the evidence of Otto's royal charters, Giselher stood in high favor. By proclaiming this papal action an outrage, historians have more or less excluded the possibility that Otto III had a part in or perhaps even instigated this proceeding.[50] Here again scholars have sifted through the scanty reports hoping to unearth an underlying rationale and plans. Part of this is based on a theory that Poland and Rome, in other words Boleslav Chrobry and Pope Gregory V, must have plotted together to put pressure on Giselher and thus to hinder the archbishop's active eastern policy. This is even more far-fetched. This attack on Giselher would have been necessary, it is argued, to promote independence for the Polish church.[51] Such an interpretation characterizes Pope Gregory V's behavior and political initiatives not only as independent of the emperor but also solidly against imperial interests. If Giselher had the emperor's confidence during this period and if Otto was not even considering refounding the bishopric of Merseburg, then Otto must have regarded as an affront this alleged alliance of Gregory with Boleslav Chrobry.

In the place of such conjectures, it is a better idea to ask what concrete sources elucidate Otto's position on the Merseburg question. First of all, there is Thietmar of Merseburg's testimony, admittedly a thoroughly partisan source. Thietmar gives a detailed report concerning Otto's position on this matter. "When the emperor grew to adulthood," writes Thietmar, " 'he put away childish things,' as the apostle says. Repeatedly he deplored the destruction of the church of Merseburg and diligently worked toward its reestablishment. For all his life he was concerned with realizing this wish, following the advice of his pious mother. As Meinswind later reported to me, she [Theophanu], according to her own account, had the following dream. In the still of midnight Lawrence, the holy champion of God [and patron of Merseburg], appeared to her with a crippled right arm. He spoke to her: 'Why do you not ask who I am?' 'Lord, I do not dare!' she replied. He however continued: 'I am———' and gave his name. 'What you now observe about me is the fault of your lord, led astray by the words of a man whose guilt has estranged many of Christ's chosen.' Thereupon she laid it upon her pious son's heart, for the eternal rest of his father at the last judgment, that he should see to the renewal of the bishopric, while Giselher was still alive or after his death."[52]

Obviously this account is intended as a moral sermon and thus unworthy of credence. But looked at another way, why should Thietmar attest to

Otto III's great efforts to reestablish Merseburg, which admittedly were not successful, if the emperor had not indeed behaved in that way? Besides, in early 997 there was a most compelling reason, barely mentioned or noticed in earlier research, to reopen the Merseburg question or at least to consider the feasibility of a reestablishment of the diocese. Bishop Hildiward of Halberstadt died in November 996. Hildiward had played a key role in all issues regarding Merseburg, because the diocese of Halberstadt had lost some of its territory to Merseburg when the new bishopric was established. Consequently, it profited from the suppression of the see by getting its property back. Bishop Hildiward had certainly played a large role in the dissolution of the bishopric of Merseburg, even though the sources only hint at it. Without the agreement of the bishop of Halberstadt a refoundation of Merseburg was out of the question.[53] So the vacancy in Halberstadt created an opportunity that had not existed before.

Otto III took action on this issue in very characteristic fashion. He rejected the candidate who was recommended by the Halberstadt chapter (Bishop Hildiward's confidant, the Halberstadt canon Hiddo). Instead he elevated to the see of Halberstadt his own chaplain Arnulf, whom historians have identified as a scion of the highest Bavarian nobility.[54] Arnulf later (in 1004) did not oppose the restoration of the diocese of Merseburg, and one must ask whether such an agreement was not a condition of his election. Pope Gregory V's initiative in Pavia to restore the bishopric of Merseburg came at exactly the same time that Otto III was heavily engaged in the Halberstadt succession. This prevented installation of a candidate chosen to guarantee that Halberstadt's position on the Merseburg question remained unchanged. So if one takes Thietmar's account of Otto III's pro-Merseburg attitude a little more seriously than earlier research has done and also pays attention to the Halberstadt vacancy and its new occupant, Otto III and Gregory V by all indications acted in full agreement on the Merseburg question. Apparently, too, they did not consider the personal consequences for Giselher. Perhaps coincidentally, Giselher's conduct, as reported in the summer of 997, seems to echo the unpleasant situation in which he found himself. For a time he had the duty of keeping military watch at Arneburg. First he was lured into a Slav ambush on the pretext of truce negotiations. Then—and more importantly—he and his garrison left the fortress before his relief, Margrave Liuthar, had arrived. Liuthar only reached the fort after the Slavs had burned it down. Giselher refused to give assistance even in this situation and returned home instead.[55] His behavior does not suggest that he was ready to expend all his powers in the service of the empire at that time. At any event, Giselher was able to hinder or delay until after his death any attempt to investigate his case in Rome. Still, the Merseburg question came up again and again. From 999 on Otto III clearly did not feel any obligation to protect Giselher from this investigation.[56]

Thus, the first expedition to Italy, with the installation of a "German" pope, resulted in a serious intrusion into Roman affairs. That these measures did not solve all problems seems self evident. The effects of power blocs already in place in Rome were also immediately apparent to Pope Gregory V. Without his emperor and the imperial army to back him up, Gregory's position in Rome was untenable. Under these circumstances it is hardly likely that this pope would have immediately attempted to challenge Otto III's power on several fronts, either by supporting old curial positions against imperial interests or by attempting a humiliating investigation of the Magdeburg archbishop without the emperor's agreement. It is therefore logical to assume that these activities, like many others, were in harmony with Otto III's wishes. In conclusion, however, one should note a particular feature of this first Italian expedition: it followed in their entirety the traditional lines of Ottonian policy for Italy. There is yet to be any trace of some sort of "Roman renewal ideology." Otto III traveled to Rome to be crowned emperor, intervened in Roman affairs, and then very quickly vanished again, without—so far as we can tell—any compelling necessity calling him back to the north.[57] Roman and Italian affairs were, as before, left to their own devices.

The Encounters with Gerbert and Adalbert

The first Italian expedition for Otto III was significant not simply for the imperial coronation and the installation of a relative on the papal throne. Besides these major events, while in Rome he became better acquainted with two men who must have made a strong impression upon him—even though their personalities were very different. The first of these was Gerbert of Aurillac. When Gerbert could not maintain his position as archbishop of Rheims, Otto brought him to court and the next year elevated him to the archbishopric of Ravenna and from there to the papacy.[58] The other man Otto met in Rome was Bishop Adalbert of Prague. The two men formed a closer relationship during the following year, the year before Adalbert was martyred by the Prussians in 997. Among other reasons and perhaps above all others, his death prompted Otto III to undertake his famous journey to

Gniezno to pray at Adalbert's tomb.[59] When Otto met both men in Rome, they each were in decidedly fraught situations, in which neither had much chance of achieving his objectives and goals.

Gerbert had been called to Rome over whether his occupancy of the arch-bishopric of Rheims was legal. This controversy had been playing out for a long time. Thanks in large part to the influence of Hugh Capet, the underage Carolingian Arnulf, an illegitimate son of King Lothar, was appointed arch-bishop of Rheims in 989. This office rewarded Arnulf's readiness to abandon Carl of Lower Lotharingia, Hugh Capet's rival for the throne of France. Despite his oath in support of Hugh, however, Arnulf delivered Rheims to Carl. After he had won victory over Carl, Hugh punished Arnulf for his bad faith by deposing him at a synod in Basle-de-Versy. He elevated Gerbert to the archbishopric in Arnulf's stead. However, at this synod Bishop Adalbero of Laon gave a speech, composed by Gerbert, that attacked the papacy in an almost monstrous fashion. Pope John XV reacted by imposing an interdict on Gerbert. Consequently Gerbert was summoned to answer for his conduct at the Roman synod of 996 and in that way came to meet Otto III.[60] Otto had already approached Gerbert in 995 and through Bishop Wilderod of Strass-burg gave him the opportunity to present a legal brief on his position. To all appearances, therefore, the young king showed a certain partiality toward Gerbert, who already had contacts with Otto's father and grandfather.[61] At the Roman synod this partiality did not help Gerbert against his enemies in the curia (among them the reform monasteries with Abbot Abbo of Fleury at their head) or those in the imperial episcopate. The synod reserved a final decision until Arnulf, who was imprisoned at the time, had been heard. But the prospects looked bleak for Gerbert. The young king's self-reliance in decision making is well displayed here. Despite Gerbert's unpromising predicament, Otto took him into his service while they were still in Rome and employed him as notary and a sort of private secretary. So it was only a few days after the synod that Gerbert composed the letter for Otto that noti-fied his grandmother Adelheid of the imperial coronation.[62] After this, to be sure, Gerbert returned to Rheims once again. In fact, he encountered so many difficulties and opponents there that he feared for his life, as one of his letters from this time reports.

By October of 996 Gerbert was again in the Mainz region and spent sev-eral weeks in the company of the emperor. This proximity is very significant because both Gerbert and Adalbert of Prague were in close company with Otto III during a period of more than six weeks in which Otto abandoned all the business of government. As Gerbert himself boasts in a letter, he and the emperor spent day and night in conversation. This statement is even more remarkable because the Roman *vita* of Saint Adalbert and a poem that praises him state that the emperor spent "day and night" with the saint and claim that Adalbert, like a trusted chamberlain (*dulcissimus cubicularius*), shared the ruler's bedchamber. Mathilde Uhlirz has calculated that the time Otto spent with Gerbert must have coincided with the time he spent with Adalbert.[63] The sources make no mention of a third partner in this conversation, who presumably was the source of information. One may nevertheless conclude that at the very least Otto spent a lot of time with both men in conversations held in an atmosphere of trust. This alone is quite unusual. We know, certainly, of medieval kings or emperors who set aside government business for a time and withdrew with their confidants from the affairs of state. But this was normally for hunting, rather than for learned and religious conversations. We know little of the content of the conversations with Gerbert. Gerbert told Queen Adelheid of France only that he had spoken at length with Otto III about a meeting the emperor urgently desired with Robert, the West Frankish king.[64]

A few months after the Mainz meeting Gerbert received an imperial invitation to enter the emperor's service as his teacher, to help him attain a Greek "subtlety" (*subtilitas*) in place of Saxon "vulgarity" (*rusticitas*).[65] Even more than this, Otto wanted Gerbert as a future *consilium summę fidelitatis;* in other words he also hoped to win him as a political advisor. Gerbert's answer followed hard on the heels of the invitation: he asserted, not without flattery, that Otto "by race Greek, by rule Roman," would win again the treasures of Greek and Roman wisdom that were his by hereditary right.[66] Otto's letter has been much discussed and widely characterized as the clearest marker of the emperor's "un-German" temperament. Percy E. Schramm has pointed out that the expression *rusticitas* was common at the time, and so tried to remove any sharpness from the antithesis, arguing that "Political activity for Saxony was very compatible with a tendency toward Byzantine intellectual culture."[67] Other interpreters have tended to see irony in the emperor's remarks, a playful self-belittling, which perhaps sardonically emphasized the all too emphatic speech of his teacher.[68] It is hard to decide. If one accepts the letter at face value, Otto's slighting reference to his earlier education is indeed surprising, since it had been directed by leading scholars. If one reads the remarks as irony, this reveals a mocking-playful relationship with Gerbert. But that would also be surprising after their few encounters, all in politically

Figure 3. Dedicatory miniature from the gospel book of Otto III: The emperor, Otto III, enthroned between two spiritual lords and two temporal lords. Bayerische Staatsbibliothek, Munich. (photo: AKG Berlin)

explosive situations. We know of too few comparable exchanges on the part of Otto III to be sure of the meaning of this text. One thing must, however, be emphasized: although we have a range of evidence about the political collaboration between these two men from the years following, there is nothing there to suggest a special relationship of personal trust and friendship. Apparently Otto and Gerbert were not "friends."[69] In any case, the emperor's invitation to enter his service saved Gerbert from personal catastrophe. When synods that met in Pavia and Rheims definitively confirmed Archbishop Arnulf of Rheims's reinstatement, thus ending Gerbert's claim to office, the former archbishop accompanied Otto III to Saxony to campaign against the Saxons.[70] As was his custom, Gerbert created a sensation with his learning and knowledge. In Magdeburg he built an astrolabe with which he could observe the movement of the stars, and led philosophical disputations that supposedly fathomed the essence of reason.[71] He spent the summer convalescing from an illness on an estate in Sasbach at Kaiserstuhl, a gift from his imperial patron. Then he accompanied the emperor on his second Italian expedition as a member of the court chapel, with the title "musician" (*musicus*).[72] Teacher and student had begun their shared path.

Adalbert of Prague was in equally serious difficulties in 996 when he encountered Otto III in Rome. When considering the details that follow, it is important to know that our only sources for Adalbert are saints' lives and a eulogy.[73] Several years before, in 989, Adalbert had abandoned his bishopric of Prague and, with the consent of Pope John XV, had entered the Roman monastery of Santi Bonifacio e Alessio on the Aventine. In Rome in 989 he met Theophanu, who through her gifts commissioned Adalbert to pray for the soul of her husband. In 992 Willigis of Mainz tried to force Adalbert to return to his diocese. This was after an embassy from Prague had lodged a complaint with Willigis in his capacity as metropolitan with jurisdiction over Prague. After even more bad experiences with the flock entrusted to him, a flock that obstinately rejected the kind of Christian life Adalbert had in mind, he returned a second time to his Roman monastery. At the Roman coronation synod, however, Willigis raised the issue again—"he sang the old song," says one of the *vitae* of Adalbert—and succeeded again in ending the uncanonical situation: Adalbert was summoned and forced to return to his office as bishop. This time, though, Pope Gregory V agreed that if the people of Prague opposed his pastoral efforts again, Adalbert could fulfill his episcopal office by conducting a mission to the non-Christian people to the east. We know nothing of Otto's contact with Adalbert during this affair. We only hear that the Prague bishop was in close contact with the emperor for several weeks in September/October 996, after the latter's return to Germany. It is not impossible that Adalbert accompanied Otto over the Alps. Certainly the bishop made no haste on his forced return to Prague. In addition to a long residence with the emperor on the middle Rhine, Adalbert also visited a whole collection of famous West Frankish monasteries.

More important is the nature of the encounter with Otto III and the quality of the relationship emperor and bishop came to enjoy on this occasion. Our only information comes from the *vitae* of Saint Adalbert, sources that distort the evidence in notable ways. Clear evidence of a close friendship between Otto and Adalbert comes from reports of the emperor's reactions upon news of Adalbert's martyrdom. As I will discuss later, Otto III founded churches dedicated to Adalbert, intensively promoted the cult of Adalbert, and not least made his famous pilgrimage to the martyr's tomb at Gniezno.[74] In light of this later evidence it has gone virtually unnoticed that the pious narratives of the saint's time in Mainz fit entirely within the hagiographical *topoi* standard for depicting such a relationship. This does not mean that these descriptions are worthless, but it is not correct simply to accept them at face value as proof of a close personal relationship. This applies to the report that Adalbert supposedly lived day and night like a "much-loved chamberlain" in the emperor's bedroom and there instructed Otto III in uninterrupted conversations. The same closeness or something very similar is reported of other saints regarding their relationships with other rulers.[75] Without a doubt, the purpose of such tales is to show that the saint had influence on the ruler and that the ruler was willing to listen to him. These stories are, however, unsuitable as evidence of a personal friendship.

The Roman *vita* by Canaparius gives some detail about the content of the conversations. However, this account too is very conventional, essentially nothing but a short composition in the genre of the "mirror of princes." Adalbert, according to this legend, taught the emperor not to regard himself as too great, to concentrate on the fact that he was a mortal man rather than on his imperial office. He should treat widows as a husband, the poor and orphans as a father, fear God, and be a just judge. He should consider how narrow is the path that leads to salvation, and how few are chosen. He should be companion to the good in humility, and restrain evildoers with the fervor of justice.[76] All these instructions are traditional in mirrors of princes. Nothing in the sources reveals a particular personal affinity between saint and ruler. Indeed it must be asked whether the literary genre of hagiography even has room for that sort of statement. Despite all conclusions drawn about the "deep impression" Adalbert made on Otto III and about their close personal friendship, the sources upon which such a valuation is based must be remembered. Thus this is also characteristic of Bruno of Querfurt's *vita* of Adalbert, which is based upon Canaparius's *vita*. While Bruno does mention meetings that lasted all day and night, it is not just teaching the emperor himself but more generally "the king's boys" (*pueri regi*).[77] More than simply a shift in emphasis, this change shows how very difficult it is to use hagiographical texts to reconstruct "reality."

Despite this problem in interpreting the sources, one thing is certain: the young emperor by all appearances was willing to invite close contact with people in great difficulties in the ecclesiastical-political sphere. This held true equally for Adalbert and Gerbert. One must wonder how members of the ecclesiastical hierarchy, especially Willigis of Mainz, reacted when the young emperor withdrew for long conversations with such men, no matter how learned and how exemplary in their rejection of the world his partners in dialogue were. The answer may seem obvious, but it is obscured, because no source speaks of the matter. The matter must rest with that conclusion, which is perhaps not completely satisfying. But the theme of Otto III's personal relations is not closed to further discussion. The encounters and contacts with Gerbert and Adalbert are only two cases among many more that will be examined systematically later in this study.[78]

‡ Chapter 3 ‡

THE "REVENGE EXPEDITION"
TO ROME AND THE BEGINNING
OF THE "ROMAN RENEWAL"

The Fight Against Crescentius and the Antipope

Gregory V had already been exiled from Rome for fourteen months when Otto III set out on his second expedition to Italy in early December 997. Time and again historians have suggested that Otto was kept from this expedition by even more urgent tasks—first by warfare against the Slavs, then by the uncertain political situation in Hungary. However, the sources are not clear about whether the emperor regarded intervention in Rome as a particularly urgent matter.[1] Further, the expedition was no different from other ventures to Rome in regard to the speed of journey and the ruler's activities along the way. Otto found time to celebrate Christmas in Pavia, to hold courts of justice there and in Cremona, and to issue charters in favor of Italians. Also, the doge of Venice apparently was not under the impression that the imperial army was in a great hurry. He sent his son to Otto III on a festively decorated ship; the emperor boarded his godson's ship and traveled in it to Ravenna.[2] We have no idea of the size of the army that marched with Otto on this second journey to Rome. Contemporary documents indicate only that a large number of secular and ecclesiastical magnates accompanied the emperor. These included Dukes Henry of Bavaria and Otto of Carinthia, Margraves Ekkehard of Meissen and Hugo of Tuscany, Bishops Notger of Liège and Wilderod of Strassburg, and also Abbots Odilo of Cluny and Alawich of Reichenau.[3] To these were added northern Italian bishops with their contingents. This information does not necessarily indicate that the levy was particularly large; it is much more likely that the force fell within the usual perimeters for imperial intervention in Italy.[4]

The imperial army found itself on the march to Rome only in the middle of February. The reaction of those concerned differed widely. The ruler of the city, the prefect Crescentius, entrenched himself in the Castel Sant' Angelo,

believed by contemporaries to be impregnable; the antipope Johannes Philagathos fled Rome and took refuge in a fortified tower. The Romans, however,
were certainly shocked by the arrival of the army. They tried to reach an
amicable settlement with the emperor, and were soon successful. The
sources do not say who the leaders of this Roman group were; that is, those
who did not want to join their fate with that of Crescentius and his followers. The *compositio*, the amicable settlement, in any case allowed the
emperor and his army to enter Rome without use of military force.[5] So it was
possible, although at first glance paradoxical, that Otto took possession of
Rome without military opposition, resided there for two months, settled a
legal dispute in the monastery of Farfa, and rewarded his followers for their
service during the Rome expedition. All the while Crescentius sat powerless,
if unassailable, in Castel Sant' Angelo. The emperor does not appear to have
been in much of a hurry to end this situation. Up to this point, therefore,
everything about this Rome expedition proceeded along lines familiar from
the visits of the emperor's Ottonian forebears.

Historical judgment that this visit to Rome was a "revenge campaign"
conducted with unusual brutality is based on the treatment of the two protagonists, Johannes Philagathos and Crescentius, after they were captured.
We must ask, therefore, the reasons behind what was in fact unusually harsh
behavior, which evoked considerable criticism even from contemporaries.
To follow the sequence of events: first a division of the army led by Count
Birichtilo was able to track down antipope Johannes in his hiding place. The
prisoner's eyes, nose, and tongue were gruesomely mutilated, and he was
brought to Rome. Even the author of the Quedlinburg Annals, who otherwise pours poison and gall over this antipope, is unhappy with this treatment. The annalist emphasizes that those who carried out this deed were
not friends of the emperor, but rather friends of Christ, who with their treatment wanted to forestall the emperor's expected mildness.[6] In light of
equally brutal treatment handed out to Crescentius, this excuse does not
stand up at a factual level. Indeed the matter did not end with Johannes's
mutilation. A synod formally deposed the antipope. In accordance with the
rituals of defrocking, the papal robes were ripped from his body and Johannes
was led through Rome sitting backward on a donkey and holding its tail as
reins.[7] The *vita* of the hermit Nilus gives full details about contemporary
reactions. The nearly ninety-year-old hermit had already set out for Rome
when he heard about the mutilation. He begged both emperor and pope to
release Johannes Philagathos to his care. Otto and Gregory received the her-

mit with honor, certainly. However, according to the description in the *vita*, the emperor would only grant the request on the condition that Nilus remain in a Roman monastery with Johannes rather than return to southern Italy. Nilus was so indignant at Johannes's defrocking and subsequent exhibition on a donkey that he left Rome and returned to his monastic settlement at Serperi. Otto III supposedly attempted to convince the hermit to remain, apparently through an eloquent archbishop, perhaps Gerbert of Aurillac (then archbishop of Ravenna). Nilus avoided the flow of words by falling asleep, but not before he issued a forceful warning to emperor and pope: "If you do not forgive him whom God has delivered up into your hands, neither will the heavenly father forgive you your sins."[8]

Interestingly the *vita* of Saint Nilus apportioned blame to emperor and pope most unequally. The author claims that for Otto III "not everything that took place was really according to his will." Gregory V, on the contrary, appears as the relentless one, who instigated the proceedings that publicly stripped the mutilated man of the office he claimed.[9] So it is not surprising that Gregory V's sudden death a year after these occurrences was linked to his brutality against Johannes Philagathos. When the *vita* of Nilus repeats the rumor that Gregory V was murdered and that his eyes were ripped out, it reflects continued bitterness concerning the treatment of Johannes Philagathos.[10] This rumor was perhaps a necessary counterpoint to the antipope's mutilation. Otto III, however, used his residence in southern Italy as an opportunity to make a barefoot penitential journey to Monte Gargano, where he also visited Saint Nilus in his monastic cell at Serperi. It has been suggested that this journey, undertaken "for the sake of penance" (*poenitentiae causa*), was to atone for his harsh conduct in Rome, even though this is not expressly stated in the sources.[11] The Italian sources especially apportion guilt to the main actors and speak of their awareness of their sin and need for penance. But there are also reports that the gruesome proceedings against Johannes Philagathos aroused no self-doubt at all in the participants. As already mentioned, the commander of the division that captured the antipope was, almost certainly, responsible for Johannes's mutilation. This was Birichtilo (Berthold), count of Breisgau, an ancestor of the Zähringers. In the period immediately following these events the sources report that he was twice singled out as the recipient of special honors and gifts. The only conclusion to draw from this is that, far from the deed discrediting him, it won him imperial goodwill to a high degree. For on 29 March 999 he received a privilege for a market, minting, and collection of tolls on his estate at Villingen in the

Black Forest.[12] The market there was given equal status to the markets in Constance and Zurich. This is the oldest surviving market privilege granted to a layman, sufficiently underscoring the significance of the gift. But this was not enough: Birichtilo at the same time was entrusted with the honorable duty of traveling to Quedlinburg as the emperor's representative. Once there, he invested Otto III's sister Adelheid as abbess of Quedlinburg. For this purpose the emperor gave Birichtilo a gold abbot's crosier as symbol of investiture.[13] Both "honors" strongly indicate that Birichtilo had earned the emperor's special thanks; there is no trace of the ruler's disapproval of the treatment meted out to Johannes Philagathos. Certainly the detailed report in the Quedlinburg Annals gives evidence about what the annalist considered the well-deserved fate of the antipope in its report of Birichtilo's journey to Quedlinburg. The annalist's account of the mutilation, so devoid of sympathy, indicates even more strongly that Otto III did not feel guilty or penitent.[14]

This evidence, however, still leaves a question unresolved: how was it that the Roman urban prefect Crescentius and the antipope Johannes Philagathos brought on themselves imperial and papal anger and to such an unbridled degree? Certainly the "merciful king," not the "angry king," accords with tenth-century ideals. Numerous cases demonstrate this ideal expressed in royal acts of *clementia*, in which opponents were forgiven in public rituals and reinstated to their offices and honors.[15] But this well-established strategy was not used to effect a peaceful resolution to the conflict in Rome. On the contrary. When the imperial army arrived in Rome, Crescentius retreated with his supporters to the Castel Sant' Angelo. He did not try by military means to prevent Otto III's entry into Rome. For a full two months we hear of no battles, suggesting that the imperial army was not prepared for a successful siege and storming of the fortress.[16] Only after Easter and the "white" Sunday following Easter do we hear that the siege intensified under the command of Margrave Ekkehard of Meissen. The sources then give special report of siege machines and towers prepared with considerable technical display. Even though some sources speak of the importance of these engines in storming the Castel Sant' Angelo, they still cannot account for the rapid success of the siege. Crescentius was captured and executed only a few days later.[17] Widely varying sources give better information on this point to explain the speedy success of the siege. Several Italian sources report that Crescentius was betrayed, that he was convinced to leave the protection of Castel Sant' Angelo and surrender himself to the emperor because he had received sworn guarantees of safety and the hope of an amicable settlement.

But once in Otto's hands he was condemned to death for treason and beheaded.[18] Two extensive descriptions of the proceedings in the *Fundatio* of the Rhenish monastery of Brauweiler and the work of the Cluniac historian Raoul Glaber expand this interpretation of events and confirm its details.[19] Both accounts are extremely valuable, since they are probably based on eyewitness reports. Raoul Glaber's informant should be sought in the circle of Abbot Odilo of Cluny, who, as a member of Otto III's entourage, was present at the proceedings in question. In fact, the abbot himself may have been the source of information. The connection is not as clear for the *Fundatio* of Brauweiler, which was first written down in the twelfth century. However, Brauweiler was founded by Count Palatine Ezzo, who was married to Otto III's sister Mathilda. Although Ezzo's presence in Rome is not attested, it is conceivable that this report too originated with a high-ranking eyewitness.[20] Both reports contain such interesting details that it is worthwhile to consider them in detail.

The Brauweiler version of the story reports that Crescentius was summoned to the emperor with guarantees of safety and then urged to submit himself and his supporters to the emperor's mercy. Supposedly he vehemently refused. As a consequence, he was allowed to return to Castel Sant' Angelo, accompanied by warriors chosen to guard his safety. But Crescentius's followers started a fight at the very moment he was entering the fortress. In the course of the struggle the emperor's men succeeded in penetrating the fortress and taking Crescentius prisoner. According to this account he was then delivered up to the emperor and sentenced to death.[21] Raoul Glaber's account is similar, but with different emphasis. According to him, when Crescentius could not find a way out of his dilemma, he decided to attempt a reconciliation, although in fact he had been allowed no access to the emperor's mercy. With the collusion of certain unnamed people in the emperor's army, he supposedly crept secretly from the fortress. He then unexpectedly (*inprovisus*) prostrated himself before the emperor, begging for his life from the emperor's mercy (*pietas*). The emperor, reports Raoul, refused with the cynical question to those around him: "Why have you allowed this prince of the Romans, chosen as emperor, who gives laws and appoints popes, to come to the wretched tents of the Saxons? Take him back to his lofty throne, until we have prepared a reception adequate for his honor." Upon this, Crescentius was returned uninjured (*inlesus*) to the entrance of the tower. After his return, according to Raoul, Crescentius announced to his followers that they could only hope to live until the enemy took the fortress. After this Raoul gives a description of the imperial troops storming the fortress and the capture of Crescentius, who had been badly wounded in the fighting. Upon receiving news of Crescentius's arrest, the emperor supposedly commanded: "Throw him publicly down from the highest battlement, so that the Romans will not be able to say that someone has stolen away their prince."[22]

Researchers have treated these reports simply—probably too simply. Some accounts have been pieced together in a simple cumulative fashion as a reconstruction of the event as it really happened, while others were rejected as "obviously legendary and rhetorical ornamentation." This patchwork approach produced the following version of the event. Negotiations for an amicable settlement of the conflict supposedly took place in the midst of fighting for the Castel Sant' Angelo. Crescentius, trusting his safe-conduct, entered the emperor's camp. The negotiations were unsuccessful. But as Crescentius returned to the fortress, fighting is believed to have broken out "for inexplicable reasons." As a result, the fortress was stormed and Crescentius taken prisoner. This chain of events prompted later Italian sources to argue that Crescentius had been deceived, and that the emperor had broken the safe-conduct he had issued.

It is necessary to raise certain objections against such a reconstruction. In the first place, it follows too closely the basic lines of the Brauweiler version of the story and discards the basic claims and particular emphases of Raoul Glaber's version. As a matter of fact, there are no methodologically acceptable grounds for such a decision. The Brauweiler version certainly attests to the accepted practice of peaceful conflict resolution in the tenth century: before or even in the middle of a siege it was normal to attempt a peaceful settlement of conflicts, either personally or through mediators. These arrangements normally included a ritual act of rendering satisfaction by the losing party. For the most part this usually took the form of a public prostration and gestures of submission associated with formal humiliation.[23] But the Brauweiler version of the story lacks credibility in reporting that Crescentius refused to perform a formal submission in hope of receiving his ruler's mercy. That, of course, would have been the most certain and logical way to achieve clemency.

Beyond this criticism—and more significantly—how could a version diametrically opposed to Raoul Glaber's in its central assertions be concocted, especially in light of the reconstruction of events surrounding Crescentius's death described above? Raoul's version asserts vehemently that Otto III refused any negotiation. This state of affairs is stressed several times in the story. Crescentius, who wanted to render satisfaction, was unable to gain access to do so. Therefore he made his prostration unexpectedly, without earlier arrangement with the emperor but instead only with the agreement of certain members of the imperial army. Otto III rebuffed this prostration and plea for mercy with a cynical comment. He ordered Crescentius back to the Castel Sant' Angelo until a fitting reception was prepared—a dramatic threat. According to the story, Crescentius understood the threat in the emperor's words and reported to his followers that there was no hope for mercy if Otto III's troops succeeded in taking the Castel Sant' Angelo. Otto III's theatrical declaration thus fulfilled a very important function. The emperor used it to make clear that he would accept no mediation leading to a peaceful settlement of the conflict, or any offer of submission. Raoul Glaber's version offers an acerbic description of imperial behavior more important than historians until now have assumed. Raoul vividly portrays that the emperor was unwilling to accept a peaceful settlement of the conflict. This was despite Crescentius's intensive efforts, extending to the point of an unexpectedly performed prostration, and despite a faction within Otto's army that advocated settlement.

Yet more evidence supports the view that Otto III and his advisors refused to consider a peaceful settlement. According to evidence in one of Gerbert's letters, the antipope Johannes Philagathos had also attempted negotiation even before the imperial army had reached Italian soil. His offer to negotiate showed that he was willing to do what Otto III wanted.[24] A formula used in this letter, which has not attracted attention, strongly suggests a *deditio*, the act of submission central to an amicable conflict resolution. With the ritual expression "do with me what you will," the submitting party to the contract appears to give himself without reservation into the hands of the victor.[25] Johannes Philagathos was signaling this willingness to submit to his enemies from the north. He did not, however, gain a positive response, as is sufficiently clear from the outcome at Rome and his own fate. Otto III and his circle did not negotiate with Johannes Philagathos either.

Hints that the urban prefect and his antipope were not considered worthy of negotiation are supported by more specific indications in the terminology used in the German sources. For example, Thietmar of Merseburg calls Crescentius a *perversus*. The Quedlinburg Annals claim that he was "deceived by the devil's wiles," and that he installed Johannes Philagathos not as pope, but as "apostate." The Hildesheim Annals assert that Otto III had to purify the

Roman *sentina*—"cesspool."[26] This sort of invective, reflecting with some certainty the opinion of people directly involved, does not suggest a desire to negotiate a peaceful settlement of a conflict with somebody spoken of in these terms. In addition, Gerbert of Aurillac (who in the period in question— 997/998—took up his position as advisor at Otto III's court and also accompanied the emperor on his Italian journey), according to some evidence, had written invective against the Roman urban prefect in quite similar terms just the year before. In the context of the schism at Rheims, Gerbert had stated that the Roman church was subjected to a tyrant and called Crescentius a "limb of the devil." It is certainly not too fanciful to propose that Gerbert saw the Roman church's subjection in 997/998 in a sharpened fashion that influenced Otto III's opinion.[27] The treatment of both Johannes and Crescentius once they were captured fits well with the kind of pejorative vocabulary directed against heretics and apostates. We have already mentioned the mutilation of Johannes. Crescentius was not only beheaded after his capture, but his corpse was also thrown from the battlements of the Castel Sant' Angelo. The body was then hung upside down on Monte Mario, along with the corpses of twelve of Crescentius's associates who had also been executed.[28] The "lust for revenge" apparently continued against the dead, just as the mutilated antipope was not spared the dishonoring procedure of unfrocking and public exhibition on a donkey. Echoes of this indignity even extend to the dating line of a charter issued on this day for the monastery of Einsiedeln: the pious donation of the emperor for his and his parents' salvation has as date the formula "given on the 4. Kal. of May, when the decapitated Crescentius was hanged" (*quando Crescentius decollatus suspensus fuit*).[29]

Raoul Glaber's account gains credence from the fact that people in the imperial camp were determined to make an example of the *perversus* and the *apostata* and not to accept any amicable reunion. That this is probably what actually happened still does not explain what provoked such harsh behavior on the emperor's part. It is by no means unique to Otto III's time that popes loyal to the emperor could not be secure in Rome and were threatened by candidates from noble factions within the city of Rome. Rather, this was a constant in papal history during the so-called German imperial age.[30] But in other cases this sort of behavior did not provoke countermeasures as brutal as Otto III and Gregory V employed. Instead, the special circumstances of the 997/998 case are key to explaining the course of events. During his first Italian expedition, after the imperial coronation, Otto III already had sentenced Crescentius to exile. This was the result of the great wrongs he had committed against the deceased Pope John XV. This sentence was revoked at Pope Gregory V's request, and Crescentius was allowed to retain his position.[31] Here, in other words, we witness an amicable resolution of a conflict mediated through Gregory V and a ruler's clemency brought into play in place of justice. Obviously, such an act could not be repeated. If an opponent renewed a conflict after he had found mildness and pardon, he instead lost any claim to the law of submission, any hope of reconciliation. In their place he could expect the harshest punishment.[32] Precisely this rule was employed in the case of Crescentius. His behavior had forfeited him the trust placed in him during the first expedition to Rome. There could no longer be a question of negotiating with him for an amicable resolution to the conflict. Understood in this way, Raoul Glaber's account accords fully with the rules of the game that applied to this sort of occurrence during the tenth century. Should somebody continue in a conflict after he had made a formal submission and thus had won mild treatment, his punishment had a parallel to those ordered by canon law for heretics and apostates. They too can be forgiven one time; the death penalty is mandatory for backsliding.[33] Perhaps the terms used in the German sources to designate Crescentius and Johannes Philagathos are explained by this analogy. The designations *perversus* and *apostata* evoke precisely these associations. This also explains the gruesome brutality against Otto's main opponents on the second Italian expedition. This came not from individual motivations such as Otto III's and Gregory V's desire for revenge, disappointment, or bitterness. Instead they followed the rules of the time for punishing such behavior, as the case of Crescentius had already shown. The person submitting to the law of clemency had the advantage of mild treatment. But it allowed no backsliding, no reliance on endless patience. Thietmar of Merseburg appears to address precisely this state of affairs when he reports the second fall of Crescentius. There Thietmar remarks that Crescentius acted "unmindful of his oath and the great mildness [*magne pietatis*] that the exalted Otto had shown him."[34] This assessment was more understandable to contemporaries than to us: a person could only hope for *pietas* (mildness) once.

Some might object that the reassessment and reconstruction of the events surrounding Crescentius's death presented here fail to explain the origin of the Brauweiler variation on the story of Crescentius's capture or the basis for the charge that Crescentius was betrayed in the independent Italian sources. Possibly these accounts had their origin in Crescentius's attempt to negoti-
:ment and its failure. But offering such an interpretation opens the
speculation. With a collection of sources such as those examined

here, pure speculations about plausibility obviously cannot be allowed. Of necessity, a number of explanations might be considered plausible and thus contribute to a reconstruction. But that is a practice from which it would be best to abstain.

Otto III's "Idea of Roman Renewal" in Older and Newer Scholarship
Sensational actions against rebels are not the only things that distinguish Otto III's second Italian expedition. According to the general opinion of scholars this supposedly was the occasion when the emperor developed and put into practice a political ideology that, under the catchphrase "Roman renewal ideology" has become the most distinctive attribute of Otto III. It is thus appropriate to consider here the issues contained in this formula, even if the subject certainly cannot be limited to the second Italian expedition. The notion of a renewal of Rome that was supposedly the heart and soul of Otto III's policies essentially derives from the work of Percy Ernst Schramm, presented in his book *Kaiser, Rom und Renovatio* (Emperor, Rome, and renewal) and in subsequent works.[35] Until recently it would have been possible to do little more here than to refer to this generally accepted belief. This situation changed in 1993, when in his doctoral dissertation Knut Görich provided a detailed and critical revision of the "Roman renewal ideology", as well as other assessments of Otto III.[36] His analysis fundamentally changed the basic terms of investigation. Central to Görich's critique is that at essential points the evidence of the sources does not support the theory of a distinct policy for Roman renewal. Either to cite and assess the historiographical dimension of this controversy or to discuss the sources in all their specifics is impossible here. By looking at key sources and their historiographical analysis, it is possible, however, to sort out the issues at the heart of different views on this subject. In that way we can evaluate the questions raised by this issue and better judge Otto III's ideas as well as his accomplishments.

Schramm's notion of a "Roman renewal ideology" described a political concept that had as its ideal the renewal of the ancient Roman Empire. Supposedly the particular political goal was to align the authority and rule of the emperor with the model of ancient Roman imperial rule.[37] This ideology was thus distinct from the Christian idea of Rome. The latter idea regarded the city of the apostles as mother and head of the Christian world, where after the Donation of Constantine the emperor had given up his share in the "residence of the apostles."[38] By contrast Otto III's "Roman renewal ideology" was a cult of secular Rome, transmitted by a literary education. Otto III purportedly was

won over to this ideal primarily by his learned advisors Gerbert and Leo of Vercelli. From 997/998 on this revival of ancient Roman rule was supposedly the
plumb line of Otto's political activity. According to this premise, other political activities such as Otto's new valuation of the Polish and Hungarian kingdoms fall into this unified plan. Percy Ernst Schramm advocated consistency
for this intellectual construct by applying very different groups of evidence to
the question. In this way he largely succeeded in introducing a necessary correction to the image of Otto III.[39]

There is no source that presents this "Roman renewal ideology" in so
many words and expounds on it as a political concept. To expect a treatise, a
report, or a comparable programmatic statement from the end of the tenth
century dealing with the idea of renewal and what it involved would certainly be anachronistic. Evidence for such an ideology, therefore, is discerned
only through analysis of relevant sources. More specifically, evidence to support Schramm's thesis appears in no source. There are only significant allusions, at least according to the interpreters who argue for its existence. The
existence of a central policy of renewal and its importance in the circle of
Otto III is assumed in every instance. But this creates a very serious problem
in interpretation. The significance of the concepts and images is by no means
unambiguous; the interpreter must first deduce the connotations, which
presents the danger of a circular argument. To put this concretely: if Rome is
celebrated as *caput mundi* ("head of the world") in the texts, this does not
prove in any way that Otto III wanted to renew the ancient imperial age.[40]
The interpreter only reaches this conclusion by means of analogy—and
analogies in general are an unsure basis for historical knowledge.

The expression *caput mundi* used there is an honorary epithet that refers
to Rome in her capacity as the city of the apostles and the head of the Christian Church. And yet this is the crux of the argument that the Roman
renewal was based on antiquity. There is, of course, the possibility that these
references are to Rome as Christian *caput mundi*, which will be restored to
its true dignity after ages of subjection by Roman noble factions. The distinction between notions of secular and spiritual renewal is Görich's central
argument against Percy Ernst Schramm's interpretation, probably rightly
because such a division in fact is anachronistic for the tenth century. Görich
himself, in his description of the content and goals of Otto's renovation policies, focuses entirely on a projected renewal of the papacy after Crescentius's
reign of terror. The possible difficulty of such an emphasis is evident in interpreting individual sources. The evidence is not any clearer than for Schramm's

theory. An analysis of the relevant sources shows that they only indirectly address the goal of reforming the papacy.

Existence of an ideology of renewal is attested primarily through the introduction of a lead seal instead of the customary wax seal used to verify Otto III's documents. The motto on this seal reads *Renovatio imperii Romanorum*—"Renewal of the Roman Empire." It appears for the first time, suggestively, on a charter issued on 28 April 998 for the monastery of Einsiedeln, the very document in which the date clause mentions the decapitation and hanging of Crescentius.[41] On its verso the seal portrays an armed figure of Roma; on the recto, the head of a bearded man copied from a seal of Charlemagne. In fact, the seal in this way subtly expresses the programmatic elements of Otto III's policy: reference to Charlemagne, and a link to Rome stressing a *renovatio* of the Romans' imperial power. Naturally enough, however, the seal does not reveal what was meant by the term *renovatio*. It is just as difficult to explain why it was no longer used after January 1001, when it was replaced by the motto *Aurea Roma* ("golden Rome"). It is almost certain that this date marks the end of Otto III's journey to Gniezno, but there is no very compelling reason why this should have led to a change in the imperial seal.[42] In other words, here again is the fundamental dilemma: the political ideology expressed in the phrase *Renovatio imperii Romanorum* must be reconstructed from widely differing sources. And even this statement on its own betrays a supposition that a single, clearly defined overarching political concept informed the device, which was known at the very least to the inner circle around the emperor. Independent of this problem, it is debatable how much of this political ideology was based on the revival of ancient Roman practices or on the renewal of the papacy in the tenth century.

This dilemma recurs in other sources at the heart of the disagreement between Schramm and Görich. The prologue to a work Gerbert of Aurillac dedicated to Otto III early in 998, the *Libellus de rationali et ratione uti*, is another early witness to an ideology of renewal and its meaning.[43] In the prologue to this philosophical tract, Gerbert extols Otto's rule, contrasting it emphatically with Byzantine claims. Thus, "fruitful Italy bestows its strength, Gaul and Germany filled with men, and the brave land of the Scythians is not lacking to us." Or: "You are our 'emperor of the Romans and Augustus,' oh Caesar, you who spring from the noblest blood of the Greeks, who triumph in power over the Greeks, you who command the Romans by lawful inheritance and surpass both in spirit and eloquence." A letter from Gerbert to the emperor, written about the same time, contains the famous exclamation: "Ours, ours is the Roman Empire" (*Noster, noster est Romanorum imperium*). According to Schramm's interpretation, this exclamation programmatically expresses the "change in mood" in the army and in the emperor's entourage: "the Roman past . . . had become a necessary part of the justification with which the Western Empire asserted its claims."[44] Görich has convincingly demonstrated that this example is much more dependent on forms of traditional praise of the ruler—to which Gerbert, only recently given a place in Otto III's court, had easy access—than a future-looking policy for renewing the glory of ancient Rome.

While this text and its interpretation demonstrate the problem with particular clarity, there are many similar cases. In fact, reference to Rome is conspicuous in panegyric and metaphor, and the use of ancient terminology was not simply present but overwhelming. Indeed, to rely on this literary mania for a reconstruction of a political ideology does not convince. A poem of panegyric written by Leo of Vercelli, the second imperial advisor, for Pope Gregory V and Emperor Otto III, further demonstrates this problem.[45] The poem begins with a call to Christ to look upon "his Rome" and renew it, so that it might bloom under the rule of the third Otto. (*Romam tuam respice, / Romanos pie renova, vires Romę excita. / Surgat Roma imperio sub Ottone tertio.*) The rest of the poem in essence praises the collaboration of emperor and pope (*Sub caesaris potentia purgat papa secula*). It also expresses the thought, important for the relationship between the two powers, that the pope is answerable for souls, while the emperor applies himself to the "care of bodies" (*cura corporum*). It is easy to derive from this a belief in the preeminence of spiritual over secular power. But such was certainly not part of Leo's intention in this work. Just as far removed is any description of an ideology guiding imperial actions. Görich has shown that the ideas expressed in the poem are much more influenced by the Christian notion of four world empires than they are by ideas "of a completely thought-out *renovatio.*"[46]

If the texts and their essential claims cannot stand in face of Görich's critique, two ruler portraits of Otto III also cannot decisively support the theoretical construct of a "Roman renewal ideology." In these portraits, four female forms, with humble demeanor, present their tribute to the ruler. Italy, or Roma, takes the first place among the serving *gentes*, preceding Gallia, Germania, and Sclavinia.[47] Even if one reads this picture as a shift in the relative importance of the "peoples of the empire," it is hardly plausible to argue that Rome takes precedence over the other personifications because of

Figure 4. Dedicatory miniature from the gospel book of Otto III: The four provinces—
Sclavinia, Germania, Gallia, and Roma—pay homage to the emperor. Bayerische
Staatsbibliothek, Munich. (photo: AKG Berlin)

ancient reminiscences and not because of Rome's significance as the capital
of Christianity.[48] So far, I agree with Görich's critique of Schramm's interpretation. Neither the motto on the imperial seal nor panegyrical texts from the
context of the second Italian expedition define the contours of a policy to
renew Rome, and certainly not with a specific linkage of either the seal or
the texts to ancient practices.

Still more concrete evidence indicates that Rome was becoming more
important in imperial policy during the second Italian expedition: Otto III

built a palace in Rome, behavior very different from that of his predecessors. This was a significant way in which he brushed aside the claims of the so-called Donation of Constantine. This text had reserved Rome for the popes "because it is not right that, where the chief of priests and head of the Christian religion has been established by the heavenly emperor, the earthly emperor should have power."[49] It is possible to connect Bruno of Querfurt's criticism of the emperor with these building activities. Bruno reproached Otto III for excessive love of Rome, charging that the emperor wished to remain always in Rome and intended to restore Rome's former greatness.[50] Clearly Otto III's activities while in Rome struck contemporaries as unusual and worthy of criticism. They echo in part the rhetoric of renovatio in the circle around the emperor. But at the same time Bruno's critique gives a closer insight into the true goals and nature of this intended renewal.

There is a further, equally contested controversial aspect of this issue. The sources report other imperial measures in Rome following the defeat of Crescentius. In older research, these measures gave substance to the view of Otto III as an unrealistic dreamer. They have a place in this discussion because the new official titles that appear for the first time in 998 suggest changes in the way Rome was organized. These unusual and in part jejune titles employed by Otto in charters have been considered evidence for a so-called "Byzantine court state" created by the emperor that in 998 resulted in mockery and scorn for Roman functionaries. Such an aping of unrealistic Byzantine titulary with no concrete association of duties to title supports the image of Otto as an "un-German" emperor. One example of such an "empty title," the imperial praefectus navalis (admiral), was a title borne by a Roman nobleman without, scholars have sarcastically remarked, a single imperial ship sailing on any sea.[51] Percy Ernst Schramm, in several preparatory studies, had already set the parameters for interpreting this evidence: some of the titles granted do not in fact belong to the period in question. They first appear in the so-called "Graphia" and in lists of Roman judges from a later time. In other cases the people so designated are papal office-holders; in yet others these titles are evidence of literary mania, similar to the appropriation of ancient concepts like that of the senate, the consuls, or the classical abbreviation S.P.Q.R.[52] After Schramm's investigations, the only major novelty that remains is the office of magister palatii (master of the palace), which first became necessary, of course, with the building of an imperial palace in Rome. Another new office, the magister imperialis militiae (master of the imperial army), appears previously as the Roman magister

militum. The only striking change in this case is the stress on the connection between the Roman militia and the emperor. The title *patricius* given to
the Saxon nobleman Ziazo involves duties long unexplained. There is no evidence of an imperial deputy in Rome; astonishingly, this *patricius* did not in
fact even remain in Rome, but accompanied the emperor on his journey to
Gniezno.[53] Such details (for the most part occurring only in a single imperial
document) allow no conclusion about reform of governmental or administrative offices, much less the creation of a "Roman" or "Byzantine" court
state.[54] So this line of investigation also fails to produce certain evidence of
the concept and content of "Roman renewal ideology."

The prime objective of the second Italian expedition was the restoration
of Pope Gregory V to Rome. Thus it seems natural to seek a concrete appli-
cation of *renovatio* policies in a reorganization of papal affairs in Rome. Knut
Görich argues that reorganization of the papacy is much more important
than any possible linkage of the renewal policy to ancient Roman practices.[55]
In this regard, too, we see little spectacular after the execution of Crescentius. Certainly the Roman rivals of the Crescentii, such as the Tusculan
counts, come to the forefront again; but the extant sources give no evidence
of far-reaching change within the Roman ruling class.[56] Both emperor and
pope were indeed involved several times in restoring alienated ecclesiastical
possessions to the authority of spiritual institutions. This motivated a campaign against a relative of Crescentius, a count of Sabina named Benedict,
who had robbed the monastery of Farfa. The struggle, by the way, came to a
successful conclusion: Pope Gregory V threatened to hang his imprisoned
son before the count's eyes, convincing the count to give in.[57] Otto III
presided over a synod at Pavia on 20 September 998 that may have been
devoted to the same goal. By agreement of that synod, all leasing agreements
in the kingdom of Italy that put ecclesiastical property into lay hands would
only remain valid during the lifetime of the bishop or abbot who had made
the contract.[58] Successors would be allowed to demand the return of all
leased land, thus preventing alienation through excessively long leases. The
concerted action of emperor and pope in this period is also clear in two synods held in Rome in May 998 and around the turn of the year 998/999, over
which they presided jointly.[59] The second synod discussed whether the dissolution of the diocese of Merseburg was legal, and gave very clear orders that
Archbishop Giselher of Magdeburg lay down his archbishopric.[60] The synod
also dealt with the consanguineous marriage of the French king Robert,
threatening him with excommunication if he did not separate from his wife,

Bertha. The bishops who had performed the marriage ceremony were anathematized until they came to Rome to justify their conduct.[61] The first synod, among other issues, had also settled a dispute over possession of the Spanish bishopric of Vich, a way in which Otto III declared himself competent to deal with questions outside of his own realm.[62] But the best sources fail to indicate whether Gregory V and the Roman curia used this synod to bring up issues regarding papal claims to secular lordship. Such issues might have brought them into conflict with Otto III, even if the emperor supposedly declined to deal with this sort of claim.[63]

It is difficult to determine if the activities mentioned here or later activities carried out by the emperor and the pope were part of a programmatically ordered policy of *renovatio*. In other words, it is difficult to reduce the policy of *renovatio* to a policy of renewal for the papacy, as Görich proposed after he rejected the notion of a "Roman renewal ideology" based on antiquity.[64] The actions of Otto and Gregory were simply too traditional and too heterogeneous to fit comfortably into this theory. The quest for a concrete program of renewal until now has been futile. Evidence for it appears only in formulaic or panegyric exchanges. It is more justifiable to ask if such a specific program existed at all. In the introduction I have already pointed out how quick modern research is to attribute underlying ideologies to medieval rulers. It is disillusioning to realize that in many cases the recorded activities of rulers are not very compatible with the ideologies theorized for them. This encourages the suspicion that theoretical constructs of this sort are often based upon anachronisms and that modern notions are attributed to medieval rulers. So it is with Otto III. One can accept, therefore, in its basic assertions Görich's critique of Schramm's thesis that renewal ideology was based upon ancient Rome. It is, however, necessary to modify his suggestion of an ecclesiastical-monastic "Roman renewal policy" to replace the earlier thesis.

The medieval centuries are filled with calls for change and improvement that could only be regarded as re-forming and re-newing, demanding the abolition of abuses that had insinuated themselves into the God-ordained order of things. And researchers always seem perplexed—as sometimes were even contemporaries—about the specific content of this reform. The eighteen-year-old emperor had only been of legal age for a few years and was confronted at exactly this period with new personalities in his entourage. Why should he have formed totally untypical guiding principles and ideologies of this sort, before he even ended the subversive activities of Crescentius and his antipope? It is much more probable that the motto *Renovatio imperii Romanorum* provided a sufficiently general and motivating formula to describe programmatically what was certainly in his mind: to take the reins of imperial rule into his hands energetically and to restrain opponents and abuses. That these abuses and opponents were concentrated in the city of Rome at this time meant that of necessity the ruler's activities were concentrated on this city and on Italy. Otto's actions in his second Roman expedition were out of compelling necessity and are comprehensible without theorizing an overarching plan that preceded or developed alongside them. Such an understanding would certainly not exclude the possibility that the incontrovertible successes of this Italian expedition were the reason for the later formula *Aurea Roma,* as they could have inspired other panegyrical reminiscences on the past greatness of Rome.

✝ 𝕮𝖍𝖆𝖕𝖙𝖊𝖗 4 ✝

THE JOURNEY TO GNIEZNO

Preconceptions and Preparations

istorians have long considered the relations of Otto III with his empire's eastern neighbors, especially Poland and Hungary, part of Otto's presumed policy of Roman renewal. Indeed they have treated Otto's Roman ideology as the very source of his eastern policy. Many scholars have seen the new relationship, indeed the independence, Otto willingly conceded to the rulers of these lands as implicit in a policy that regarded the emperor as overlord of a family of kings. In other words, it was part and parcel of an attempt to apply ancient and Byzantine models and influences to tenth-century political realities.[1] This complex of themes forms part of a broader scrutiny of the goals of Ottonian eastern policy, an issue that has sparked intense controversy in both German and East European research. This discussion has never moved beyond the subjectivity of historians influenced by their own political environment, whether they were writing in the nineteenth or the twentieth century. In the end, these arguments always seem to reduce themselves to a concern with reinforcing claims and rights of modern states based on events long past.[2] These modern political concerns alone make comprehensible the energy with which every detail of Ottonian eastern policy has been thrashed out.

The entire debate over Ottonian eastern policy might be summarized in the efforts to understand Otto III's journey to Gniezno in the year 1000 and to uncover what precisely happened there. The question of how much independence Otto III granted to Duke Boleslav Chrobry of Poland lies at the heart of the problem. If, as the German side of the debate has argued from Heinrich Zeisberg to Albert Brackmann, Otto named Boleslav *patricius*, then Boleslav was a deputy. As such he was a subordinate of Otto's, and Poland was a part of the empire. If Boleslav was elevated to the kingship in Gniezno, then Otto III had effected Poland's "declaration of independence."[3] With hardly any exceptions, historians have employed methodological techniques already criticized often in this work. They still do so up to the present. In all cases, underlying motives and larger plans were deduced on the basis of a few events. In reality, even the few events in the sources are reported in widely differing form. The form of transmitted sources upon which the reconstruction and evaluation of events are based must be continually kept in mind. This will prevent attribution of all too plausible motives to the people involved, and the reconstruction of entire policies from the few extant reports. Doing so, of course, will provide some certainty, especially about the limitations of our knowledge.

As early as the summer of 997 Otto III learned that Adalbert of Prague had been martyred during his mission to the Prussians. Adalbert died on 23 April.[4] Supported by Boleslav Chrobry, the Prague bishop had dedicated himself to evangelizing the Prussians, and had been killed by them. After Adalbert's death, Boleslav ransomed the body and brought it to Gniezno. Some of Adalbert's companions survived the event, among them his half-brother Radim-Gaudentius. They made sure that the imperial court knew what had happened. As a result, Otto commissioned a written description of Adalbert's deeds and death. This work was justified specifically as an important preparation for Adalbert's canonization.[5] Composition of the *vita*, though, is the only known direct reaction to news of the death. In 997 Otto first traveled from Aachen to Saxony, where he campaigned against the Liutizi. There is no evidence that Otto used this opportunity to contact Boleslav Chrobry about the uncertainties Adalbert's martyrdom created. Then late in the year Otto set out on his Italian expedition discussed above. Only from the autumn of 999 are there concrete reports that the emperor planned to travel to Gniezno to visit the tomb of the martyr.

Certainly, researchers have surmised other reasons for Otto's decision to visit Gniezno. Already early in 997 Pope Gregory V held a synod at Pavia, since he had been driven from Rome. There he ordered an inquiry into the so-called Merseburg question. As a result Archbishop Giselher of Magdeburg was ordered to appear in Rome to defend himself against the charge of uncanonically abandoning his see (Merseburg) and taking over another (Magdeburg). Pope Gregory V sent a letter outlining this issue to Archbishop Willigis of Mainz. However, nothing in the correspondence suggests any connection between the Merseburg inquiry and recent developments, not to mention possible ecclesiastical-political maneuvering in Poland. Despite this, scholars have continued to postulate such a connection. They do so by juxtaposing different reports in an adventurous fashion and blending them into a theory of a great conspiracy. Boleslav Chrobry and Pope Gregory V emerge as the chief actors in this plot. The father of the former had formally donated his land to the Holy See in 990/992.[6] Now his son Boleslav supposedly worked systematically to found an independent ecclesiastical province in Poland. According to this argument, Boleslav and the curia—whatever is meant by this institution in the tenth century—countered expected opposition from Magdeburg by raising anew the issue of Merseburg's dissolution. This was intended to divert and otherwise occupy Archbishop Giselher.[7] Allegedly they also had won over Pope Gregory V, and later even Otto III, to this diversionary tactic. Otto subsequently became personally concerned with reestablishing the bishopric of Merseburg, in effect unwittingly furthering Boleslav's aims. Giselher, gravely threatened on all sides, was unable to articulate opposition to Boleslav's plans or to organize resistance. This accomplished an important step toward freeing Poland from dependence on the German empire.

This is not the place to scrutinize the research tradition that produced such views.[8] It is, however, important to point out a completely different and compelling reason to raise the issue of Merseburg at the beginning of 997, a reason often overlooked by historians.[9] Bishop Hildiward of Halberstadt had died late in 996. He had been one of the people working behind the scenes to dissolve the diocese of Merseburg in the first place. His death thus created an opportunity to consider a refoundation of the bishopric, since the agreement of the bishop of Halberstadt was necessary to do this. Consequently, when the Halberstadt cathedral chapter quickly elected Hildiward's confidant as his successor, Otto III would not accept the election. Instead, Otto imposed his chaplain Arnulf as bishop, and Arnulf was ready to agree to cede Halberstadt territory to Merseburg. That these measures did not immediately succeed in reestablishing Merseburg was due to Archbishop Giselher's delaying tactics. Using all the weaknesses inherent in this sort of decision-making process, he postponed any decision in this matter. It was still unresolved when Giselher died on 25 January 1004. In short, discussion about restoring Merseburg was completely separate from Boleslav Chrobry's political plans. According to clear testimony in various sources, the new concern over Merseburg resulted from a realization that the "sin" of abolishing the bishopric in 981 caused the catastrophes at Crotone in 982 and the Slav rebellion of 983.[10]

Otto III's journey to Gniezno did not therefore originate out of the sup-posed plots of Boleslav Chrobry and the curia. Instead, there was another motivation, even though the sources may not give specific information about the reasoning behind it. Why should not personal friendship combine with religious and political motives to inspire this certainly unusual journey? In other words, could not Otto have undertaken a pilgrimage to pray at the tomb of the martyr and also have used the opportunity to deal with issues of both ecclesiastical and political relations with Boleslav Chrobry? In the year 999 there is almost no hint that Otto III planned to travel to Poland. He found time for a penitential pilgrimage to Monte Gargano in Benevento, which the hermit Romuald supposedly enjoined upon him as penance for his sin against Crescentius and Johannes Philagathos.[11] The *vita* of Romuald reports that the emperor set out barefooted from Rome. Then came a decisive moment when Pope Gregory V died, apparently unexpectedly and suddenly. Not surpris-ingly, wild rumors circulated quickly after his death. One chronicler specu-lated that the pope had been poisoned. Another reported that his eyes had been ripped out, a likely reference back to the mutilation of the antipope.[12] Neither account had much relationship to reality.

After his return from Monte Gargano, Otto III decided to elevate Gerbert of Aurillac, whom he had already made archbishop of Ravenna, to the see of Saint Peter. As pope, Gerbert adopted the certainly programmatic name Sylvester II. Sylvester I had been pope at the time of Constantine and was the supposed recipient of the Donation of Constantine. Otto presided jointly with his new pope over a Roman Easter synod. Gregory V had earlier sum-moned this synod and ordered Archbishop Giselher of Magdeburg to appear there. Giselher, however, claimed illness. He sent one of his clerics to repre-sent and defend him, thus obtaining a postponement.[13]

The emperor was also engaged in several other personal matters both in and out of Rome. He promoted close confidants to several bishoprics, some of them of considerable importance. For example, Otto made his chaplain Leo bishop of Vercelli, in this way bestowing on him a bishopric so problematic that his predecessor Peter had been murdered by Margrave Arduin of Ivrea and his followers.[14] When the archdiocese of Cologne came vacant with the death of Archbishop Everger, Otto named his chancellor Heribert as successor. According to the *vita* of Heribert, the ruler announced his decision to the recipient in a short letter displaying a spark of something like imperial humor: *Otto imperator sola Dei gratia, Heriberto archilogotetae gratiam et Coloniam ac pallii cubitum unum* ("Otto, emperor by God's grace alone, presents to the

Figure 5. Seal of Otto III. The emperor is shown with scepter, orb, and imperial robes, and wears a closed crown. The inscription is OTTO(D)IGRATIAREX (Otto, king by the grace of God). The seal is reproduced here in its original size of 73 mm. Staatsarchiv Frankfurt am Main.

archilogothete Heribert his favor and Cologne and a yard of pallium").[15] In this case too, it is significant that Otto elevated a person in whom he had confidence to an important see.

The *Vita Heriberti* gives another piece of significant evidence: the new archbishop entered his episcopal city barefoot, after sending the episcopal insignia and pallium before him.[16] This behavior, unlike Otto III's on the road to Monte Gargano, was not an act of penance for a sin, but a ritual display that the new archbishop was conscious of his unworthiness and humility. Both cases, though, testify to the prevalence of demonstrative ritual actions in the ruler's circle, including the emperor himself. Further examples include the penitential exercises Otto III performed in Rome in the same year, in the company of his faithful follower Bishop Franco of Worms. In penitential garb and with bare feet, the two men secretly sought out a cave (*spelunca*) near the church of San Clemente and remained there fasting and praying for fourteen days.[17] This demonstrative penitential behavior was directed toward winning God's mercy, not a public result— nevertheless it is evidence of how significant such demonstrative behaviors were to Otto III's self-definition.

In this period Otto III also decided on the succession to the archbishopric of Ravenna, the elevation of Otto of Lomello to the office of count palatine of Pavia, and that of the Saxon Ziazo to the position of Roman *patricius*.[18] What this office of "patrician" meant is unclear and contested; scholars have debated whether Ziazo's authority was limited to the city of Rome or included the whole empire.[19] Whichever the case, the *patricius* Ziazo accompanied Otto III to Gniezno, at any rate suggesting that his authority was not confined to Rome.[20] In February Otto's aunt Mathilda, the abbess of Quedlinburg, also died. It was she whom Otto had made regent in Germany before he set out for Rome and whom he later called *matricia* in an epitaph he wrote himself.[21] Her successor as abbess was Otto's sister Adelheid. The emperor had invested her in her office with a golden crosier that Count Birichtilo brought from Rome to Quedlinburg.[22]

Also significant is an imperial intrusion in north Alpine affairs during the year 999 that casts a unique light on Otto III's powers as ruler. At the Easter synod in Rome, Otto turned over to the bishopric of Worms, and thus to his trusty bishop Franco, the old, venerable, and rich imperial monastery of Lorsch. Its status in that way was changed or reduced from imperial to episcopal monastery.[23] Certainly such transfers of imperial monasteries occurred at other times, especially during the minority of kings like Louis the Child and Henry IV. But such a measure was highly unusual and frequently received with indignation and opposition by those concerned.[24] This appears to be what occurred in this case, since in the same year Otto III took the monastery back under direct imperial control. He even permitted Pope Sylvester II to confirm Lorsch's old liberty. The document cites the intervention of Archbishop Willigis of Mainz and all the bishops of his ecclesiastical province, a clear indication of what forces gathered to reverse the original gift of Lorsch.[25] This is a good example of the kind of opposition the emperor encountered when he made decisions perceived as arbitrary. It also shows that he had to take this opposition into account.

In the fall of the same year Otto III encountered certain difficulties arising from a legal conflict between the abbots Hugh of Farfa and Gregory of Saints Cosmas and Damian in Rome. The latter failed to appear on several appointed court dates, and the emperor summoned him several times in vain.[26] Only on 2 December 999 did a judicial decision in Rome settle the matter in question. The verdict is recorded in the register of Farfa, dating from the late eleventh century. The record of this decision also gives key testimony to Otto III's preparation for his journey to Gniezno. Gaudentius, half-brother of Saint Adalbert, appears among the signatories, with the title "archbishop of Saint Adalbert the martyr" (*archiepiscopus sancti Adalberti martyris*).[27] Historians have inferred from this that Gaudentius had already been consecrated as archbishop, even if he still did not have a fixed see. This circumstance supposedly accounts for the unusual title given to the archbishop in lieu of a place name. Now, it is not easy to believe that a foundation of an archdiocese should have been planned and even an archbishop consecrated for this purpose, without deciding where the center of the archdiocese should be. Gaudentius's descriptive title in the document clearly refers to the location of Adalbert's tomb—Gniezno. At the same time it is possible that Gaudentius received archiepiscopal consecration without a fixed see, since this was the case a few years later with the Saxon missionary Bruno of Querfurt. Theoretically, the new "archbishop of Saint Adalbert the martyr" could also have been assigned to the mission field.[28] Scholars have even postulated successful negotiations leading eventually to the foundation of a Polish ecclesiastical province from the unusual manner of designating Gaudentius in the Farfa document. This gave rise to the notion that Gaudentius traveled to Rome under orders from Boleslav Chrobry, and there negotiated with emperor and pope. At the same time he supposedly arranged the details of Otto III's visit to the tomb of the martyr. Johannes Fried recently suggested a variation on this: that Prague, not Gniezno, was originally intended to be Gaudentius's see. This, however, has already been refuted.[29]

In light of these controversies, it is again necessary to clarify which sources support these assertions. Our only source about the preparations and negotiations, as I have stated, is the signature of *archiepiscopus* Gaudentius on the legal judgment cited above. The sources give no information about who sent him to Rome, who negotiated with whom about what. On the contrary, the evidence we have available raises questions we cannot answer. We have only inferences from subsequent events. Although Gaudentius's role is unclear, however, contemporary annalists do make declarations about Otto III's motives for traveling to Gniezno. The emperor went to Gniezno to receive the relics of Adalbert, say the hagiographical texts about the life and martyrdom of Adalbert.[30] Thietmar cites "for the sake of prayer" (*orationis gratia*) as a further reason for the journey.[31] The Polish populace, who flocked to Gniezno to protect their new saint, supposedly thwarted the plan to take the relics.[32] It is impossible to decide whether these statements in the hagiographical sources are believable or if they were intended to underscore the relics' value. At any rate there is no sign that Otto III was annoyed at not attaining his supposed goal, the acquisition of the body. It is equally impossible to assess what political purposes motivated the journey from its beginning. The sources say nothing on the subject. On the other hand, it seems natural to suggest that political plans were carefully prepared and firmly established before Otto began the journey. Historians assume that what happened in Gniezno brought an earlier agreement to fruition, and this assumption has something to recommend it. But what the sources have to say about what actually happened at the end of the journey does not provide consistent evidence.

The Journey

Sometime around Christmas 999 Otto III set out from Rome on this journey to Gniezno. He crossed the Brenner Pass in January. He is reported north of the Alps (in Bavarian Staffelsee) for the first time on the seventeenth of that month.[33] There he made a gift in return for prayers for the soul of his grandmother Adelheid, who had died on 17 December. This gift went to the archdiocese of Magdeburg, whose archbishop Giselher had met the emperor at Staffelsee. This is not surprising in light of the measures the Roman synod took against the archbishop regarding the matter of Merseburg. According to Thietmar, Giselher had obtained the emperor's favor (*gratia*), although this imperial favor could not be relied upon.[34]

It was in Staffelsee that the famous addition to Otto III's imperial title appeared for the first time: *servus Jesu Christi et Romanorum imperator augustus secundum voluntatem Dei salvatorisque nostrique liberatoris* ("servant of Jesus Christ and emperor augustus of the Romans, in accordance with the will of God and of our savior and redeemer").[35] Scholars have used this to deduce the intentions and the goals of the journey. This devotional formula, which puts the emperor into the apostolic tradition as a propagator of the Christian faith, appeared as part of the imperial title throughout the entire trip. After his return it was changed to the formula, just as ambitious, *servus apostolorum* ("servant of the apostles").[36]

In general, contemporaries saw the trip to Gniezno as something entirely different from the barefoot penitential pilgrimage to Monte Gargano that had taken place the year before. The sources instead emphasize the honor accorded to the emperor from all sides once he was north of the Alps. Thietmar of Merseburg describes the emperor's reception in Regensburg, where Otto spent several weeks in January and February, as splendid: Bishop Gebhard supposedly received the emperor "with magnificent honor" (*magnifico honore*). Overall, Thietmar asserts, an emperor never left Rome and returned there more gloriously.[37] The Quedlinburg Annals improved on this by reporting that all of Gallia, Francia, and Suevia flocked to the emperor by horse and by foot. So did the emperor's sisters Adelheid and Sophia.[38] As the journey continued, the reception in the episcopal cities was similarly spectacular and fully appropriate for an emperor. In Meissen, the regional bishops and also Margrave Ekkehard were responsible for this.[39] According to Thietmar, all these receptions, however, were overshadowed by the welcome that Duke Boleslav prepared for Otto in Eulau on the Bober, and more still by the escort he gave the emperor to Gniezno. This, remarks Thietmar, was simply incredible and indescribable.[40] Thietmar was certainly not favorably inclined toward the Polish ruler, so his compliment to Boleslav also supports the conclusion that the journey was well planned out beforehand and that this was done with full agreement between the duke and the emperor. The reports of the *translatio* and miracles of Saint Adalbert and the description of the Gallus Anonymus do not differ at all from the German accounts. All praise the honor with which the emperor was received.[41]

The receptions to honor the emperor only changed their nature in Gniezno itself. Before entering the city, the emperor again transformed himself into a barefooted pilgrim. In this guise, Bishop Unger of Poznán led him into the church to the tomb of Adalbert, where Otto in tears prayed for Adalbert's intercession with Christ.[42] On this point, there is no disagreement between the various reports. Rather, they tend to corroborate one another, despite some differences in details. About what happened after this, however, the reports of the "German" and the "Polish" sources (represented by the Gallus Anonymus) diverge. With a clearly critical tone, Thietmar reports (with the doubting rider "as I hope legitimately") that the emperor then established an archbishopric in Gniezno, which he gave to Gaudentius-Radim. The emperor subordinated Bishops Reinbern of Kolberg, Poppo of Cracow, and Johannes of Breslau to the new archbishopric. According to Thietmar, Poznán was exempted from the arrangement because its bishop had refused his consent.[43] This reflects well the contemporary power relations also at the heart of the troubles over the archbishopric of Magdeburg: nobody could found bishoprics without the consent of all of the other bishops concerned.[44] Thietmar is silent, however, about any sort of contact between Otto III and Boleslav during that time. He only reports that, after the completion of all business, Boleslav returned to Germany with the emperor. There Boleslav was highly honored and presented with rich gifts by his host.[45] The Quedlinburg Annals, too, give little information. The annalist reports only that Boleslav wanted to honor the emperor with rich guest-gifts, which Otto allegedly declined, saying that he had not come "for robbing and taking, but for giving and prayer."[46]

The chronicle of the Gallus Anonymus, written only in the twelfth century, is more informative.[47] There is a serious question about whether it was based on older accounts no longer extant. It does, however, provide a coherent and consistent account. Above all, it betrays its polemic: praise of Boleslav and the glory of his reign. Since the context of the contested passages is important for any evaluation, a whole section of the chronicle is given here:

We also regard it as worthy of mention that in his time Otto the Red came to Saint Adalbert to pray and to win him [as advocate], and at the same time to become acquainted with the fame of the glorious Boleslav, as one can find in more detail in the passion account of the martyr. Boleslav received him as honorably and grandly as it is proper to receive a king, a Roman emperor, and so noble a guest. For at the emperor's arrival Boleslav displayed exceptionally marvelous works, especially diverse battle lines. Then he had the "choir" of princes arrange themselves in rows in a spacious field, and their clothing of different bright colors in their clear divisions gave a glittering appearance to the individual lines. And there was not any cheap color displayed, but everything [that was most valuable] that could be found among the Polish people. For in Boleslav's time all knights and ladies of the court wore fur mantles instead of linen or wool clothing, and such costly furs, even if they were new, were not worn at court without trimming and gold brocade. Gold in this time was considered by all to be as common as silver, while silver was regarded as straw. When the Roman emperor observed his renown, his power, and his riches, he said, marveling: "By the crown of my empire, what I see is greater than I could have imagined from reports." And on the advice of his magnates he added before everyone: "It is not fitting that such a great and important man as this should be called duke

or count by the princes, but that he, honorably encircled with a diadem,
should be raised upon a royal throne." And he took the imperial diadem
from his head, setting it as a pact of friendship upon Boleslav's head. He
gave him, in place of a triumphal banner, a nail from the cross of the Lord
and the lance of Saint Mauritius as a gift, in return for which Boleslav gave
him an arm of Saint Adalbert. And on this day they had come together in
such high opinion of each other that the emperor made him brother and
helper of the empire [fratrem et cooperatorem imperii constituit] *and named*
him friend and ally of the Roman people. Beyond this, he turned over to him
and his successors power over ecclesiastical offices in the kingdom of
Poland and in the other barbaric lands conquered by him or still to be con-
quered that belonged to the empire. With a privilege of the holy Roman
Church, Pope Sylvester confirmed the decree recording this agreement.
After Boleslav was so spectacularly elevated to kingship by the emperor, he
exercised the generosity nature gave him by celebrating the three days of his
installation in a manner fit for a king and emperor. Each day he had
changed all the containers and tableware, replacing them with different
ones of even greater value. Then at the end of the feast he had the cupbear-
ers and waiters gather together the gold and silver containers—there were
no wooden ones—and all the cups and goblets, bowls, plates, and drinking
horns from all the tables from the three days. He gave them to the emperor
as a gift of honor, not as princely tribute. Similarly, he had the chamberlains
assemble and place in the emperor's chamber broad weavings and wall
hangings, tapestries, blankets, tablecloths, handcloths, and all that is
needed for service. Besides this he also gave a great number of other con-
tainers of gold and silver of various workmanship, brightly colored cloaks,
ornaments of unknown workmanship, jewels, and so many and so great a
variety of such things that the emperor was astonished by these gifts. He
gave such generous presents to the princes with the emperor that he won
them as his best friends. But who is able to relate what and how great the
gifts were that he gave to the people of rank, so that not a single servant out
of so great a number returned home without a present? The emperor
returned joyfully to his own land with great gifts; Boleslav, however, now as
king renewed his old wrath against his enemies.[48]

The *Passio S. Adalberti,* to which the Anonymus refers at the beginning
of his report, has not survived. Much of what is reported here can therefore
no longer be verified by accounts contemporary to the events. Textual criti-

cism of the Gallus Anonymus and evaluation of his reports thus must proceed differently. First it is particularly noteworthy that in this passage the chronicle records the elevation of a king, an event the other sources either know nothing about or let go by in silence. It is simply not plausible to assume that the Saxon authors, who do not restrain their criticism of Otto III and even less of Boleslav, would have been silent about an event with such profound consequences just because they did not like it. Even writers well inclined toward Boleslav, like Bruno of Querfurt, take no notice of his kingship.[49] This report of the royal coronation also loses credibility in light of the angry report of "German" sources from about 1025 that Boleslav laid claim to the royal title then.[50] Why this fuss, if he had already been raised to this honor by the emperor himself in the year 1000?

In addition to that problem, the royal elevation, as it was described, is also remarkable. It consisted of a single act alone: the emperor set his own crown on Boleslav's head. Such an occurrence is highly unusual, earning the description a measure of mistrust.[51] Especially striking is the fact that no ecclesiastical acts or ceremonies are mentioned. Historians have tried to explain this by linking it to the disagreement with Bishop Unger of Poznán over the foundation of the archdiocese of Gniezno. This had led to such deep-seated animosity that churchmen refused to participate in Boleslav's elevation to the kingship.[52] This is not convincing. Bishop Unger's protest was in fact completely unsuccessful in preventing the foundation of the archbishopric, so how could he have hindered ecclesiastical participation at the coronation of the duke of Poland, especially if both the emperor and Boleslav desired it? Herbert Ludat has already commented on this in a rather obscure passage. Besides all this, the Gallus Anonymus expressly conveys his sense that the coronation act was extraordinary: Boleslav was not crowned in a royal elevation, but in *foedus amicitiae*—a "pact of friendship."[53] The setting of the crown on Boleslav's head took place within the bounds of a treaty of friendship; in this context, it was a symbolic act. This sort of act is evidenced nowhere else, although we do possess many reports of friendship alliances that kings and emperors concluded with other persons.[54] It is, therefore, worth asking whether the report in fact recounts the sealing of a friendly alliance. Many other details in the account match customary ceremonies for forging a friendly alliance. These include the honorable reception, the exchange of gifts and the multiday feast, at which each participant sought to outdo the other in rich appointments and gestures of honor.[55] Much of the account cited above can in this way be read as describing the lavish celebration of a friendship treaty. Later interpreters, however, might have understood such an account as an elevation to kingship, especially if the event included the unusual act of "coronation" with the imperial crown.

The Anonymus's belief that these events signified Boleslav's elevation to kingship is discussed above. Beyond that, the account contains little that would appear to have been a later addition. There are only the remarks imputed to Otto III that a man such as Boleslav should not be duke or count, but should be raised to a royal throne. The lavish celebration of the friendship treaty between Otto III and Boleslav described in original sources also mentioned a "crowning" as ceremonial high point of the treaty making. The account in the Gallus Anonymus shows how this could later have been understood as the elevation of Boleslav to kingship. And such an understanding would not be completely mistaken. Boleslav was friend of the emperor, *cooperator imperii* and *amicus populi Romani*. An independent province of the Church was established in his territory. In these ways the ruler of Poland was in a position in reality little different from that of a king. Thietmar of Merseburg was certainly right in claiming that Otto III transformed Boleslav from a *tributarius* (tributary) into a *dominus* (lord).[56] The Gallus Anonymus too emphasizes that Boleslav had given gifts of honor to the emperor, rather than pay a demanded tribute.[57] The alliance was consolidated through a marriage pact between Boleslav's son and a niece of Otto III, a marriage that actually took place later.[58] But such agreements on many levels were not unique to the "family of kings," as they were known from Byzantium; in the west, too, such double and even threefold commitments were sealed with an oath of homage as well as friendship and kinship.[59]

In general, many questions about events in Gniezno have no certain answers. But the sources leave no doubt about this: Boleslav received and treated Otto III with such great honor so as to have stuck in the memory of many witnesses, whatever else they may have thought about the event. Beyond this the sources indicate no deterioration in the relationship between the emperor and the duke of Poland. Otto III, therefore, must have fulfilled all of Boleslav's expectations. Certainly the emperor acknowledged and honored the Poles, as the gift of a replica of the Holy Lance makes clear[60] and as was required and customary in arranging treaties of friendship. The friendly alliance, which indeed transformed Boleslav from "tributary" to "lord," was quite likely central to the political proceedings in Gniezno. Friendship with the emperor signified an elevation in rank, but it certainly did not make Boleslav independent of Otto III and his imperial authority. However, holding such a high and honorable rank substantially raised his social standing and that of his rule. It certainly also promoted his self-reliance. A proprietary church province created in his domain was the religious-ecclesiastical counterpoint to this elevation in rank. Historians have long argued that, for the sake of this agreement with Boleslav, Otto III abandoned one of Otto the Great's long-term goals in his eastern policy, that Otto III sacrificed the jurisdiction of Magdeburg over the east, which was not yet Christianized.[61] That Otto the Great had mission plans of such a scope in the first place is more a construct of modern research than any real policy of the tenth century. At least there is scant evidence in the sources that Magdeburg was accorded such a wide jurisdiction.[62] Founding the new ecclesiastical province of Gniezno in fact impinged on Magdeburg's status much less than scholars have long assumed, largely because they worked from a nationalist perspective. After the Liutizi rebellion of 983, after all, the archdiocese of Magdeburg had more urgent duties and worries than the ecclesiastical infiltration of Poland. For Boleslav, however, the ecclesiastical rank raised him above the dukes of the empire. While these dukes had once had a similar discretionary power over the imperial church early in the Ottonian period, they had lost that right by the end of the tenth century.[63]

All of Otto's steps were likely planned well in advance and perhaps with the agreement of Pope Sylvester II. The extant sources, however, give no insight into stages of preparation and motivations. It is unknown who among the ecclesiastical and secular magnates of the empire took part in preparations for the journey to Gniezno, or which of these magnates were present in Gniezno at the time of the visit.[64] The sources name no one from the ranks of the great nobles. On the other hand, there is also no evidence that this event in Gniezno was regarded with suspicion, or protested, in the empire. After Gniezno, the emperor did not avoid contact with the man who was supposedly most affected, Archbishop Giselher of Magdeburg. Instead Otto hastened directly to Magdeburg, accompanied and guided on his route by Boleslav Chrobry. Boleslav, on his departure, gave a further present of three hundred armored horsemen, which sources report especially pleased the emperor.[65]

From Gniezno to Aachen

The emperor followed Ottonian tradition by celebrating Palm Sunday in Magdeburg. On the next day he strongly urged Archbishop Giselher to return again to his old see of Merseburg. It is impossible to tell if this request was

connected in any way with events in Gniezno. Some have conjectured that
Giselher made himself disliked by siding with the annoying Bishop Unger of
Poznán and protesting against the foundation of the archbishopric of
Gniezno.[66] But this assumes that the emperor could manipulate synods and
their decrees as if he were playing chess. Such a power is not at all likely.
Energetic adherence to legal positions, even against imperial wishes, is
attested in numerous cases. Moreover, Otto III's conduct toward Giselher is
not consistent. It was affected by the measures the synods of Pavia and Rome
enacted to deal with the Merseburg question.[67] Thietmar reports in detail and
with no sympathy the subterfuges Giselher used to evade the threatening
snare. He is certainly not overly concerned to do justice to Giselher. First
Giselher supposedly achieved a week's delay by offering a large bribe to mid-
dlemen. When the postponement was over and Giselher was obliged to
answer before a synod in Quedlinburg on Easter Monday, he again excused
himself on grounds of ill health and sent the provost Walthard to defend him.
Later a synod in Aachen was appointed to deal with his case. According to
Thietmar, the archbishop did appear on this occasion, but demanded the
right to have his case heard by a general council. By this means he again
obtained a postponement.[68] Giselher's behavior is a fine example of how
someone could hinder or protract ecclesiastical decisions. It shows how
strictly all parties felt themselves bound by legal custom, even when it was
not in their own interests.

Aachen was Otto III's next destination, and Boleslav Chrobry apparently
accompanied him there. This unusually long companionship of the two main
actors at Gniezno might cast further light on their political relationship; that
is, if we can believe the report that while in Aachen Otto III presented
Boleslav with Charlemagne's throne.[69] But this account must be interpreted
in context. More occurred in Aachen than the synod mentioned above, which
deliberated concerning Archbishop Giselher. While in Aachen Otto III also
acted in a way that would have long-term consequences for his reputation. He
found and opened the grave of Charlemagne, with his own hands and with
only a few companions. Almost immediately, contemporaries branded this
deed a desecration of the grave, for which God punished the emperor with an
early death.[70] Modern scholarship has enthusiastically interpreted the grave
opening as evidence that the youthful emperor was a fanatical dreamer, while
some have added praise for the seriousness with which Otto III introduced
himself into the tradition of Charlemagne.[71] One of the participants, the Italian count Otto of Lomello, left a detailed report of the opening of Charle-

magne's tomb. Count Otto had already accompanied the emperor from Rome to Gniezno, and he, along with two bishops, was considered worthy to witness the event. His report, preserved in the *Chronicon Novalinciense,* is generally considered the standard description of the event:

So we went in to Charles. He did not lie, as the dead otherwise do, but sat as if he were living. He was crowned with a golden crown and held in his gloved hands a scepter; the fingernails had penetrated through the gloves and stuck out. Above him was a canopy made of limestone and marble. As we entered, we broke through this. At our entrance, a strong smell struck us. We immediately gave Emperor Charles our kneeling homage, and Emperor Otto robed him on the spot with white garments, cut his nails, and put in order the damage that had been done. Emperor Charles had not lost any of his members to decay, excepting only the tip of his nose. Emperor Otto replaced this with gold, took a tooth from Charles's mouth, walled up the entrance to the chamber, and withdrew again.[72]

Using this as the basis, scholars have tried to understand the proceedings, a struggle since none of the sources indicate what motivated Otto. Scholars often have digressed widely from the sources in trying to determine what actually occurred. The extent of this digression is clear in Mathilde Uhlirz's attempted summary of the state of scholarship: "Recent research has generally proven that Otto III by no means wanted to disrupt the state of reverence [that surrounded Charlemagne]. Rather he wanted to lay an account before his great predecessor and beg for his help in his further undertakings. He did so in a state of high tension about the agreement reached with Poland, in his new imperial power, and in western Christendom. Perhaps he also wanted to prepare his own resting place, since at this time he was already distressed by premonitions of death."[73] Every single point made here is an assumption with no basis in the sources.

Very recently Knut Görich has located the proceedings within an entirely different tradition. His interpretation of the tomb opening has the advantage of being grounded in the accounts of the various sources. He pointed out how many of the statements used the mode of description familiar from accounts of discovery and elevation of the relics of saints.[74] This is true of those parts of the account in which the location of the grave had been forgotten; the search for, and opening of, the grave took place secretly with few companions; all had prepared themselves with three days of fasting; they found an uncorrupted body; and they reverently took away small parts of the body.[75] Details of the description closely match hagiographical descriptions of opening the tombs of saints. Görich's conclusion, therefore, has much to recommend it: that Otto III's goal was to canonize his great predecessor, a plan that apparently fell through only because the ruler died shortly afterward. This view of affairs has decided advantages. It is based on clues in the sources, and moreover it puts the proceedings into a tradition that removes the impression that they were spectacular to the point of sacrilege. Such an interpretation is clearly preferable to the older one, which emphasized political issues and motives. This new perspective on the proceedings also explains why Boleslav Chrobry received Charlemagne's throne in return for an arm of Saint Adalbert. The exchange only makes sense if the throne, too, had, or would soon receive, the character of a relic.

In an imperial journey already filled with events, Aachen was the last stop at which something unusual occurred. From Aachen, Otto set out for Italy—his last expedition there. One last thing is striking about this long journey from Rome to Gniezno and (by way of Magdeburg) to Aachen, however. The emperor had been in Italy for several years by this time, and yet we hear astonishingly little during the entire trip about any measures and consultations dealing with problems in the "German" part of the empire. We also know virtually nothing about who sought him out and accompanied him for longer or shorter periods. Certainly cardinals such as the oblationary Rotbertus were with the emperor when he left Rome and were still with him in Aachen. The same is true of Count Otto of Lomello, the count palatine of Pavia.[76] But we simply cannot say which German magnates were with the emperor in Gniezno. With the exception of attacks against Archbishop Giselher, we also hear nothing of deliberations concerning problems in the empire north of the Alps. Apparently Otto III did very little "ruling" in this region. Nor does the impression change when one considers the documents Otto's chancery issued during the journey for a wide array of recipients.[77] These grants leave no trace of splendidly attended court assemblies at which emperor and magnates met together. In the same way, it was clearly not necessary to hold intensive consultations concerning issues left unresolved or postponed. This insight is an important basis for assessing rulership in the tenth century. It reveals how inextensive this rule was. Even after an absence of several years, there was no backlog of questions and problems requiring the ruler's decision or the ruler's action in consultation with the magnates. The Quedlinburg annalist reinforces this strong impression. This author characterized Otto III's ruling activities during this period as follows: Otto returned to his palace in Quedlinburg after he had satisfied the expectations of his magnates and the people (*totius senatus ac plebis expectationi satisfacturus*). He spent a week there carrying out his royal duties—"ruling, granting, giving freely, and rewarding" (*regendo, indulgendo, largiendo ac remunerando*).[78] It would be hard to describe the "essence" of rule in this period more plainly and clearly. Because this was the case, Otto III could soon return to Rome, without being criticized for neglecting his duties as ruler by leaving Germany.

✝ Chapter 5 ✝

THE LAST EXPEDITION TO ROME

"Government Business" on the Way

As remarked in the last chapter, there is strikingly little evidence for Otto's actual rule of the empire, even though signs of such activity would be expected after his long absence. This clearly underscores one of the main themes of this book: how effective rulership actually was in the tenth century, how wide the sphere of political activity, and whether the king could shape the events of this era. Did he spend his time outlining political strategies in the widely diverse realms of church and monastic policy, the policies of the west, east, and Italy? Did he try to reach accord among the powers concerned? Did he then formulate final plans, and oversee their implementation? Or are these activities anachronisms? Did a tenth-century king understand his duties differently? To answer this question, it would be instructive to observe for a while longer Otto III's activities as ruler and to note where and how he acted as a ruler on his new journey to Italy.

To anticipate the conclusion: signs of Otto's rulership are relatively meager. Charters alone are almost the only evidence for stops along the way and contacts made. Historians and annalists did not make note or comment during this period about the emperor's activities. Furthermore, the documents reveal no main points of policy evident in who received Otto III's grants or in who intervened on their behalf. One of the few notable grants is the nunnery of Hilwartshausen, hitherto subject to Mainz, to Bishop Bernward of Hildesheim. As we will see below, this measure is striking in light of the Gandersheim controversy.[1] Furthermore, Bishop Henry of Würzburg appears both as a recipient of royal gifts and as someone who intervened. He must have been among Otto III's special circle. After all, he was the brother of the chancellor and archbishop Heribert of Cologne, himself a confidant of the ruler.[2] Several other monasteries, bishoprics, and laypeople also received gifts or privileges in this period. But those gifts are not concentrated geographically, nor do they reveal any royal political strategy.[3] Of course, transmission of documents was accidental and many were lost. What has survived, though, attests to a "normal" level of royal activity in granting gifts and privileges.

The same is true of the places Otto III chose to stop on his way south and the contacts he made there. A meeting between Otto III, the Burgundian king Rudolf III, and his wife in Bruchsal is an exception, even though only a single document attests to it. It is impossible, however, to attribute a purely political motivation to this meeting. Bruchsal was very close to the monastery of Selz, where Empress Adelheid had been buried the year before.[4] Otto III more likely went to his grandmother's tomb to pray, and Adelheid's Burgundian relatives—King Rudolf was her nephew—were there for the same reason. This certainly does not exclude the possibility that the visits were coordinated and the opportunity seized for political discussions. From Bruchsal the emperor proceeded to Lake Constance, evident from charters issued in Hohentwiel. Here, too, there is no hint of his activities. Yet in this period the famous so-called Liuthar gospel book was produced on Reichenau, including the royal portrait of Otto III that until recently has been the subject of controversy.[5] It is attractive to imagine that during his residence the emperor discussed and planned the program of illustration with the masters of the Reichenau school of painting. But this must remain pure conjecture. As in other cases, here too we quite simply know nothing about whether rulers helped to plan the works of art that depicted them.

These few events complete the list of all the important activities Otto III conducted in the empire after his return from Gniezno, or at least those activities transmitted in the sources. To return once more to the point at issue here: after several years of absence in Italy and a carefully planned trip to Gniezno, the emperor returned to his holdings north of the Alps for less than half a year before departing yet again for Rome. During these months, he held synodal assemblies in Magdeburg, Quedlinburg, and Aachen on the question of reestablishing Merseburg, but did not come to a decision. He opened the tomb of Charlemagne, probably visited his grandmother's grave, and then headed back over the Alps to Italy, traveling by way of the Lake Constance region and through Chur. Certainly, he issued other documents on the way from Magdeburg via Aachen, Tribur, Bruchsal, and Hohentwiel. But there is no sign of court assemblies to deliberate political decisions or appearances to demonstrate the emperor's authority. Further, no one found this striking or worthy of criticism. This has parallels in many other cases, and leads to the following conclusion: We must be careful when describing and evaluating kingship in this period, and we must use careful reflection to guard ourselves from projecting notions from later centuries about the extent of rulership, spheres of involvement, and areas of duty into these earlier times.

The patterns described here repeat themselves to a certain extent after Otto arrived in Italy. In Como and Pavia, Otto III met a Venetian emissary, the deacon Johannes. Johannes first reported to the emperor concerning the early stages of a campaign by a Venetian fleet against the cities on the Dalmatian coast, and then later announced the great success of this action.[6] The emperor's response was most unusual: he announced his intention to meet Doge Peter II Orseolo face-to-face, to whom Otto III was already bound as godfather to the doge's son. To achieve this goal—and this is what makes the proposal extraordinary—Otto wanted to enter Venetian territory secretly. Since who came to whom for a meeting was crucial in establishing rank and honor, the importance this offer had for the doge is easily apparent. It is harder to understand why Otto III proposed a secret meeting. There are comparable cases in which secret meetings took place under specific circumstances.[7] What at first glance appears a Venetian chronicle's added frill or an emperor's unconventional fancy thus in this way assumes another meaning. The meeting really did take place in the manner the emperor proposed. To be sure, the meeting only occurred after nearly a year had passed. However, for the sake of continuity we will consider it here.

In April 1001, Otto III, pleading illness, proceeded with a handful of trusted companions from Ravenna to the monastery of Saint Mary in Pomposa on Lake Comacchio.[8] There the emissary Johannes sent a ship at night to bring Otto to Venice. When he arrived, the doge personally received Otto in the dark of the night. The Venetian description of this meeting paints the scene in broad strokes, reporting that the emperor and the doge could not even see each other for the darkness. Still, after embraces and kisses of greeting they supposedly agreed that Otto would first go to the monastery of Saint Zacharius and then come before dawn to the doge's palace.[9] The emperor is even supposed to have disguised himself (*sane vili . . . habitu indutus*) to avoid recognition. Then in the early morning the doge officially greeted Count Hezelin, one of Otto III's companions, as though Hezelin had come to Venice as the emperor's emissary. Only later did the doge go secretly to the emperor in the east tower. So as not to arouse any suspicion, the doge returned to the others at meal times. Doge and emperor, however, passed the evening in feasting and discussion (*dapibus colloquisque*). As ceremonial climax of the meeting, Otto III stood as godfather at the baptism of the doge's daughter, strengthening their alliance (*ad perfecte namque fidei vinculum confirmandum*) in this way. When the doge tried to offer rich presents at the emperor's departure, Otto refused them, claiming that he had not come to Venice because of avarice, but out of love for Saint Mark and the doge. The Quedlinburg Annals put similar words in Otto's mouth during his visit to Gniezno. The secrecy of the meeting was further emphasized at the emperor's departure. Count Hezelin and the other companions remained in Venice for another day to maintain the fiction of an embassy. Three days later, though, the doge called together the people of Venice and told them about the event, praising the fidelity of the emperor as well as the wisdom of his *senior*, by which term he meant the emperor. Otto III behaved similarly. After his return to Ravenna, he also announced to all that he had been in Venice. People could scarcely believe this, and marveled greatly.[10]

This visit has attracted great attention from scholars, who focus specifically on its significance for the relationship between Venice and the empire.[11] If Otto III had already based his relationship with Boleslav in Gniezno on the *foedus amicitiae* (friendship pact), a quite similar agreement was apparently reached at Venice: that of spiritual kinship, compaternity based on baptismal sponsorship.[12] Note that, even according to Venetian accounts, compaternity did not exclude the doge's dependence, since he still applied the title *senior* to Otto.[13]

That this meeting was planned and conducted in secrecy, however, has attracted little attention and has not been explained. The sources almost force us to the conclusion that people of the time saw this secrecy as the emperor's whim and did not take it very seriously. But the secrecy makes sense, and also is part of a tradition. Certain circumstances led other persons in the Middle Ages to hold secret discussions.[14] These invariably took place whenever issues were not clear and the success of discussions was in doubt. In other known cases, it was not the meeting itself that was secret, but the content discussed. Such meetings made it possible to seek solutions confidentially. In our case the content was kept secret, as initially was the meeting itself. This is best explained by proposing that the discussions were about the relationship of Venice to the empire, and that of the doge to the emperor. In view of Byzantine claims to overlordship of Venice, such a discussion would be highly sensitive. Therefore secrecy was probably designed to avoid any disagreeable consequences from failed negotiations on an official visit.

Such a failure would have required each side to cling to its public position, and perhaps eventually to demand satisfaction for suffering loss of honor or even affront. When Otto III insisted on silence, it thus was far from a "boyish" idea. Instead it was a strategy that made it possible to deal personally with the doge at all. Here the emperor paid careful attention to contemporary rules of the political game, and used them to their full extent. The trip to Venice, like that to Gniezno, was a visit to territory under foreign rule. The emperor's visit was a grand gesture that elevated the status of the person visited. Despite the friendships and compaternities established at these meetings, it must be noted, the participants remained conscious of the emperor's superior status. Otto III clearly demonstrated this at both Gniezno and Venice by taking few or none of the gifts offered him. In this way, he conducted himself as the participant of higher rank.[15]

Let us return from this excursus on Venice to Otto III's journey to Rome in the year 1000. We have already followed the journey as far as Pavia. In Pavia, Otto III apparently was occupied again with a conflict in northern Italy between Margrave Arduin of Ivrea (later elected king of Italy) and the bishops of the region around Ivrea. This had reached a climax in 997 with the murder of Bishop Peter of Vercelli.[16] The Roman synod of 999 had already found Arduin guilty of the crime and ordered his goods and supporters seized. Efforts to carry out this judgment can be seen in privileges the emperor either issued in Pavia or dealt with there and later had written down.[17] They addressed the bishoprics concerned: Novara, Ivrea, and Vercelli. One of these documents remarks that Ardicinus, Arduin's son, had been summoned to judgment in Pavia, but that he had fled on the night of the proceedings. This must have occurred when Otto was residing in the city.[18] Seen as a whole, the documents reveal that the emperor took strong measures to improve the legal position of these bishops in their territories. From Pavia Otto then continued on to Rome without any long stops. Once he reached the city, he stepped into a conflict that echoed from Saxony to the Roman metropolis, that occupied several synods and emperors, and that can be regarded as a prime example of tenth-century "conflict culture."

The Gandersheim Conflict

This conflict originated in the year 989, when Otto III's sister Sophia received the veil as a canoness in Gandersheim. This was discussed in an earlier chapter.[19] Before examining the conflict and its background, it must be stressed that our only evidence about the facts, arguments, and course of this controversy come from a source concerned with the outcome and supporting Hildesheim. This is the *vita* of Bishop Bernward of Hildesheim, in which a "memorandum" on the affair gives detailed evidence.[20] Since the controversy did not involve a clear question of right or wrong, such one-sided information does not necessarily prejudice our interpretation. The course of the squabbling and the ways and means used to resolve it exemplify the way tenth-century society understood law, even if in this case it was primarily canon law. Although the Hildesheim description was clearly partial, it makes clear how very important consensus was in reaching legal decisions. That consensus was established through consultation among the participants in synods. Opposition based on recognized legal custom had every opportunity to gain a hearing. In addition, the course of the conflict makes clear how little the Church in this period was hierarchically structured with Rome at the apex. Roman synods under the presidency of pope and emperor simply did not have the authority to force compliance with their decisions, especially if those decisions concerned an archbishop of Mainz. Indeed this conflict makes clear that nothing took the place of physical presence. The controversy could not be steered by letters, instructions, or legates from Rome, even though the legates without doubt brought with them insignia and vestments "as if the pope himself were coming."[21]

The commotion that arose at Sophia's consecration as canoness, as discussed earlier, was resolved with considerable effort and bother. Sophia was veiled by both the bishop of Hildesheim and the archbishop of Mainz. In the period following, Sophia led a very unrestricted life as a canoness, at least according to the Hildesheim account. She spent several years at the imperial court. While there, she had established a close relationship with Archbishop Willigis, a friendship that raised all sorts of suspicions.[22] In the meantime, the fundamental conflict over rights in and over Gandersheim had not really been settled. It broke out again over who should consecrate the monastic church that Abbess Gerberga had had built. Because of her age, the abbess had given Sophia the burden of preparing for the consecration, and Sophia had arranged the event in consultation with Archbishop Willigis. Bishop Bernward of Hildesheim, the diocesan who in the normal course of events would have had full authority over this affair, did indeed receive an invitation to the consecration. But then later he was informed that the archbishop of Mainz had decided to delay the consecration by a week. Bernward became stubborn; he sent a letter informing Willigis that he could not attend at the later time because of imperial orders. Bernward then appeared in Gandersheim on the first date arranged. The nuns rightly feared that he intended to bless the church imme-diately and alone, and they responded by treating the bishop with marked dis-respect. At the celebration of mass a commotion broke out:

When the offering was reached, they threw down their offerings angrily and with incredible fury, and uttered savage curses against the bishop. Deeply shocked by this unusual commotion, the bishop, weeping, did not think of the injury done him. Instead, thinking of the example of the true shepherd who prayed for his persecutors, he deplored the ignorance or rather malevo-lence of the raging women. So he returned to the altar and brought the mass to its usual conclusion in deep contrition of spirit.[23]

We misunderstand the scene if we do not see it in the context of how demonstrative behavior functioned in the Middle Ages. Dissent and conflicts had their established arsenal of symbolism, because invariably one used overt behavior to express disagreement with a position. The sisters made clear beyond any possible misunderstanding that they considered protection of their legal position more important than the peace of the holy space. On the other side, Bishop Bernward's mass expressed his episcopal rights over Gander-sheim, which he publicly defended as the lawful diocesan bishop.

When Willigis came a week later to consecrate the church, Bernward sent as his representative his fellow bishop Eggehard. Eggehard was a refugee from Schleswig who had taken up residence in Hildesheim. In company with other dignitaries of the Hildesheim church, Eggehard formally requested that the archbishop desist from the planned ceremony and first take counsel with his fellow bishops concerning the contested claims. And in fact this inter-vention did prevent the consecration and did convince the archbishop of Mainz to summon an assembly for two months later, supposedly to decide the conflict. Bernward, however, felt his claim would only succeed if he set out for Rome to demand his legal rights from emperor and pope. The recep-tion the two gave the bishop is described in the *Vita Bernwardi*. It serves well as a paradigm for demonstrative behavior toward a close confidant:

When the pious and humble emperor heard this [that Bernward had arrived in Rome], he could not wait, because of his longing to see his old teacher. Because he did not want him to have greater effort, the emperor himself hur-ried from the palace almost two miles to the church of Saint Peter, received him with great love, embraced and kissed him like his best friend, and accompanied him to his lodgings. There the emperor spoke a long time with him and bade him come to the palace the next day. And he would not allow the bishop to pay anything for his needs out of his own pocket; instead, for six weeks, as long as he remained, the emperor cared richly for all his needs. The following morning the emperor invited the pope to receive his beloved guest. As the bishop approached, both met him in the entry hall and welcomed him. Nor would they permit him to return to his lodging, but the emperor instead placed at his disposal a splendid apartment next to his own chambers. Then they sat side by side, sometimes in the emperor's chamber and sometimes in the bishop's, and discussed the legal dispute and the concerns of the state. For the emperor did not need details about the archbishop and the Gandersheim conflict, about which reports had already reached him, so that before Bernward's arrival all was already known. Therefore he only needed to answer briefly certain small questions of the emperor's.[24]

Notably the author gives a vivid description of how confidential conversation functioned as a sign of particular esteem. In addition to this, though, there are many other signs and gestures bestowing honor: going to meet Bernward at his arrival, the embrace and kiss, and the prepared chambers, as well as the assumption of all costs.

A consequence of Bernward's journey was that two synods now met at almost the same time to deal with the Gandersheim controversy: a regional synod in Gandersheim itself over which Willigis presided, and a general synod in Rome under the presidency of pope and emperor. In Gandersheim a commotion arose when the archbishop asked the bishops present to immediately reach a decision about this problem under penalty of excommunication. The bishops responded that this was impossible in the absence of Bernward, a legal point already raised by Bishop Eggehard, acting as Bernward's representative.[25] At this point, many left the assembly. The only honorable solution for Willigis—as always according to the Hildesheim description—was for him and his supporters to raise the question of boundaries. In fact that had the desired result. In Rome, by contrast, the conference went smoothly and without dissent. Above all, the *vita* credits Duke Henry of Bavaria, who worked eagerly to restore peace and concord, with summoning the council. His interest is certainly understandable, since his aunt was abbess of Gandersheim and his father was buried there.[26] After Bernward had presented his complaint to the synod, the pope asked those present "if what the archbishop had held could be understood as a synod, conducted as it was with the people he himself had brought together, in a church that had always been the possession of the bishops of Hildesheim and moreover held in the absence of the bishop while the bishop was on his way to the Roman see because of this very issue. Or if not, what ought one to call such a conventicle?"[27] The panel met publicly, but the participants asked to discuss the question in private. The pope agreed. The Roman bishops then withdrew for deliberation, and after this closed-door session their answer was unequivocal. All the archbishop of Mainz had enacted in his mockery of a "synod" at Gandersheim was declared void. Bernward was confirmed in his rights over the convent in all respects. Further, the Saxon bishops were summoned to meet in Pöhlde, and a papal emissary was to attend the meeting. Chosen for this purpose was a Saxon named Frederick, a cardinal priest of the Roman church, "still young in years, but with the habits of a mature man."[28] Everything possible was done to strengthen his authority as a papal representative: "he was ornamented with the papal insignia, as if the pope himself was coming. His saddle, like that of the pope, was covered with purple in the Roman fashion. At the same time, papal and imperial letters were sent to the bishops and the other princes, bidding them to receive the Roman legate with suitable honors and to give his legation unqualified obedience, as if they saw the pope himself before them."[29] All this was not sufficient to cause Willigis's party to recognize Frederick. They expressed their rejection unmistakably and demonstratively:

The archbishop, indeed, and those of his party spurned him [the legate] with unbelievable indignation and curses. Bishop Bernward, though, along with Archbishop Lievizo of Hamburg and many others, treated him with reverence and showed him special honor. When the council assembled, indescribable conflict and tumult arose. For the pope's vicar was not even granted a place to sit. A horrible racket broke out, law and right were ignored, canonical order was brought to nothing. The pope's vicar, sitting between Bishops Lievizo and Bernward, announced that he had with him a papal letter and legation to the bishops and asked that he might carry out his duties. When silence had finally fallen, the legate admonished the bishops with mild words about peace, love, and harmony. Then he produced the pope's letter to the archbishop and asked that it be read publicly in the hearing of all. When the archbishop refused to touch or look at it, the letter was publicly read at the demand of the bishops.[30]

Then people on all sides tried to get Willigis to concede and to render satisfaction in accordance with the advice or judgment of the assembled brethren. This led to further tumult. The doors of the meeting room were wrenched open. Laymen stormed in, issuing threats against the papal plenipotentiary and of course also against Bishop Bernward. The assembly was postponed until the next day. The papal legate commanded on pain of papal ban that the archbishop appear before the synod again the next day. This too failed, for Willigis secretly left early in the morning with his entourage. As a result the legate suspended him from all exercise of his office until he answered at Christmas before a synod held in the pope's presence. In addition to sending this summons to Willigis in writing, the legate also commanded the other bishops to appear in Rome. The archbishop of Mainz apparently was not very impressed by this legatine proceeding. His followers next undertook an assault on the monastery of Hilwartshausen, which Bernward had received as a gift from Otto III and where he celebrated special feast days. They smashed everything there to pieces and took Bernward's people there captive. Such activity was typical feuding behavior by the laity, which coerced the enemy to yield by damaging his goods. There was defensive activity at Gandersheim itself: they prepared for a visit by the bishop of Hildesheim as for a possible siege.

The failed meeting in Pöhlde and the papal representative's summons of the parties in the conflict to a Roman synod, combined with the archbishop's suspension, did not prevent the other bishops in the empire from taking further steps to resolve the conflict. With this goal in mind, a synod was called in Frankfurt. Bernward did not appear there, excusing himself because of illness. This again postponed the judgment until the next appointed assembly in Fritzlar. Apparently Willigis sought a resolution of the squabble during this period through regional or imperial synods, where he could demand presidency or copresidency. Bernward, on the contrary, appealed to Rome—understandable in light of the archbishop's preeminence in the empire. Besides, in Rome Bernward could be sure of the emperor's support. And so it happened again. Pleading ill health, Bernward sent his confidant Thangmar to Italy in his place. This representative found a hearing for his petition before an assembly in Todi, in the presence of emperor and pope. The legate Frederick was also received there. He confirmed the Hildesheim version of events and raised serious complaints against Willigis. Despite this, the only decision by the synod was to wait for more imperial bishops to arrive.[31] The death of Otto III put further activities and decisions on a back burner. In the following years, the conflict would engage several more emperors and synods.[32]

It is remarkable how shadowy a role Otto III played in this conflict, despite all the details in the Hildesheim account. Despite all the esteem and friendship that he felt for Bishop Bernward and despite the fact that Archbishop Willigis had fallen somewhat into disfavor by this time, the emperor did not intervene in the conflict. At least he did not do so effectively.[33] The sources do not explain this. The most probable reason is that he could not do so, because legal customs did not allow the emperor a dominant role in this sort of affair. This is all the more striking because the case concerns a family monastery of the Ottonian dynasty and the monarch's sister was the protagonist of Willigis's party. This indicates that Otto's informal and private channels for exerting influence were not sufficient to convince the most important archbishop in the empire and his own sister. Resolution was further complicated or hindered in this case because one of the parties—the archbishop of Mainz—claimed the traditional right to preside over regional and imperial synods. This created a problem of "partisan presidency," against which the legal norms of the time apparently had no recourse. Certainly it explains Bernward's multiple evasions and appeal to Roman courts. This was a way out, but most of the imperial episcopate in this era did not accept it as a true solution—or they would not have more or less ignored the Roman judgments and looked for their own resolution to the conflict. Viewed in this way, the Gandersheim conflict marks, or rather manifests, a systemic weakness, which would later play itself out in a similar fashion in royal courts and their judgments, particularly when the king himself was party to the conflict.[34]

The "Ingratitude" of the Romans

Let us return to Otto's last journey to Italy. Without making long stops along the way, the emperor traveled from Pavia to Rome in the summer of 1000. He remained there for the entire second half of the year, without performing any notable acts of rulership. Action only became necessary at the beginning of 1001, when the inhabitants of Tivoli, a city near Rome, rebelled against imperial rule. They killed the commander (*dux*) of the city, Mazelinus, whom the sources call a "familiar" (*familiaris*) of the monarch.[35] Otto responded by besieging Tivoli with an army under his personal leadership. We know details of this incident because Bishop Bernward was with the emperor's army at this time and played an important role in easing tensions. At any rate, his *vita* asserts that the bishop played a prominent role. The city was encircled. Considerable technical expertise was expended to build machines and earthworks designed to interrupt the water supply. When that appeared unlikely to succeed:

Several days later Lord Bernward and the pope appeared before the city gates. The citizens joyfully received the servants of God as they approached and led them with reverence into their city. Neither gave way until with God's help they submitted peacefully to the emperor's command. On the next day the bishops returned to the emperor, followed by a noble triumphal procession. All the leading citizens of the city followed them, naked but for loincloths, carrying in their right hands a sword and in their left a rod, and proceeded thus to the palace. They surrendered themselves and all their possessions to the emperor, excepting nothing, not even their lives. Whomever he regarded guilty he might execute with the sword, or if he preferred to show mercy, he might order them to be beaten at the whipping post with the rod. If he wished the walls of the city to be leveled, they would carry it out promptly and willingly. Never again in their lives would they oppose his majesty's command. The emperor gave the highest praise to the peacemakers, the pope and Bishop Bernward, and at their request pardoned the guilty. Having taken counsel, they decided not to destroy the city. The inhabitants were again admitted to the emperor's favor and admonished to be peaceable and not to fail the emperor again.[36]

We have here a classic description of a *deditio*, an act of submission, as we have already seen in another form in the cases of Henry the Quarrelsome and Crescentius.[37] This act is the most typical form of rendering satisfaction, with which conflicts were concluded in the Middle Ages. In this period there was what almost amounted to an *ordo deditionis*, a specific fixed ritual for acts of submission. In other words, its essential components were of a ritual nature. Several indispensable deeds and gestures were prescribed, even though it was possible to tailor the submission to each specific situation. Among these necessary elements was appropriate clothing: one had to appear barefoot and in penitential garments. Objects such as the sword and rod in this case, as well as verbal self-accusations, publicly acknowledged that punishment was merited. In general, the high point of a submission was the prostration. While not specifically mentioned in this source, it is a logical conclusion to the parade as it was described. Then followed the judgment of the humbled offenders for better or for worse, which is reported here. Not unusually, but rather as a rule, people who renounced all their rights in that way found forgiveness. Here, however, we touch on a point essential for understanding the proceedings: this was by no means an event whose conclusion was left open to chance. Instead, mediators, in this case Pope Sylvester and Bishop Bernward, would deal with the specifics and then act as guarantors of the agreement. Those submitting were assured of forgiveness in return. In other words, this event was staged. All the participants played fixed roles. However, the purpose of such productions was to make the behavior displayed in this way binding. The public was, so to speak, made to witness and thus guarantee what had been promised through submission and forgiveness.

An imperial charter, issued in the same month as the siege of Tivoli, was addressed to Pope Sylvester II. This document expresses, as no others do, Otto's understanding of his own position as well as his relationship to Rome and the popes. Not surprisingly, this document has received most intensive scrutiny from historians.[38] Leo of Vercelli is considered the author, and it is also thought that the recipient himself, Pope Sylvester II, influenced its composition.[39] The title of the emperor already attests to the intended programmatic message: *servus apostolorum et secundum voluntatem dei salvatoris Romanorum imperator augustus* (servant of the apostles and, in accordance with the will of God the savior, emperor augustus of the Romans). We encounter the designation *servus apostolorum* here for the first time, a change from the formula *servus Iesu Christi* used on the journey to Gniezno. The closing formula of the document was partially anticipated by an expression that Otto used on 18 January 1001 in a document for Vercelli: *secundum voluntatem Iesu Christi Romanorum imperator augustus sanctarumque ecclesiarum devotissimus et fidelissimus dilatator* (emperor augustus of the Romans by the will of Jesus Christ, and most devoted and most faithful enlarger of the holy churches).[40] A variant of the title also appears on 23 January 1001 in a document for Hildesheim. Its author was once considered to have been Thangmar, also the author of the *Vita Bernwardi*. Recently, strong arguments have suggested that the document was the work of the emperor himself. He named himself thus: *Otto tercius Romanus Saxonicus et Italicus, apostolorum servus, dono dei Romani orbis imperator augustus* (Otto III of Rome, Saxony, and Italy, servant of the apostles, by God's gift emperor augustus of the Roman world).[41] After this, its first appearance, the designation of *servus apostolorum* became standard in the chancellery as an invariable component of the *intitulatio*. This devotional formula certainly expresses more than piety. Like the description of the emperor as "enlarger," it attests to the monarch's efforts to spread the Christian faith. This was displayed concretely in the proceedings during Otto's journey to Gniezno and in the case of Hungary.[42]

The *intitulatio* follows a similarly programmatic confirmation of Rome's position: *Romam caput mundi profitemur, Romanam ecclesiam matrem omnium ecclesiarum esse testamur* ("We declare Rome to be the head of the world, we avow that the Roman church is the mother of all churches"). There are difficulties in interpreting this. One cannot be sure whether the two parts of this declaration refer to Rome twice—first to the ancient imperial capital and then to Christian papal Rome. Certainly this has been assumed since Percy Ernst Schramm's times. Knut Görich has opposed this view, arguing that the formula *Roma caput mundi* can refer equally to Rome as city of the apostles.[43] One can certainly not exclude this possibility. But praise for the Roman church as mother of all churches directly precedes what has been called a "philippic in diplomatic form."[44] And this philippic is aimed against the popes, the predecessors of the recipient. It proclaims that their carelessness and incompetence had darkened "their distinguished title" (*sue claritatis tituli*). Both in Rome and beyond they had sold and alienated rights and granted away titles. Later they misappropriated imperial rights. Some sentences follow that are very hard to understand, but that historians have long felt declare the Donation of Constantine to be false. This assertion was then lost until the fifteenth century.[45] After several thorough analyses in recent years, however, scholars now understand these sentences differently. They were a polemic against the Ottonianum—Otto the Great's donation to the Roman church—but without naming the donor himself. They were also a polemic against a copy of the Donation of Constantine, claiming special authenticity, that was part of an attempt to extend its powers. Finally they were a polemic against a donation of Charles the Bald to the Roman church. Charles supposedly made this grant long after he had lost the imperial office and been expelled. Otto III would accept none of these as support for papal and curial claims. On the other hand, as he makes clear in the positive part of the document, he wants "to give to Saint Peter what is his own [the emperor's] from his own generosity, not give what belongs to him [Saint Peter] as if it were his [the emperor's]."[46] Scholars have emphatically stressed that the gift here is not given to the pope or to the Roman church, but to Saint Peter. Gifts to the patron saints of churches or monasteries are certainly not unusual. But in this case, the formula about free power to dispose of the property once it had been received, the *libera potestas vendendi, commutandi*, etc., is missing. This supports the assumption that the grant was made most specifically to Saint Peter, whose steward Otto III could lawfully regard himself. According to this interpretation the emperor himself subtly and implicitly retained rights to dispose of the property in question.[47] It also gives particular support to the theory that the transfer would also have strengthened Otto's rule.[48]

Apart from the problem of how to understand this unusual stress on Saint Peter, the document provides important evidence for collaboration of emperor and pope at this time. It not only asserts imperial rights, but it also rejects the curia's strategies for restoring a secular papal territory. It is also impressive testimony to the overarching significance of Rome in the area of imperial-papal collaboration.

However, the Romans were not greatly impressed by these plans for their city. This much is clear from an incident during the exact weeks in which this diploma was issued: the "uprising" of the citizens, which in many respects thwarted these plans. Sources about the uprising are numerous, but do not agree well enough to allow a conclusive picture of how serious the revolt was and what danger it posed to the emperor and his entourage. At any rate the revolt certainly came as a complete surprise. Certainly, too, not enough military contingents were in the city to provide the emperor security. Contemporaries attributed the rebellion to Roman resentment over Tivoli's pardon, and named Count Gregory of Tusculum as the ringleader. Count Gregory had held a position of trust with Otto III and had become his *praefectus navalis*—the commander of that famous imperial fleet that never had a ship on the sea.[49] Other sources also claim that the so-called *bacularii*, stick-carriers, took part in the outrages. These were members of the city's lower social classes, thought to be hirelings of the nobility.[50] Some—and in fact the most detailed—accounts, however, raise doubt about the intensity and danger of this tumult, and certainly about the intention of the rebels "to make his [Otto's] residence in Rome and a further consolidation of his rule impossible."[51] The already often-cited *Vita Bernwardi*, for example, portrays Bernward as a central figure in the entire course of events, and also describes his behavior during the revolt:

Now the Romans, indignant that the emperor had reached an agreement with the people of Tivoli, closed the gates of their city and barricaded the streets. They did not allow people to enter or leave Rome freely, and also forbade the free buying and selling of goods. Some of the king's friends were unjustly murdered. Those in the palace, however, accepted the salutary advice of Bishop Bernward: they purified themselves with confession and strengthened themselves with the sacred viaticum of the mass. Then they armed themselves for a sally and brave onslaught against the enemy. Bishop Bernward seized the Holy Lance, signed himself and all the others with the protecting sign of the life-giving cross, and publicly gave the blessing. While he encouraged the bravery and strength of the others, he armed himself to set out as standard-bearer with the Holy Lance at the forefront of the column. On the following morning after the solemn mass the venerable bishop strengthened the emperor and his people with the heavenly sacrament and pious admonitions. Then they set out for battle, with the bishop in the foremost line, the Holy Lance glinting terribly in his hand. In his heart, however, he constantly begged for peace from the author of all peace. And truly, upon the prayer of his pious servant, soon Christ himself, the prince of peace, was present, at whose nativity already the joy of peace was announced, and who afterward in his gospel calls the peacemakers the children of God. Through his mercy all the fighting and strife was calmed. The enemies begged for peace, threw down their weapons, and promised to come to the palace the next day. Through God's mercy, in the morning they really did appear, asked for peace, renewed their oaths, and promised eternal fidelity to the emperor.[52]

The purpose of this account certainly was to place Bernward's role in the best possible light. However, it is notable that the author also attests to the Romans' immediate readiness to see reason and to suspend hostilities. This account does not speak at all of military engagements. Otto's speech to the Romans and its consequences, discussed below, is best understood by remembering that the Romans had agreed to meet again on the following day to arrange peace. To a degree, Thietmar of Merseberg confirms this view of events. His account is certainly different in emphasis, but shares the same overall attitude:

After that Gregory, whom the caesar held very dear, sought to bring him into his power by treachery, and laid a secret trap for him. Unexpectedly the conspirators gathered together and rose against him. The emperor escaped through the gate with a few followers, but the majority of his people were shut up inside. The common people, never content with their lord, repaid his ineffable goodwill with evil. Now Caesar by means of a messenger urgently ordered all his friends to gather there, demanding of each that, if he cared for his honor and his safety, he should come quickly with armed force to avenge him and secure his safety. The Romans, though, now regretted the fault of the offense brought to light and reproached one another greatly. They let all those who had been shut up depart unharmed and humbly begged for mercy and peace from the emperor. But, distrustful of their falsehood, the emperor harmed them and their possessions wherever possible. All of the regions of the Romans and Lombards remained faithful to his rule except only Rome, which he loved above the others and always cared for.[53]

This account also does not include any mention of serious military conflicts. Instead, Thietmar gives the impression that this incident was much the same as others that often broke out in Rome whenever the "German" army was encamped in and around the city.[54]

The famous speech the emperor supposedly addressed to the citizens from the battlements of a castle at this time also suggests an atmosphere certainly tense and hostile to the emperor, but by no means intent on contesting Otto III's lordship in and around Rome. Once again, our source is the *Vita Bernwardi*, which was crafted according to ancient rhetorical rules. How much of this speech is authentic is contested even today.[55] To understand it, one must look at the function such addresses had in that sort of situation. And when considering the situation one should remember that the people had met again to make peace. Fundamentally, verbal exchanges in the context of conflict settlement serve one of two distinct purposes: there was either an unconciliatory or a conciliatory form of address. The first was intended to signal readiness and willingness to decide the conflict by armed force; the latter served as a prelude to a peaceful solution. *Verbis compositis lenire studiit*—"with reconciling words he studied to be gentle"—is a phrase used elsewhere to describe such a proceeding. Otto III's speech to the rebels, according to this report, was characterized by these same concerns:

Meanwhile, the mild and gentle emperor climbed with a few companions to a tower and addressed them, saying: "Listen to the words of your father, pay attention, and diligently ponder them in your minds! Are you not my Romans? For your sake I left my homeland and my kinsmen, for love of you I have rejected my Saxons and all Germans, my own blood. I have led you to the most remote parts of our empire, where your fathers, when they subjected the world, never set foot. Thus I wanted to spread your name and fame to the

ends of the earth. I have adopted you as sons, I have preferred you to all oth-
ers. For your sake I have made myself loathed and hated by all, because I
have preferred you to all others. And in return now you have cast off your
father and have cruelly murdered my friends. You have closed me out,
although in truth you cannot exclude me, for I will never permit that you,
whom I love with a fatherly love, should be exiled from my heart. I know the
ringleaders of this uprising and can see them with my eyes; however, they are
not afraid, although everyone sees and knows them. However, I find it mon-
strous that my most faithful followers, in whose innocence I triumph, are
mixed together with the evildoers." Moved to tears by these words of the
emperor's, they promised satisfaction. They seized two men, Benilo and
another, beat them cruelly, dragged them barefooted up the stairs, and threw
them half dead at the emperor's feet.[56]

The Romans' reaction to the speech shows that they understood it as an
offer of peaceful agreement, as discussed above. The Romans certainly made
an equally vigorous demonstration of their readiness to make a settlement.
As strange as such behavior may appear to us, it was perfectly typical behavior in the Middle Ages to express a change of mind visually. Publicly shed-
ding tears or self-denunciation could demonstrate a change of heart, or even
the ritual segregation of individual wrongdoers. Finally, the *Vita Bernwardi*
describes the next stage of these events in such a way as to make clear that
these ritual gestures were the steps toward harmonious settlement of the
hostilities: "After the uprising was calmed, the venerable father Bernward
visited the church of Saint Paul to pray."[57]

Considering the purpose of the speech, however, does not free us from the
task of analyzing its content and putting it against the background of Otto
III's Roman policy. This will involve a study of contemporary opinions.
Regarding the speech as a demonstrative expression of readiness to reach a
peaceful agreement yields only one new insight: that the factual content of
such speech-acts was not the central point; what counts is the formal elements of the speech.[58] This does not make interpretation any easier. The
author may have been stylizing the remarks to fit an ideal model for such
events. But even more important, Otto III could not be expected to generate a
comprehensive exposition of his notions of rule or of Rome in this situation.
Strikingly, however, the emperor's words correspond closely to contemporary
criticism of his policy to make Rome a capital city and his political behavior:
partiality for the Romans and disregard for "his" Saxons and Germans.[59]

Whatever Otto actually said here, chroniclers constructed the content of his speech around a real problem to his contemporaries, and not simply the Saxons. This suggests that the formulations in the speech rested on the evidence of Thangmar, who had seen and heard it. Despite this, the speech is too specific to a single event to interpret as an expression of the monarch's general policy. The precarious situation in which he found himself did not call for major policy statements but for what facilitated a reconciliation without loss of face for either side.

Otto III apparently did not regard the satisfaction given by the citizens as sufficient. He and the pope left the city without really bringing the conflict to an end. Despite the pacific gestures, both sides of the conflict felt strong distrust. Advisors urged the emperor to remove himself from the insecure situation and to wait outside the city for military reinforcements. Otto himself, from the evidence of various sources, was driven to avenge himself on the Romans for what they had done.[60] It is not so certain that the rebellion was really "a stab in the heart" for Otto, as scholarly opinion commonly has it.[61] The uprising, after all, ran along lines very familiar in this era. Further, there was evidently a wide range of efforts to reach peaceful settlement. The situation was entirely different from that which led to the execution of Crescentius a few years before. Moreover, the idea of retribution, which supposedly drove the emperor, appears only in those sources trying to explain Otto's early death as God's punishment for his sins in the final part of his life. That purpose does not make their statements more believable.

The Death of Otto III

Thus emperor and pope removed themselves from the rebellious city and traveled north toward Ravenna. The departure had none of the character of a precipitate flight. The *Vita Bernwardi* attests to this specifically, reporting the tears of the Roman citizens at their departure. It also describes in detail how Bernward accompanied the emperor on the first two days of the journey and then took his own equally tearful departure—heavily laden with gifts, relics, and also messages.[62] From Ravenna Otto III undertook his journey to Venice, discussed above. During Lent he also visited Romuald's hermitage in Pereum—the swamp region at the mouth of the Po. There he fasted and did penance. Only sources originating here—Peter Damian's *vita* of Romuald and the *Life of the Five Brothers* by Bruno of Querfurt—give us a picture of a monarch spiritually devastated during these months.[63] These accounts culminate with the claim that the emperor promised to renounce all worldly

things and to become a monk. He supposedly qualified this intention by stat-
ing that first he wanted to spend three years correcting the errors of his rule.
The sources do not say what errors he had in mind.[64]

It is very hard to assess the truthfulness of these accounts. Some have
objected, and probably correctly, that at this same time Otto III sent an
embassy to Byzantium to bring back his bride. This hardly suggests solid
plans to become a monk and to abdicate his throne.[65] On the other hand, we
should not take his ascetic inclinations too lightly. In earlier years this side
of his personality had already inspired him to both demonstrative and secret
penitential efforts.[66] Then too, during Lent, he wore a penitential garment,
hidden under the imperial purple robes.[67] Otto's endowment of a monastery
in honor of the martyr Adalbert at precisely this time attests to his close contact with the hermits around Romuald. Duke Boleslav of Poland sent a
request that also occupied Romuald and Otto III during these days.[68] Boleslav
asked for missionary monks from Romuald's community who would dedi-
cate themselves to spreading the Christian faith in Poland. Two volunteers
from the hermit's circle eventually stepped forward to undertake this duty,
and immediately started to learn the Slavic language.[69]

During these days in Pereum and Ravenna more work was done toward
the political, as well as the ecclesiastical, reordering of the east. But evidence
on this point is sparse in the sources. There is an account of a judicial session
in the monastery of Saint Apollinare in Classe written by an *Anastasius
abbas monasterii sancte Marie Sclavanensis provincie.*[70] Scholars have spec-
ulated that he was the leader of a Hungarian embassy that supposedly
arranged with emperor and pope the event Thietmar of Merseburg describes
in a single sentence: "Through the favor and admonition of the aforementioned emperor, Waic, the brother-in-law of Duke Henry of Bavaria, erecting
bishoprics in his kingdom, received crown and unction."[71] Historians have
argued intensively about the meaning of that sentence.[72] Certainly Otto III
agreed to Hungary's elevation to the status of a kingdom, and he supported it.
Otto was also connected in some way with the creation of an independent
church province in Hungary. These new creations leave traces that display
many parallels to the proceedings in Gniezno already extensively discussed.[73]

The emperor, meanwhile, was in no hurry to have his revenge on Rome.
This may be because it took a long time for levies from Cologne, Würzburg,
Mainz, Worms, and Fulda to reach the emperor in Italy. They arrived only
after Otto had already fallen seriously ill and it was too late for military
action. Several sources attest to Otto III's plans for revenge, even if the long

delay of considerably more than a year raises doubts about his urgency. This speculation also does not accord well with Otto's efforts, discussed above, to bring about a peaceful resolution to the Roman uprising.[74] Bruno of Querfurt's description of the emperor's death is our major source for Otto's overwhelming obsession with revenge.[75] And the author's intent to present the death as a consequence of the monarch's offenses left its very clear mark on the account:

In this winter time, as the emperor led a force of men from the empire and a chosen army of strong men against the city of Remus without the right omens, the mild Otto died without children, alas. He died not as was expected of a great emperor, but in a small castle. Although he had done much good, in this point he had fallen into error, for he forgot the Lord's word that says: "Vengeance is mine, I shall repay," and did not give honor to God or to him who bears the keys of the kingdom of heaven, his precious apostle Peter, following the words: "honor your holy Lord, Israel." For since Rome alone pleased him and he favored the Roman people above all others with gifts of money and honor, he wanted to remain in Rome always and with childish games wanted to raise the city to its earlier dignity. You need not search long to find proper words in the Bible, for in the words of the psalmist you find: "human thoughts are vain." This was the king's sin: he did not wish to see the land of his birth, dear Germany, again, so great was his desire to remain in Italy, where in a thousand cares, a thousand risks of death, a savage scourge hurried armed [against him]. At his side fell chaplain, bishop, count; the servants died in great number, of the fighting men not just one but the best among them. The sword raged in the blood of the noble; dripping greatly with the death of those dear to him, it horribly wounded the emperor's heart. His empire did not help him, nor his cumbersome treasures, nor the mighty army that had assembled; neither the lance nor the sharp sword availed to escape the hand of Death, who alone knows no awe of kings. The good emperor found himself not on the right way when he thought to throw down the mighty walls of great Rome. For even though the Roman citizens had repaid his good deeds only with evil, still Rome was the seat given to the apostles by God. And even there love for his birthplace, desirable Germany, did not awaken in him; the land of Romulus, wet with the blood of those dear to him, still pleased him better with its lecherous beauty. Like an ancient pagan king, who only with difficulty gives up his own will, he labored to no purpose to restore the faded beauty of aging Rome.

This chapter is hardly a realistic description of the supposedly fierce battles with the Romans in the year 1002.[76] Instead it summarizes with a clearly negative slant Otto III's entire Italian policy, particularly when it argues, as did the Donation of Constantine, that the Eternal City is the home of the apostles. Any right of the emperor to rule there thus could be contested. In addition, emphasizing plans for revenge provides a way of proving—suitable to the biblical "Revenge is mine"—that Otto's early death was predetermined: because the emperor had given way to a wrongful craving for vengeance, God took a hand in events and fulfilled the Bible's word. To express it in another way, focusing on Otto's plans for Rome could have resulted from a need to explain the course of events, necessary because of the early and unexpected death of the emperor. Since all of the sources were written after this occurrence, of course, such attempts to explain can neither be confirmed nor excluded as a possibility.

His death was unexpected. Certainly, Otto had already admitted his attacks of fever to Thangmar, the departing confidant of Bishop Bernward, but he was still, as they say, "in the field." He had gone to the castle of Paterno near Cività Castellana, not far from Rome. There the sickness rapidly grew worse, called in the sources the *morbus Italicus*, in other words an unknown, perhaps epidemic illness. The various reports emphasize the peaceful, Christian death of the ruler.[77] In the presence of his loyal followers, surrounded by relics, he is said to have confessed his faults, received the Eucharist, and then passed away as gently as if he were falling asleep. It is only later texts that connected the death to poison. They also single out a candidate as poisoner: Stephania, the widow of Crescentius, who like another Kriemhild is supposed to have taken revenge for the execution of her husband.[78] But this is a later invention, unconnected to reality.

However, the position of the German troops was doubtless very precarious immediately after the emperor's death. Otto's followers kept the death a secret until their own troops had been informed and gathered together. Then the army, constantly threatened by enemies, withdrew from Italy, in order to carry out the emperor's request to bury him in Aachen at the side of Charlemagne. Later sources embroidered this funeral journey, too, in typical fashion. They tell that the emperor's corpse was tied to a horse to ride along with the army, in order to keep the Romans ignorant of his death.[79]

When the retinue reached Bavaria, it was immediately obvious that the emperor's death created great difficulties here as well as in Italy. Certainly, Duke Henry of Bavaria paid the last honors to the departed in Polling, moving

Figure 6. Lothar Cross. Cathedral treasury, cathedral (Palatine Chapel), Aachen. (photo: Erich Lessing/Art Resource, New York)

all those present to fresh tears. Then, however, he demanded that Chancellor Heribert of Cologne surrender the royal insignia. When Heribert would not turn over the Holy Lance, which he had already reverently sent on in advance, Henry forced the Cologne archbishop to swear an oath supporting Henry's claim to the throne.[80] The battle for the succession had begun. In Italy it went a step further. On 15 February 1002 in Pavia the Lombard magnates had already elected Arduin of Ivrea, Otto III's inveterate opponent, as king of Italy.[81] By way of Cologne, the funeral procession proceeded to Aachen, where Otto III was buried in the middle of the choir on Easter Sunday. The funeral, too, in which numerous princes took part, did not lack political implications. During the solemnities the participants agreed to support Duke Hermann of Swabia, who was present, in his bid for the succession.[82]

The dead man left behind him much unfinished work. How could it be otherwise after less than twenty-two years of life? For historians, the answer to the question "what would have happened if . . . ?" is just as alluring as it is futile. This is especially true in any judgment of Otto III. Any assessment of a life can only be based on what has been done and accomplished, not what could have been. So much is clear: Otto III decisively influenced both his empire and beyond. He did so as scarcely any ruler of his epoch did before or after him. In a matter of days, he had made changes that took on the guise of renewing what was good and old. His ideas might have been the expression of carefully planned policies or, as Bruno of Querfurt believed, "childish play" (iocus puerilis). They might have had a chance of winning acceptance. Otto might have possessed enough perseverance and creative will to maintain them. But the last emperor of the short Ottonian line was not granted enough time to prove himself. This makes it almost impossible to do him justice. Every assessment, however, must also take into account what was conceivable and possible in his epoch, the limitations with which people thought and judged, and what scope there was for deviation from the tried and true. Only thus can we avoid crude anachronisms.

Chapter 6

BUILDING BLOCKS FOR AN
ASSESSMENT OF OTTO III
Observations, Insights, Open Questions

he assessments of Otto III, as they were presented in the introduction, whether positive or negative, certainly provide no basis for a fair judgment about this ruler. Only current scholarship can do that. The scholars surveyed there appraised the emperor too much from the perspective of their own times. One must avoid this danger, without however denying that his or her own appraisal is a judgment of the late twentieth century, not of the late tenth. To do so one must take into account the parameters of ruling activity in the tenth century, the rules of play for political and social interaction of that time. Those should be the starting point of any assessment. Stated in another way: modern assessment should have its foundation not in what of the emperor's deeds appears extraordinary to us, but rather in what is original when viewed in the context of the conditions of his own age. Only by paying heed to activities extraordinary in their own context is it possible to develop an individual profile for the emperor. Then, as a next step, we can ask whether these activities unusual in their own time should be categorized as political fantasies or as forward-looking innovations. Two areas especially demand such an examination, since they have already been used as critical evidence for this ruler's personality. First, there are Otto III's apparently original and spectacular gestures of humility and self-abasement, and second, the emperor's pronounced inclination to establish relations of personal friendship with widely varying sorts of people. How much was the ruler's behavior in these areas due to the conventions of his age?

Demonstrative Ritual Behaviors

Modern historiography largely based its picture of Otto III on a series of public acts he performed. These appeared nearly eccentric to modern observers and were accepted as firm indicators of a high level of emotion. Among these are his penitential and fasting practices both public and private. Here Otto showed himself barefoot and in penitential garments and—according to the dominant scholarly opinion—he ruined his health by performing such gestures. His barefoot entry into Gniezno, and certainly also the public tears that he shed in Regensburg after his encounter with the abbot of Saint Emmeram's, are cited as evidence.[1] His secret visit to Venice, with its accompanying masquerade, also appeared to be unusual, displaying his personal idiosyncrasy alone.[2] At first sight the emperor also seemed moved solely by personal impulses and temperament in the many friendships he established. This seemed particularly true in the way he gave them expression, by showing demonstrative partiality toward his friends, whether with all-night conversations or with choice gifts, or promoting them to offices that came vacant.[3] Among such spectacular acts of individual sentiment, historians have singled out particularly Otto III's famous speech from the battlements of a tower with which he reproached for their ingratitude the Romans standing below.[4] When judging all these acts and the supposedly inherent eccentricities of the emperor, scholars have used modern behavior as their measure. Historians have praised or blamed Otto according to whether the behavior he displayed corresponded to modern demands and values. They have stigmatized his ritual displays of religiosity as overly scrupulous and argued that because of this he could not have been aware of what practical politics demanded. What seemed an open reliance on people who impressed him was considered a positive trait. Historians credited him with a "genius for friendship." Nobody, however, has weighed the evidence by asking and considering how the emperor's actions fit into the framework of the era's communication style. Against this background of his own time are they really as unusual and eccentric as they seem from the perspective of our own customs of communication? When posed in this way, the central question becomes the markedly demonstrative and ritualistic style of communication in the tenth—and not only the tenth—century.[5] When, in medieval public life, politically significant forces interacted in an open arena, more was shown than was spoken. Many events in public life were intended for this sort of public display, which we subsume under the terms "ritual," "ceremonial," or "staging" and which we describe with their own particular "language" of nonverbal communication displayed in gestures, behaviors, and ritual acts. In medieval politics, coronations, royal entries, homage, investitures, submissions, peace agreements, and many other occasions of state fell within the sphere of demonstrative gestures and acts. Otto III's behavior should be judged against the background of these specific forms of communication. When one does so, it quickly becomes clear that his behavior was based on this sphere's rules of behavior as they were customary in his own age. This sort of demonstrative behavior applied not only to the emperor himself or his immediate circle. Surveying comparable proceedings during the age of Otto III reveals clearly a common language and, as it were, a component of custom.

We know of several such public displays from as early as the struggle with Henry the Quarrelsome for the throne. Henry the Quarrelsome publicly celebrated Easter in Quedlinburg as king and had himself honored there with royal *laudes:* in this way he publicly declared his ambitions for the royal office. As a counterpoint to this behavior, he had to pay public homage to the underage Otto III in Frankfurt—"humble in clothing, humble in act" (*humilis habitu humilis et actu*). Afterward he had to serve at the child-king's table at a feast in Quedlinburg.[6] With these acts he relinquished his claims to the throne. He signified as well his willing loyalty to the king in whose favor the majority of the magnates had decided. The sources do not report any sort of verbal proclamation accompanying this ritual. This may not be an accident in transmission, but rather the expression of a style of communication that consisted of actions, not speech. People did not argue in public. Instead they informed the public of the state of relationships or of decisions made by meaningful actions. Henry the Quarrelsome's behavior was not alone in revealing this understanding of communication and its functions. The entire monastery of Saint Emmeram's lay on the ground to await the ruler, using a form of prostration. Similarly, the Roman urban prefect Crescentius attempted to communicate with just such a prostration before the emperor. In this case it failed because it was *improvisa*, in other words carried out without previous agreement. Still, by prostrating himself Crescentius invoked, and gambled on, established customs for settling a conflict amicably. The act of submission with prostration at its center was the proper means for rendering satisfaction to the opponent.[7] In any case, one had to agree beforehand on procedures and the parameters of the ceremony. Crescentius left this out for reasons specific to him.

Accounts of the Gandersheim conflict include a demonstrative prostration by the archbishop of Mainz before his fellow bishop of Hildesheim, his opponent in the controversy.[8] The bishop of Hildesheim, interestingly, responded to the prostration by throwing himself to the ground before the prostrate archbishop of Mainz. In this way he evaded the result usually dictated by the

Figure 7. Otto III by Joseph Anton Settegast (1813–90). (photo: AKG Berlin)

prostration. This urgent form of wordless imploring made it hard for the person so beseeched to reject the request. We know of no case in which Otto III personally prostrated himself before someone of lower rank. But we are nevertheless aware that other kings did not shy away from prostrating themselves before magnates when, in especially important circumstances, they needed their assistance. Through several prostrations, Emperor Henry II forced a favorable decision from an episcopal synod not at all inclined to agree to the foundation of the bishopric of Bamberg.[9] Apparently convention had it that one could not refuse a request someone of higher rank made kneeling. Examination of various prostrations shows that the semantics of gestures took many forms. In prostrations by people both higher and lower in rank the gesture functioned as an urgent request. Or, in the context of a submission, it became a symbolic self-renunciation. A person appeared to surrender himself for better or worse to another, but fully aware the whole time that the scales of the decision were weighted beforehand toward a positive outcome.

Penitential clothing and going barefoot are related to prostration and its larger realm of expression. These are found in religious as well as secular contexts. The attire of ecclesiastical penitents and of those in the secular sphere demonstrated a submission very similar or indeed identical. On various occasions Otto III displayed the garments of a religious penitent and sometimes on these occasions also went barefoot: publicly on his pilgrimage to Monte Gargano and for his entry into Gniezno. He also did so privately in his penitential practices with Franco of Worms in a cave in Rome and in Pereum in the circle of hermits around Romuald. On the latter occasion indeed he wore penitential garb under the imperial purple robes.[10] But this difference between private and public generally applies only to the public of this world. None of the imperial penitential practices remained secret from the heavenly public, and this audience was certainly the primary target of Otto's demonstrative behavior. There is no more evidence of this demonstrative form of penitence on the part of Otto III than of other rulers. One should remember that other German rulers performed public penance—Louis the Pious before Otto III's time, and later Henry II and Henry III.[11]

During Otto's lifetime Archbishop Heribert assumed office in Cologne with a quite comparable demonstration: he entered the city barefoot, thus certainly emphasizing publicly his humility and unworthiness for such an office. Also, the Halberstadt tradition, probably dating from the tenth century, reports that Otto's grandfather, Otto I, entered Halberstadt barefoot and in penitential garments to end a conflict with Bishop Bernhard of Halberstadt.[12] The idea of a penitential ruler cannot, therefore, have been alien to contemporaries.[13] Otto III's penitential activities, to all appearances highly spectacular and self-willed, had parallels both before and after his time. These other acts had equally pronounced characteristics. Among them are also included the royal tears, with which Otto III, for example in Regensburg, publicly bemoaned his sins.[14] This is not a unique case either. Kings, like other Christians, demonstrated their repentance with weeping among other means. When kings did so, it moved spectators to tears of joy at their public piety.[15] All in all, Otto III's behavior, when he demonstratively placed the sinner before the ruler, should be evaluated in the context of the similar behaviors sketched out here. All were available in the period's arsenal of demonstrative nonverbal means of expression. Perhaps Otto emphasized his role as sinful and repentant human being more strongly than other rulers of his era. Perhaps this impression derives from the sources whose authors sought evidence for the holiness of their protagonists and had more reason to draw attention to such behaviors.[16] In any case it is absolutely essential to understand the communication style of this era before making any judgment on this issue.

Understanding the tenth-century context is equally necessary when analyzing the numerous reports and stories in which Otto III particularly honored his loyal followers and friends. Most certainly, every lord had to honor and reward his people. There was an entire arsenal of appropriate acts and signals for this purpose.[17] When he gave gifts that honored and distinguished vassals and friends, Otto III was really no different from other medieval rulers. While the *Vita Bernwardi* speaks of choice gifts the emperor either personally presented to Bishop Bernward or gave to his emissary Thangmar,[18] these presents remained within conventional practice. Nor was Otto III clearly different from other rulers in the pattern of gifts and grants to churches and monasteries; his successor Henry II is more notable in this area.[19] Despite this, scholars of Otto III have accepted as true that Otto followed an original path and made very personal decisions when he honored and distinguished confidants and friends. This impression arose from a failure to consider or find out the rules and customs of Otto's time.

Scholars have also misunderstood why Otto III granted so many and such extraordinarily intimate conversations to his confidants. True, widely varied sources emphasize this aspect of his behavior. In the *Vita Bernwardi*, for example, the confidential and confiding tête-à-tête conversations between emperor and bishop are taken to indicate their very close relationship.[20] The *vitae* of Saint Adalbert also stress that the bishop supposedly engaged in long discussions "day and night" with the young emperor. Interestingly, during that same period there are accounts that many different people spent day and night in conversation with the emperor. Gerbert of Aurillac specifically states that he himself did so.[21] These reports are valuable only if one considers that conversation in this period was a demonstrative proof of favor. Conversations possessed such a character no matter how confidential they were. In fact, at the precise moment when one individual was singled out to confer alone with the ruler in his apartments, contemporaries jealously noted the whereabouts of all the others, who did not share such an honor. In periods such as this, access to the ruler was by no means unrestricted; instead it was subject to strict rules and restrictions. The possibility of gaining an unlimited hearing was an important form of political capital and at the same time a reliable indicator of influence.[22] The sources reflect precisely this situation—not by accident mostly in the *vitae* of bishops. There authors confirmed their protagonists' influence by describing them engaged in intensive and confidential conversation with the ruler. To provide only one example for comparison: the two known bishops' *vitae* from the time of Otto the Great—those of Ulrich of Augsburg and Bruno of Cologne—also describe and stress the bishops' influence with the ruler in the same way, by emphasizing that he discussed everything with them in intimate conversation.[23]

With regard to this evidence, we have no reason to doubt that Otto III indeed established relationships of trust and that these also took concrete form in intensive conversations. Nevertheless, we should realize that emphasis on intense conversation was a chronologically defined topos for closeness and influence. This is by no means to suggest that this was an "empty" topos. Nearness and trust, which guaranteed influence, were indeed a highly important form of capital in the political economy. This is to suggest only that in this area Otto III's royal conduct was no different from that of his predecessors and successors. Otto's behavior was also closely connected to this on several occasions when he himself received gifts. The sources report this especially during his visits to Gniezno and Venice.[24] On both occasions, Otto accepted only a few of all the gifts offered him—that, at least, is what a variety of sources say. Only the general description of the Gallus Anonymus would seem to contradict this. The author reports that Boleslav lavished Otto and his entourage in Gniezno with gifts (including tableware and the used drinking goblets), without remarking that the emperor might have refused anything. Understanding customs in this sort of interaction makes it easier to understand such reports: in fact, by tradition, a lord who received gifts only chose out a part from what was offered.[25] Otto's behavior, or at least the way it was described, is thus in complete accord with the conventions of his time. Such demonstrations offered a lord an opportunity to show that he was generous, not rapacious.

If one surveys all reports of Otto III's behavior in the sources with an eye to establishing how far they followed contemporaneous customs in demonstrative ritual actions, the result is ambiguous. In many spheres of activity the behavior described follows these rules precisely. But it is not difficult to name actions outside the prescribed customs of the time. One example, discussed above, is Thietmar's claim that Otto restored an old Roman custom by dining separately on a raised table shaped in a half circle. Thietmar remarks on this occasion: "different people thought different things [about the matter]" (*diversi diverse sentiebant*).[26] One should not take this statement too lightly. Thietmar was well-disposed toward Otto and thus might be reporting a prevailing attitude.

The emperor was most willing to leave his own territory to visit neighboring princes of lower rank, as he did with the visits to Gniezno and Venice. This too might be considered unusual and unconventional. Enough is known about meetings between rulers, as well as the protocol and ceremonial connected to them, to be able to say with certainty that neither visit observed conventions and that in fact they offended customary usage.[27] In both these cases, from the viewpoint of demonstrative ritual behavior, the emperor ceded something important. He disregarded the claims and rights he held by virtue of rank. Whether this was politically justifiable and intelligent is another question that does not have to be addressed here. Nor does the question addressed above of whether Otto's behavior was motivated at all by political considerations. In the case of the journey to Gniezno, at least, that doubt is certainly reasonable. On this trip to Gniezno, according to the Gallus Anonymus, the emperor engaged in yet another action without traditional precedent: he set his own crown on Boleslav Chrobry's head.[28] If one assumes that this action took place in the way described (and this cannot be confirmed), it would be a significant additional piece of evidence for Otto III's "unconventional" notions. Since parallels are lacking, however, the meaning of this act remains unclear today: was it an elevation to kingship or a gesture of honor within the bounds of a pact of friendship?

The question of how much Otto III's behavior as ruler overstepped the bounds of convention therefore has no definite answer. But this much is nevertheless clear: this evidence does not support arguments that he was a heedless innovator making light of all conventions, or a dreamer basing his behavior only on his own personal vision. On the other hand, the sources do report actions not in accordance with traditions and customs. So any sweeping judgment must remain equivocal.

"Friends" of Otto III and His Interaction with Them

Many scholars from widely different perspectives have explored the young emperor's friendships. They search for a key to Otto III's personality, and to understand his erratic and inconsistent actions and decisions. They have created a picture of a ruler who easily opened himself to others and who tended toward "ardent" veneration of men whose ideas or lifestyles impressed him. Historians have also believed that Otto easily made friends and that his friends had a decisive influence on his political concepts. When assessing Otto's character, this emphasis on friendship in particular raises the question of how extensive the emperor's independence or pliability was. The emperor has been portrayed as oscillating back and forth between widely varying influences, as the plaything of very different interests. It is not always simple to show that he often might have been more than "a tool in the hand of clever advisors."[29] Others oppose this skeptical view, asserting "that the emperor in this many-sided society of his 'friends' always remained the leader."[30] Certainly it is always difficult to trace the origin of ideas and political concepts when they themselves can be seen only in fragments and are transmitted through very heterogeneous sources. Apart from this problem, however, we must make an important point when examining the emperor's numerous "personal" friendships: the early Middle Ages certainly knew friendship. It was one of the most important forms of alliance in political life in this period. But typically such friendship lacked the quality we would characterize with the adjective "personal."[31] Such friendship was much more by nature a contract and regulated a fixed canon of rights and duties. Feelings were not foremost, if indeed they were necessary at all. But it is precisely this level of personal feelings and sentiments that apparently distinguishes and characterizes many of Otto III's friendships, if one can trust the portraits in modern research. Here some doubts are reasonable.

There is a second important problem in studying the issue of rulers' friendships. In the Middle Ages it was a sign of successful rulership "to be obeyed like a lord and loved like a friend," but medieval people were also well aware that difficulties arose when a lord or king was friendly with his magnates.[32] There certainly was a conflict between the duty to give preferential treatment to friends and the postulate to follow the dictates of justice toward all—and not just theoretically. The question about Otto III's "friends" thus also raises a significant issue in constitutional history. Two fundamental assumptions need attention in this regard: belief in this emperor's apparent heavy investment in the sphere of friendship and the impression that in the conduct of friendship he would naturally follow his personal feelings and inclinations. In the first place, these friendships are not declared or mentioned in Otto III's own testimony, but in writings from the circles of his friends. It is mostly *vitae* of holy men from his "circle of friends" that convey this sense of a monarch deeply immersed in personal friendships—more precisely, the *vitae* of Bernward of Hildesheim, Heribert of Cologne, Burkhard of Worms, Adalbert, Nilus, and Romuald, to name only the most important. The second qualification is perhaps even more important: subsuming Otto III's various relationships under the catchword "friendship" results from modern research. Scholars have taken Otto III's behavior toward people close to him as evidence of friendship, but do not give a precise definition to this term. In the sources, on the contrary, the relationships are mostly described without any sort of statement that implies personal friendship. They reflect relationships ranging, as do modern friendships, in a spectrum from *familiaritas* (an intimate nearness) to honorable treatment, to casual forms of interaction. Thus, when modern scholarship apostrophizes Otto III as a "genius for friendship," it does not refer to the more specific early medieval "institute" of *amicitia,* but instead collects under this term all of Otto III's closer relationships.[33]

The sources provide two distinct sorts of evidence about such friendly intimacy. They can be categorized as conventional and very unconventional. "Conventional" includes the statements in the *vitae* that the emperor supposedly did nothing without the advice of the bishop or abbot concerned. In the *vita* of Bernward of Hildesheim, this claim is the leitmotiv that several times characterizes the relationship between emperor and bishop with the term *familiarissime.* Thus, "robbed of both his parents, the king entrusted himself entirely to the guidance of his true teacher. On his advice, he examined for flattery everything of which the others tried to persuade him." Or: "Then they sat next to each other, sometimes in the emperor's apartments, sometimes in those of the bishop, and spoke about legal controversies and the affairs of the state." Similarly, "As is usually the case, some believed that they should intensify the siege, while others thought . . . it would be better to break it off. . . . Thereupon the emperor took Bishop Bernward to one side and asked him what he ought to do." Yet again, "What the pious emperor hesitated to trust to writing or to a messenger, he entrusted to the deep silence of his loyal teacher, who weighed it on the scales of wisdom."[34]

The *vita* of Bishop Burkhard of Worms attributes a similar intimacy with the ruler to Franco, Burkhard's predecessor as bishop of Worms (and also Burkhard's brother). It reports: "and there for more than a year he occupied himself with fainting spirit in the emperor's service, playing a great role in his secret matters, and when something important was to be dealt with he had such a nearness [*familiaritas*] to the emperor and such prestige with him, although he was still young, that rarely was anything decided without his advice . . . and he was highly honored by the emperor and valued above others. On his advice he punished the evildoers and ruled over the realm in peace."[35] Finally, the *Vita Heriberti* describes the relations between the archbishop of Cologne and the emperor in the same way: the emperor had desired that Heribert "be first with his secrets" (*secreti sui esse . . . primum*).[36] According to the *vita*, the emperor greeted Heribert before the latter was elevated to the archbishopric of Cologne in the following way: "When he came to the emperor he was received with boundless love, embraced, kissed with intimate affection [*familiarissima devotione*], like one upon whose unwavering loyalty nearly everything depended and to whom he had especially commended the well-being of his soul."[37] The *vita* describes still more proofs of their intimacy. So, for example, they are supposed to have promised each other that whichever of them lived the longer would found a monastery, dedicated to the Virgin Mary, to pray for the other's soul.

Bruno's *vita* of Saint Adalbert at one point also describes the extraordinary warmth with which Otto III honored the bishop of Prague during their only extended encounter: "While he [Adalbert] spent several days with him, he was only allowed to take his rest under the gaze of the emperor."[38] Sharing the imperial bedchamber ratcheted up a notch the intimacy implicit in reports of the other *vitae* that the hero took a place at the emperor's side, shared in secrets, and had his advice heeded. Bishop Bernward, too, enjoyed an almost identical distinction. He had the apartments next to those of the emperor, and they visited each other in turn.[39] This intimacy occupies a border between the conventional forms of closeness a ruler was expected to accord and those more personal forms of interaction attested only for Otto III. One should note, though, that in other sources a willingness to share the royal bedchamber gave evidence of the ruler's virtue: for example, Henry IV, according to his *vita*, opened his apartments to the poor, the sick, and lepers, whom he cared for there.[40] In addition, it is advisable to pay heed to the broader context when judging the reports. Adalbert's nightly activities at the emperor's court are reported in the following way: "At night he also secretly took the sleepers' shoes and washed them with water. The disciple of humility removed the dirt with his own hands, and then restored them cleaned to their place. While he rested there a little in the night on the soft couch, he saw the desired end to his life."[41] Here we are dealing with the genre of hagiography and need to pay particular attention to the place of the statements in the author's larger point. They aim to make Adalbert's holiness manifest. This is as true of the tales of the hero's humility and selflessness as it is of reports of his esteem among the mightiest people of the temporal world.

In summary, this section of our survey of the forms Otto III's friendships took allows the conclusion that all the cases cited above involve *familiaritas*, an intimate closeness to the ruler. Every ruler of the Middle Ages granted this closeness to a circle of people, and the circle of *familiares* fulfilled an important function in the praxis of medieval rule. This inner circle served as a filter. It sealed the ruler off and at the same time carried reports, wishes, and petitions to him confidentially. In light of this task and the opportunities to exert influence linked to it, winning a place in this circle, and if possible becoming the *familiarissimus* within the circle of *familiares*, was not surprisingly a most desired goal of the medieval ruling class.[42] At least part of Otto III's alleged cult of friendship from this perspective reveals itself as merely part of the conventional requirements of medieval rule.

Aside from these customary forms of interaction, however, other reports do not fit so easily within the traditions of the time. Petrus Damiani, for example, in his *Vita Romualdi* describes Otto III's relationship with his follower Tammo (a brother of Bishop Bernward of Hildesheim) quite briefly: "he [Tammo] was, it is said, so intimate and dear [*familiaris et carus*] to the king that they wore each other's clothing and often used a single spoon when eating."[43] It is of course impossible to determine whether these reports are true, but they doubtless concern personal friendship. At one level, they are conventional, as is the report that the two often celebrated *convivia* together, an arrangement with friendship-granting power.[44] However, other elements, especially the mention of a clothing exchange, signal something quite different. Here conventional nearness has very clearly been abandoned. Instead, this is a level of personal friendship using unconventional signs to assure its strength and to invest it with demonstrative expression. There is no doubt here which of the two friends was the giver and which the recipient. The young emperor gave a sign through the exchange of clothing. This must have drawn attention, even though he certainly would not have exchanged "imperial" items of clothing with his friend. The *vita* of Romuald reports a second close personal relationship that attests to an unconventional state of affairs. It says of Bruno of Querfurt, who was a Saxon nobleman and member of the court chapel, monk in Romuald's monastery, and later missionary bishop and hagiographer: "This man was a relative of the king and so dear to him that the king called him by no other name than *anima mea.*"[45] People would have understood this term "my soul" as meaning an alter ego. Such a nickname was an unusual way in which Otto III gave expression to his intimacy with his chaplain and distant relative. If it is indeed true that the emperor never used any other name for his relative, it is a direct piece of evidence about a personal and relaxed communication. That communication found expression in intimate address including pet names, and it was indulged in before a limited audience at least. We do not have examples of such behavior from other rulers of this period. It is, of course, impossible to judge the accuracy of this report. Still, it belongs with others that equally bear witness to Otto III's very personal (in modern terms one might almost say casual) dealings with his intimates.

One possible example of this is the note with which Otto III informed his confidant and chancellor Heribert of his appointment to the archbishopric of Cologne. It read: *Otto imperator sola Dei gratia, Heriberto archilogotetae gratiam et Coloniam ac pallii cubitum unum* ("Otto, emperor by God's grace alone, presents to the archilogothete Heribert his favor and Cologne and a yard of pallium").[46] Percy Ernst Schramm has rightly pointed out that this is not simply a "parody of the pomposity of diplomatic style," but was also a joke. A pallium only a yard long would have been laughably short.[47] Someone who gave away archbishoprics in this fashion was assuredly unconventional.

The emperor's reaction to news of Margrave Hugo of Tuscany's death (who had been a loyal adherent of Otto III) has long been considered an attempt at a joke, although unsuccessful. After receiving the report the emperor supposedly quoted a verse of the psalm: "the rope is sundered and we are freed."[48] The sort of restrictive connection from which the margrave's death allegedly freed Otto III is unknown. The emperor also included personal notes in his letters to Gerbert of Aurillac. This is not so much the case with the famous letter in which he emphasized his Saxon *rusticitas,* as it was with the verse he wrote and sent to his teacher:

> *"I have never composed verses*
> *Nor studied the art.*

Still will I carry it so far
And with such vigor:
That I will send you as many songs
As there are men in Gaul."[49]

It must be emphasized that either there are no examples at all for such behavior by other rulers of this period, or there are only very isolated cases. The widely varied fragments of extant evidence allow no doubt: when in the circle of his intimates, Otto III inclined toward exchanges and activities that reveal a very personal relationship and go far beyond the customary demonstrative communication style toward friends and confidants. In fact, he gave his *familiares* extraordinary honors and signs of his esteem. Thus, in Otto III's "friendships" we encounter not only *amicitiae* that seem contractual in nature, but also relationships that were forged at a personal level. This, by the way, does not mean in the slightest that the emperor was too accommodating toward these "friends." Indeed, Bruno of Querfurt remarks, among other criticism, that "he [the emperor] only gave up his own will with difficulty."[50] In the *Vita Romualdi* Petrus Damiani describes one of Otto's strategies to impose his will even on his intimates. When the hermit Romuald doggedly refused to assume leadership of a monastery Otto III had entrusted to him, the emperor threatened him with excommunication and ban through a synod, and in that way imposed his will. At least he did so temporarily. When Romuald saw that he could not bring the monks to what he felt was the right path, he hurled his abbatial crosier in Otto III's face and left the monastery.[51]

One must view the evidence discussed in this chapter against the background of the emperor's other unusual behaviors, be they his journeys to Gniezno and Venice, or his penitential acts, or the opening of Charlemagne's grave. One must also remember that this evidence of Otto III's dealings with his *familiares* comes from a period of about seven years. This is an extremely short span of time in light of how scarce the sources are for this era. If one takes this into consideration, the personal image of the emperor becomes more focused. As ruler he was indeed different in many respects from his predecessors and successors. It is no wonder that in an age so firmly committed to custom and tradition, as Thietmar of Merseburg said, "different people thought different things" about this emperor and his style of rule and communication. That widely varying reaction has not changed even today.

Dealing with the Heritage

The pictures historians present of Otto III have been strongly affected by views about the reign of his successor Henry II. Belief that Henry II made an abrupt change of course in all essential spheres of policy is seen as clear evidence of what he thought about his predecessor's principles and plans.[52] Instead of friendship and cooperation with Boleslav Chrobry came enmity— given concrete form in Henry II's protracted wars against Boleslav. Italy and Rome apparently again moved to the periphery in royal policy. Henry II undertook three expeditions to Italy without staying there longer than his affairs demanded. Indeed, it was more than a decade before he drove the Italian antiking Arduin of Ivrea from his throne. In other words, no more was heard of the dashing plans for a *renovatio* of the Roman Empire and a family of kings around the emperor. Instead, historians have believed that they could detect for the first time "the icy breath of national-interest politics" in Henry II's activities and in his priorities.[53] Scholars found programmatic expression of this change in policy, once again in a motto. Henry II's seal now read: *Renovatio regni Francorum* (renewal of the kingdom of the Franks)—the renewal of the Roman Empire was no longer the goal.[54] But this is the only explicit evidence for a fundamental change in political direction. Everything else has been inferred from the course of events.

The belief that Henry II reacted against Otto III's policies should be challenged in many regards. First it must be stressed again that kings in the late tenth and early eleventh centuries were most unlikely to conduct their policies on the basis of preestablished conceptions and plans and that they strove to put those established programs into place.[55] Their activities were determined by their unchanging duties as Christian rulers by the grace of God rather than by any predetermined program. They were answerable for peace and justice; they were obligated to protect the weak and defenseless and, of course, the churches. In this central role there was no room for a change in political direction. It is not at all improbable that new events, situations, or developments led to changes. But these changes were not, and did not necessarily have to be, a conscious departure from earlier principles. Clearly, Henry II's relationship with Boleslav Chrobry experienced strains not foreseeable in Otto III's time. Dealing with the inheritance left by Margrave Ekkehard of Meissen was just such a severe stress.[56] As a relative of the deceased margrave, Boleslav made demands Henry II, for unknown reasons, was not prepared to honor. Boleslav's victorious expedition against Bohemia added another tension that had not existed before. A third point of stress was an assault against Boleslav's warriors in Magdeburg, for which Boleslav held King Henry responsible.[57] Even without a conscious change in policy beforehand, such stresses could turn friendship into enmity. Henry II's behavior at the same time does not signal a return to older principles of Ottonian policy, as his alliance with the non-Christian Liutizi should make sufficiently clear.[58] In addition, the divided reaction among the Saxon nobility to the new situation shows that people who were part of different networks of power could imagine different outcomes. Reactions ranged from open support of Boleslav to forms of neutrality and attempts at mediation, to active support of the king. This suggests clearly that the conflicts had nothing to do with a "national" German policy toward Poland. Much more, they were conflicts among the members of the ruling class, who were bound to one another in multifarious ways. It is not an accident that Boleslav Chrobry too, as a prince of the empire, was present among the Saxon magnates in Merseburg at Henry II's so-called "after-election," when the nobles ratified what was in effect Henry's seizure of power, and there paid homage to him. There is no evidence here of a fundamental change in political direction.[59]

The same insight comes from comparing the Italian policy of the two rulers. In spite of everything, Henry II reestablished the limited rule of the empire over Italy, defeated the antiking, and forced him to enter a monastery. True, the people of Pavia destroyed the royal palace in their city after Henry's death, and others attempted to provide Italy with a non-German king—but without success.[60] Certainly Henry II spent less of his time in Italy than Otto III had. But to conclude from this a fundamental change in Italian policy is merely hypothetical, all the more so because there is no agreement about the goals of Otto III's policy in the first place.[61] At the same time, continuities are also clear. Henry II continued his predecessor's policy in a number of regards, further intensifying the advancement as well as the utilization of the imperial church, and completing the incorporation of the south German duchies into the royal sphere of activity.[62]

More important for a complete assessment, though, is the complete lack of evidence that Henry II ever criticized his predecessor. On the contrary! In the year 1001, before becoming king, he refused to support a group of Saxon magnates who, in collaboration with bishops, had conspired against Otto III.[63] After Otto's death, the charters of his successor divulge only that he did not avoid his duty to the *memoria* of his relative and predecessor. He or his chancellery designated Otto III in these charters with expressions for the most part conventional.[64] The behavior of his successor, therefore, and changes he effected are not decisive evidence of judgment on either Otto III's policies or his personality.

Let us at this point return to the start of our investigation of the next to last Ottonian emperor. In the course of the centuries—especially in the modern era—he has had as many vehement opponents as enthusiastic admirers. Both groups characterized the emperor's life and deeds, illumining or darkening the history of Otto III using criteria that were for the most part anachronistic. Some anachronism is always unavoidable, if we ask what a particular historical individual has to say to *us*. But Otto did not live and act to say something to us. Therefore let us attempt to understand him within the context of the possibilities or limitations of his own era, without forgetting the fact that we are very far removed from these circumstances.

Applying these criteria, the following characteristics of the life and deeds of Otto III stand out in relief. He was just as ready to accept novelty as he was responsive to ideas and influences. These qualities on their own marked him as unconventional in a period that lived in accordance with custom and convention. In fact this emperor introduced or brought about a whole series of novelties and displayed behaviors that contemporaries marveled at, admired, or criticized. In other words, he used and indeed expanded the creative playing field the period offered him. Despite this openness to the unconventional, many of his actions were doubtless more dependent on the conventions of his era than his modern admirers and critics have noted. It is impossible to judge the long-term effectiveness of his deeds, because his life was too short to do him justice in this regard. This unalterable fact makes every judgment difficult. Still, in his seven years as adult ruler he gave more clues and evidence about himself as an individual than those before or after him who ruled for many decades. Sometimes one almost has the impression that Otto himself gave an individual stamp to the conventions, even when he conformed to them. We should not be surprised that already among his contemporaries "different people thought different things."[65] That is still permissible today. But certainly those who speak of the individuality of Otto III glimpsed behind all the conventions cannot be too far wrong.

Abbreviations ‡ ‡ ‡

ADipl.	*Archiv für Diplomatik, Schriftsgeschichte, Siegel- und Wappenkunde*
AK	*Archiv für Kulturgeschichte*
AKG	*Archiv für Kirchengeschichte*
Annales ESC	*Annales: Économies, sociétés, civilisations*
BDLG	*Blätter für deutsche Landesgeschichte*
BG	Böhmer and Graff, *Regesta Imperii* II, 4: *Die Regesten des Kaiserreiches unter Heinrich II.*
BU	Böhmer and Uhlirz, *Regesta Imperii* II, 3: *Die Regesten des Kaiserreiches unter Otto III.*
BZ	Böhmer and Zimmermann, *Regesta Imperii* II, 5: *Papstregesten, 911–1024*
DA	*Deutsches Archiv für Erforschung des Mittelalters*
EHR	*English Historical Review*
FMSt	*Frühmittelalterliche Studien*
FSGA	*Freiherr vom Stein-Gedächtnisausgabe*
FSI	*Fonti per la storia d'Italia*
HJb	*Historisches Jahrbuch*
HRG	*Handwörterbuch zur deutschen Rechtsgeschichte*
HZ	*Historische Zeitschrift*
JbKGV	*Jahrbuch des Kölnischen Geschichtsvereins*
MGH	*Monumenta Germaniae historica* (with the following divisions)
Const. I	*Constitutiones et acta publica imperatorum et regum* I
Epp. DK	*Die Briefe der deutschen Kaiserzeit*
Epp. Selectae	*Epistolae selectae*
DD	*Diplomata*
DH II	Charter of Henry II
DO II	Charter of Otto II
DO III	Charter of Otto III
SS	*Scriptores*
SSrG	*Scriptores rerum Germanicarum in usum scholarum*

MIÖG	*Mitteilungen des Instituts für österreichische Geschichts-forschung*
MPH	*Monumenta Poloniae historica*
NA	*Neues Archiv der Gesellschaft für ältere deutsche Geschichtskunde*
NDB	*Neue deutsche Biographie*
NdsJb	*Niedersächsisches Jahrbuch für Landesgeschichte*
SaAn	*Sachsen und Anhalt: Jahrbuch der landesgeschichtlichen Forschungsstelle für die Provinz Sachsen und Anhalt*
ZGO	*Zeitschrift für die Geschichte des Oberrheins*
ZOF	*Zeitschrift für Ostforschung*
ZRG	*Zeitschrift der Savigny Stiftung für Rechtsgeschichte*
GA	*Germanistische Abteilung*
KA	*Kanonistische Abteilung*

Notes ‡ ‡ ‡

INTRODUCTION

1. On this subject in general, see the articles in Peter Wapnewski, ed., *Mittelalter-Rezeption: Ein Symposion* (Stuttgart, 1986); Gerd Althoff, ed., *Die Deutschen und ihr Mittelalter* (Darmstadt, 1992).

2. The three quotations are from Wilhelm von Giesebrecht, *Geschichte der deutschen Kaiserzeit,* 5th ed. (Braunschweig, 1881), 1:719, 720–21, and 759. They have been translated by Phyllis G. Jestice, as have all further translations unless otherwise noted.

3. Albert Hauck, *Kirchengeschichte Deutschlands,* 8th ed. (Berlin, 1954), 3:257.

4. Ferdinand Gregorovius, *Geschichte der Stadt Rom im Mittelalter vom 5. bis zum 16. Jahrhundert,* new ed., ed. Waldemar Kampf (Tübingen, 1953), 1:687–88.

5. Percy Ernst Schramm, *Kaiser, Rom und Renovatio* (Leipzig and Berlin, 1929), 2:9 ff., which includes an astonishingly short analysis of the earlier research. And yet, a year before, Menno Ter Braak, in *Kaiser Otto III.* (Amsterdam, 1928), 13 ff., had attempted a new assessment of Otto based on extensive analysis of the state of previous research. His assessment, however, did not prevail against Schramm's view.

6. This interpretation will be discussed in detail in Chapter 3, in the section titled "Otto III's 'Idea of Roman Renewal' in Older and Newer Scholarship."

7. Karl Hampe, *Das Hochmittelalter* (Berlin, 1932), 61–62.

8. Karl Hampe, "Kaiser Otto III. und Rom," HZ 140 (1929): 513–33.

9. Albert Brackmann, "Der 'Römische Erneuerungsgedanke' und seine Bedeutung für die Reichspolitik der deutschen Kaiserzeit," in *Gesammelte Aufsätze* (Weimar, 1941), 130; see more generally 117 ff.

10. Robert Holtzmann, *Geschichte der sächsischen Kaiserzeit (900–1024)* (Munich, 1941), 381–82.

11. Carlrichard Brühl, *Deutschland—Frankreich: Die Geburt zweier Völker* (Cologne, 1990), 623–24.

12. Mathilde Uhlirz, *Die Jahrbücher des Deutschen Reiches unter Otto II. und Otto III.* (Berlin, 1954), 2:412–13.

13. Josef Fleckenstein, "Das Reich der Ottonen im 10. Jahrhundert," in *Gebhart: Handbuch der deutschen Geschichte,* ed. Herbert Grundmann, 9th ed. (Stuttgart, 1970), 1:269–70, 273, and 278.

14. Helmut Beumann, "Otto III.," in *Kaisergestalten des Mittelalters,* ed. Helmut Beumann (Munich, 1984), 97.

15. For the latest survey of the literature, see Eduard Hlawitschka, *Vom Frankenreich zur Formierung der europäischen Staaten- und Völkergemeinschaft* (Darmstadt, 1986), 145 ff., 223 ff.; on the problem of judging the emperor as an individual, see especially Knut Görich, *Otto III., Romanus Saxonicus et Italicus* (Sigmaringen, 1993).

16. Concerning this issue, see the extended discussion in Chapter 6.

17. For an assessment of Otto III's portrayal in literary works, see Albert Morgenroth, "Kaiser Otto III. in der deutschen Dichtung," Ph.D. diss., Breslau, 1922; Elisabeth Frenzel, "Otto III.," in *Stoffe der Weltliteratur* (Stuttgart, 1992), 608–10.

18. August von Platen, *Werke* (Leipzig, 1895), 1:32 n.

19. Ibid., 32 ff. Translation by Margarita Yanson.

20. Compare to this Christoph Gradmann's recent analysis of the controversy about historical literature, in *"Historische Belletristik": Populäre historische Biographien in der Weimarer Republik* (Frank-

furt am Main, 1993). This discussion, however, does not include any works with medieval themes.

21. Ricarda Huch, *Römisches Reich, deutscher Nation* (Berlin, 1934), 66 ff.

22. Gertrud Bäumer, *Der Jüngling im Sternenmantel* (Munich, 1949).

23. Ibid., 95.

24. Henry Benrath, *Der Kaiser Otto III.* (Stuttgart, 1951), 5.

25. On this issue, see Karl J. Leyser, "Ottonian Government," EHR 96 (1981): 721–53; idem, *Rule and Conflict in an Early Medieval Society: Ottonian Saxony* (London, 1979); and especially Hagen Keller, "Reichsstruktur und Herrschaftsauffassung in ottonisch-frühsalischer Zeit," FMSt 16 (1982): 74–128; idem, "Grundlagen ottonischer Königsherrschaft," in *Reich und Kirche vor dem Investiturstreit*, ed. Karl Schmid (Sigmaringen, 1985), 17–34; idem, "Zum Charakter der 'Staatlichkeit' zwischen karolingischer Reichsreform und hochmittelalterlichem Herrschaftsausbau," FMSt 23 (1989): 248–64.

26. See Gerd Althoff, "Colloquium familiare—colloquium secretum—colloquium publicum," FMSt 24 (1990): 145–67. This article attempts to establish the significance of confidential resolution prior to open decisions and the staged character of public consultations.

27. On this confidence in a consensus about "correct" behavior, see Gerd Althoff, "Ungeschriebene Gesetze," in *Spielregeln der Politik im Mittelalter* (Darmstadt, 1997).

28. The standard in this area certainly remains Carlrichard Brühl, *Fodrum, gistum, servitium regis* (Cologne and Graz, 1968), which exhibits the necessary comparative perspective. Ongoing work by the Göttingen Akademie der Wissenschaften offers useful and specific information. For rulers nearly contemporary with Otto III, see the methodologically progressive work by Eckhard Müller-Mertens, *Die Reichsstruktur im Spiegel der Herrschaftspraxis Ottos des Großen* (Berlin, 1980); Eckhard Müller-Mertens and Wolfgang Huschner,

Reichsintegration im Spiegel der Herrschaftspraxis Kaiser Konrads II. (Weimar, 1992).

29. For a critique of Otto III's supposed plans, see Görich, *Otto III.*, 263–67; see also, in Chapter 3, the section titled "Otto III's 'Idea of Roman Renewal' in Older and Newer Scholarship."

30. On this issue, see especially Keller, "Reichsstruktur und Herrschaftsauffassung," esp. 85–100, with an investigation of such changes under Otto III.

31. See Brühl, *Fodrum, gistum, servitium regis*, 127–32.

32. Among the older scholarship, see Leo Santifaller, *Zur Geschichte des ottonisch-salischen Reichskirchensystems*, 2d ed. (Vienna, 1964); Timothy Reuter, "The 'Imperial Church System' of the Ottonian and Salian Rulers: A Reconsideration," *Journal of Ecclesiastical History* 33 (1982): 347–74, especially the critical debate over the systemic character of the "system"; as well as Josef Fleckenstein, "Zum Begriff der ottonisch-salischen Reichskirche," in *Ordnungen und formende Kräfte des Mittelalters* (Göttingen, 1989), 211–21, and Rudolf Schieffer, "Der ottonische Reichsepiskopat zwischen Königtum und Adel," FMSt 23 (1989): 291–301.

33. Fundamental to any consideration of this issue is Josef Fleckenstein, *Die Hofkapelle der deutschen Könige* (Stuttgart, 1966), 2:52 ff.

34. See, for example, the case of reestablishing the bishopric of Merseburg, with associated difficulties, discussed in Chapter 4.

35. Such as what Otto III granted to his *amicus*, Margrave Ekkehard of Meißen; see Thietmar of Merseburg, *Chronicon*, ed. Robert Holtzmann, MGH SSrG, n.s., 9 (Berlin, 1955), v. 7, p. 228.

36. For this, see Gerd Althoff, "Königsherrschaft und Konfliktbewältigung im 10. und 11. Jahrhundert," FMSt 23 (1989): 265–90; idem, "Genugtuung (*satisfactio*): Zur Eigenart gütlicher Konfliktbeilegung im Mittelalter," in *Modernes Mittelalter*, ed. Joachim Heinzel (Frankfurt am Main,

NOTES ‡ 153

1994), 247–65. During the reign of Otto III, the cases of Henry the Quarrelsome and the Roman Crescentius are particularly interesting in their demonstration of this issue. See the sections titled "Henry the Quarrelsome and the Disturbances over the Succession," in Chapter 1, and "The Fight Against Crescentius and the Antipope," in Chapter 3.

37. On this, see Gerd Althoff, *Verwandte, Freunde und Getreue* (Darmstadt, 1990), 119 ff.

38. See, in Chapter 6, the section titled "Dealing with the Heritage."

39. Symptomatic of this perspective are assessments such as those of Karl Hampe (*Das Hochmittelalter*) and Robert Holtzmann (*Geschichte der sächsischen Kaiserzeit*). An example of the persistence of this viewpoint in recent research is the title of Hans K. Schulze's work *Hegemoniales Kaisertum: Ottonen und Salier* (Berlin, 1991). Schulze himself reflects on the problems of this perspective in the prologue (9 ff.). Entirely within the same perspective is, most recently, Egon Boshof, *Königtum und Königsherrschaft im 10. und 11. Jahrhundert* (Munich, 1993). On the problem, see principally Keller, "Grundlagen ottonischer Königsherrschaft," 17 ff.; idem, *Zwischen regionaler Begrenzung und universalem Horizont* (Berlin, 1986), esp. 356 ff.

40. One example of this is the description of Otto III's ruling activities in the *Annales Quedlinburgenses*, ed. Georg Pertz, MGH SS 3 (Hannover, 1839), a. 1000, p. 77: "Unde in ipsis horis matutinalibus ad curtem suam totius senatus ac pebis expectationi satisfacturus redit, illamque septimanam regalibus impendens officiis, regendo, indulgendo, largiendo ac remunerando transegit."

41. Older works often declare this perspective up front, in their titles; for example, see Victor Domeier, *Die Päpste als Richter über die deutschen Könige von der Mitte des 11. bis zum Ausgang des 13. Jahrhunderts* (Breslau, 1897), esp. 5 ff.; Walther Kienast, *Die deutschen Fürsten im Dienste der Westmächte bis zum Tode*

Philipps des Schönen von Frankreich (Utrecht, 1924/31), esp. 1:1–41.

42. On this issue, see the articles collected by Hedda Ragotzky and Horst Wenzel, eds., *Höfische Repräsentation* (Tübingen, 1990), and Gerd Althoff and Ernst Schubert, eds., *Herrschaftsrepräsentation im ottonischen Sachsen* (Frankfurt am Main, 1998).

43. This issue has recently been the theme of several collections of essays; see Hagen Keller, ed., *Pragmatische Schriftlichkeit im Mittelalter* (Munich, 1992); Gert Melville, ed., *Institutionen und Geschichte* (Cologne, Weimar, and Vienna, 1992).

44. See the lectures given at a section of the Hannover Historikertag in 1992 under the title "Spielregeln in mittelalterlicher Öffentlichkeit" and published in FMSt 27 (1993): 27–146.

45. Preliminary studies on this issue are found in Althoff, "Colloquium familiare"; idem, "Huld: Überlegungen zu einen Zentralbegriff der mittelalterlichen Herrschaftsordnung," FMSt 25 (1991): 259–82; idem, "Genugtuung (*satisfactio*)."

46. On Thietmar, see Helmut Lippelt, *Thietmar von Merseburg* (Cologne, 1973), 139 and 162 ff.; Patrick Corbet, *Les saints ottoniens* (Sigmaringen, 1986), 251; Görich, *Otto III.*, 62–85; Gerd Althoff, *Adels- und Königsfamilien im Spiegel ihrer Memorialüberlieferung* (Munich, 1984), 228–36. On the *Annales Quedlinburgenses*, see Althoff, *Adels- und Königsfamilien*, 187 ff.; Ernst Karpf, "Von Widukinds Sachsengeschichte zu Thietmars Chronicon," in *Settimane di studio del Centro Italiano di studi sull'alto medioevo* 32/2 (Spoleto, 1986), 577–78.

47. On Bruno, see Reinhard Wenskus, "Forschungsbericht: Brun von Querfurt und die Stiftung des Erzbistums Gnesen," ZOF 5 (1956): 524–37; idem, *Studien zur historisch-politischen Gedankenwelt Bruns von Querfurt* (Münster, 1956), 171–85. On Bernward, see Knut Görich and Hans Kortüm, "Otto III., Thangmar und die *Vita Bernwardi*," MIÖG 98 (1990): 1–57; Görich, *Otto III.*, 26–51, 92 ff. On Nilus, see Jean-Marie Sansterre,

"Les coryphées des apôtres: Rome et la papauté dans les 'Vies' des Saints Nil et Barthélemy de Grottaferrata," *Byzantion* 55 (1985): 516–43; idem, "Otton III et les saints ascètes de son temps," *Rivista di storia della chiesa in Italia* 43 (1989): 377–412; idem, "Saint Nil de Rossano et le monachisme latin," *Bollettino della Badia Greca di Grottaferrata* 45 (1991): 339–86. On Romuald, see Jean Leclerq, "Saint Romuald et le monachisme missionnaire," *Revue bénédictine* 72 (1962): 307–23; Giovanni Tabacco, "Romualdo di Ravenna e gli inizi dell'eremitismo camaldolese," in *L'eremitismo in Occidente nei secoli XI e XII* (Milan, 1965), 73–119; Hans Laqua, *Tradition und Leitbilder bei dem Ravennater Reformer Petrus Damiani* (Munich, 1976); Giuseppe Fornasari, "*Pater rationabilium eremitarum:* Tradizione agiografica e attualizzezione eremitica nella Vita beati Romualdi," in *Fonte Avellana nel suo millenario* (Urbino, 1983), 2:25–103.

48. For this, see principally František Graus, "Der Heilige als Schlachtenhelfer," in *Festschrift für Helmut Beumann zum 65. Geburtstag,* ed. Kurt-Ulrich Jäschke and Reinhard Wenskus (Sigmaringen, 1977), 330–48; Friedrich Lotter, "Methodisches zur Gewinnung historischer Erkenntnisse aus hagiographischen Quellen," HZ 229 (1979): 298–356; Pierre Sigal, "Le travail des hagiographes aux XIᵉ et XIIᵉ siècles," *Francia* 15 (1987): 149–82.

49. Gerbert of Aurillac, *Briefsammlung,* ed. Fritz Weigle, MGH Epp. DK 2 (Berlin, 1966). [English: *The Letters of Gerbert, with His Papal Privileges as Sylvester II,* trans. Harriet Lattin (New York, 1961).]

50. On irony, see Brackmann, "Der 'Römische Erneuerungsgedanke,'" 115 n. 36; on suffering from Germanness, see Giesebrecht's formulation on pages 0–0.

51. See Percy Ernst Schramm, *Kaiser, Rom und Renovatio,* 4th ed. (Darmstadt, 1984), 97–100; Kurt Zeillinger, "Otto III. und die Konstantinische Schenkung," in *Fälschungen im Mittelalter* (Hannover, 1988), 2:512ff.

CHAPTER 1: A CHILD ON THE THRONE

1. Thietmar, *Chronicon,* III, 26, p. 130: "completo hoc officio, mox legatus tristi nuncio tanta perturbans gaudia advenit."

2. Eccles. 10:16; see Theo Kölzer, "Das Königtum Minderjähriger im fränkisch-deutschen Mittelalter: Eine Skizze," HZ 251 (1990): 291–324.

3. See Uhlirz, *Jahrbücher des Deutschen Reiches,* 2:176–79.

4. On the Slav uprising, see Thietmar, *Chronicon,* III, 17–18, pp. 118ff.; Wolfgang Brüske, *Untersuchungen zur Geschichte des Liutizenbundes* (Münster and Cologne, 1955), 39–45; Wolfgang Fritze, "Der slawische Aufstand von 983—eine Schicksalswende in der Geschichte Mitteleuropas," in *Festschrift der landesgeschichtlichen Vereinigung für die Mark Brandenburg zu ihrem hundertjährigen Bestehen,* ed. Eckart Henning and Werner Vogel (Berlin, 1984), 30–38; Christian Lübke, *Regesten zur Geschichte der Slaven an Elbe und Oder* (Berlin, 1984–88), vol. 3, nos. 220–24, pp. 14–22, with further references.

5. Thietmar, *Chronicon,* III, 24, p. 128: "Omnes nostri principes, comperta tam miserabili fama, conveniunt dolentes et, ut eum sibi liceret videre, per epistolae portitorem unanimi supplicatione poscebant." See also Wolfgang Giese, *Der Stamm der Sachsen und das Reich in ottonischer und salischer Zeit* (Wiesbaden, 1979), 127.

6. See the thesis in Mathilde Uhlirz, "Der Fürstentag zu Mainz," MIÖG 58 (1950): 267–84; for an opposing view, see Wenskus, *Studien zur historisch-politischen Gedankenwelt Bruns von Querfurt,* 45ff.

7. Thietmar, *Chronicon,* III, 26, p. 130: "Huius inclita proles, nata sibi in silva, quae Ketil vocatur, in die proximi natalis Domini ab Iohanne archiepiscopo Rawennate et a Willigiso Magociacense in regem consecratur Aquisgrani . . ."; see Franz-Reiner Erkens, ". . . *more Grecorum conregnantem instituere vultis?*" FMSt 27 (1993): 273.

8. On Henry the Quarrelsome's activities between 974 and 985, see Uhlirz, *Jahrbücher des Deutschen Reiches*, 2:10–66; Rudolf Kohlenberger, "Die Vorgänge des Thronstreits während der Unmündigkeit Ottos III. 983–985" (Ph.D. diss., Erlangen, 1931); Kurt Reindel, *Die bayerischen Luitpoldinger* (Munich, 1953), 232–54; Winfrid Glocker, *Die Verwandten der Ottonen und ihre Bedeutung in der Politik* (Cologne and Vienna, 1989), 179–83; most recently Erkens, ". . . *more Grecorum conregnantem instituere vultis?*"

9. For example, the regular renewal of the *pacta* between the popes and the Carolingians after the death of one of the treaty partners makes this clear; on this, see Anna Maria Drabek, *Die Verträge der fränkischen und deutschen Herrscher mit dem Papsttum von 754 bis 1020* (Vienna, Cologne, and Graz, 1976), esp. 31–34. See also the discussion of the length of time the Concordat of Worms remained valid: Peter Classen, "Das Wormser Konkordat in der deutschen Verfassungsgeschichte," in *Investiturstreit und Reichsverfassung*, ed. Josef Fleckenstein (Sigmaringen, 1973), 413–16; Fritz Trautz, "Zur Geltungsdauer des Wormser Konkordats," in *Geschichtsschreibung und geistiges Leben im Mittelalter*, ed. Karl Hauck and Hubert Mordek (Cologne, 1978). In general, see also the article "Vertrag" in HRG, vol. 36, esp. cols. 842 ff.

10. See Helmut Beumann, "Zur Entwicklung transpersonaler Staatsvorstellungen," in *Wissenschaft vom Mittelalter* (Cologne and Vienna, 1972), 135–74.

11. *Annales Quedlinburgenses*, a. 984, pp. 64 ff.: "Heinricus . . . simulans se primo ob ius propinquitatis partibus regis infantis fidelissime patrocinaturum, regem tenuit . . ."; on this, see Johannes Laudage, "Das Problem der Vormundschaft über Otto III.," in *Kaiserin Theophanu*, ed. Anton von Euw and Peter Schreiner (Cologne, 1991), 263–68; Erkens, ". . . *more Grecorum conregnantem instituere vultis?*" 279 ff.

12. Adelheid, Theophanu, and Mathilde only returned to Germany in May or June 984; see BU, no. 956c/2, p. 429, and Uhlirz, *Jahrbücher des Deutschen Reiches*, 2:22 ff. The imperial ladies therefore did not personally intervene in the first phase of the throne struggle.

13. Thietmar, *Chronicon*, IV, 1, p. 132: "Qui cum palmarum sollemnia in Magadaburg celebrare voluisset, omnes regionis illius principes huc convenire rogavit atque precepit, tractans, quomodo se suae potestati subderent regnique eum fastigio sublevarent." *Annales Quedlinburgenses*, a. 984, p. 66: "dein accrescentis avaritiae stimulis agitatus, quorundam etiam persuasione male illectus, regnum tyrannice invasit, atque in id elationis usque prorupit, ut et rex dici et in regem benedici appeteret."

14. See the evidence in BU, no. 956a/1, p. 421; no. 956d/1, p. 422; and especially Richer of Rheims, *Histoire de France*, ed. Robert Latouche (Paris, 1937), III, 97, p. 122: "Quod dum a Lothario expetendum cogitaret, eumque concessa Belgica sibi sotium et amicum facere moliretur, legatos praemisit, apud quos sacramentum commune negocium firmaretur. Quo etiam sacramento utrique reges sibi pollicerentur sese super Rhenum loco constituto sibi occursuros." III, 98, p. 124: "Hezilo sese metuens in suspitionem principum venire si Lothario occurreret, acsi eum in regnum recipere vellet, periurii reus, occurrere distulit." Most recently, see Pierre Riché, *Gerbert d'Aurillac* (Paris, 1987), 84–87; Brühl, *Deutschland—Frankreich*, 576 ff.

15. Adalbero warns against appointing a coruler with Otto III ("Ne consortem regni facias, quem semel admissum repellere nequeas"), and calls Henry the Quarrelsome "rei publicae hostis: Germanum Brisaca Rheni litoris Francorum reges clam nunc adeunt, Henricus rei publicae hostis dictus kal. febr. occurrit." Gerbert, *Briefsammlung*, no. 39, pp. 67–68.

16. Like Otto II, Lothar and Henry the Quarrelsome were direct grandsons of Henry I. On the kinship connections, see

Kohlenberger, "Vorgänge des Thron-streits," 24ff.; Hlawitschka, *Vom Franken-reich zur Formierung der europäischen Staaten- und Völkergemeinschaft*, gene-alogical table 2, pp. 292–93; Brühl, *Deutschland—Frankreich*, 576.

17. See Walther Kienast, *Deutschland und Frankreich in der Kaiserzeit* (Stuttgart, 1974–75), 104–13; Brühl, *Deutschland—Frankreich*, 577–78; most recently Bernd Schneidmüller, "Ottonische Familienpoli-tik und französische Nationsbildung im Zeitalter der Theophanu," in *Kaiserin Theophanu*, ed. Euw and Schreiner, esp. 354ff.

18. Thietmar, *Chronicon*, IV, 1, pp. 130ff.: "Prefatus vero dux cum Poppone venerabili episcopo, sub cuius potestate diu tenetur, et cum Ekberto comite unióculo Agripinam veniens, regem patronus legalis de Warino, ut predixi, archipresule suscepit, eiusdemque auxil-ium cum omnibus, quos ad sui gratiam convertere poterat, firmiter est adeptus. Dispositis autem, prout sibi placuit, cunc-tis dux ad Corbeiam cum eis venit ibique Thiedricum et Sicconem comites ac con-fratres nudis pedibus veniam postulantes dedignatur suscipere."

19. A formulation of Gerbert's in a let-ter he wrote in the name of Carl of Lower Lotharingia inspired recent discussion of this possibility; *Briefsammlung*, no. 26, p. 49: "Forte quia Grecus est, ut dicitis, more Grecorum conregnantem instituere vultis?" See the extensive treatment by Erkens, ". . . more Grecorum conregnan-tem instituere vultis?" 283–88, with fur-ther references.

20. See Thietmar's statement in note 18 above; on ritual, see Althoff, "Genug-tuung (*satisfactio*)," esp. 261ff.

21. Thietmar continues from the pas-sage cited in note 18 above, *Chronicon*, IV, 1, p. 132: "Quod hii egre ferentes abierunt, cognatos suimet et amicos a ducis ministerio toto mentis nisu amo-vere studentes."

22. Widukind of Corvey, *Res gestae Saxonicae*, ed. Paul Hirsch and Hans Eberhard Lohmann, MGH SSrG 60 (Han-nover, 1935), preface to bk. 1, p. 1; see also his references to the importance of *clementia* in the prefaces to books II and III, also addressed to Abbess Mathilde (pp. 61 and 100–101), as well as the admiring epithet of Otto the Great: "vicina sibi semper clementia" (clemency was always near him), II, 29, p. 91.

23. On this issue, see Gerd Althoff, "Demonstration und Inszenierung: Spiel-regeln der Kommunikation in mittelalter-licher Öffentlichkeit," FMSt 27 (1993): 27–50; on *clementia*, see esp. 31ff.; on the ritual of prostration, 33–39 and 41ff.

24. See Thietmar, *Chronicon*, IV, 2, pp. 132ff.: "Multi ex his fidem violare ob timorem Dei non presumentes paululum evaserunt et ad civitatem Hesleburg, quo consocii eorum adversus ducem iam palam conspirantes conveniebant, festina-vere. Quorum haec sunt nomina. . . . Con-provincialium autem Thiedricus et Sibert confratres . . ."

25. Ibid., IV, 1, p. 132: "Huic consilio maxima pars procerum hoc dolo consen-sit, quod licenciam a domino suimet rege, cui iuraverat, prius peteret postque secura novo regi serviret."

26. Ibid., IV, 2, p. 132: "Hac in festivi-tate idem a suis publice rex appellatur laudibusque divinis attollitur. Huc Mis-eco et Mistui et Bolizlovo duces cum cae-teris ineffabilibus confluebant, auxilium sibi deinceps ut regi et domino cum iura-mentis affirmantes."

27. On the destruction of Hamburg by the Abodrites, see Lübke, *Regesten*, vol. 3, no. 223, pp. 19ff.; Thietmar, *Chronicon*, III, 18, p. 120: "Mistui, Abdritorum dux, Hômanburg, ubi sedes episcopalis quon-dam fuit, incendit atque vastavit. Quid vero ibi mirabilium Christus operaretur e cçlis, attendat religio tocius christianitatis. Venit de supernis sedibus aurea dextera, in medium collapsa incendium expansis digi-tis, et plena cunctis videntibus rediit. Hoc admiratur exercitus, hoc stupet Mistuwoi timoratus. Et id mihi indicavit Avico, capellanus tunc eius et spiritualis frater meus postea effectus. Sed ego cum eodem sic tractavi: reliquias sanctorum itinere in

caelum divinitus collatas abisse hostesque terruisse atque fugasse. Post haec Mystuwoi in amentiam versus in vinculis tenetur; et aqua benedicta inmersus: 'Sanctus', inquid, 'me Laurentius incendit!' et antequam liberaretur, miserabiliter obiit." On the assembly in Quedlinburg, see Lübke, *Regesten*, vol. 3, no. 228, pp. 27–28; Wolfgang Eggert and Barbara Pätzold, *Wir-Gefühl und Regnum Saxonum* (Weimar, 1984), 238ff.

28. Kohlenberger, "Vorgänge des Thronstreits," 10–11; Dietrich Claude, *Geschichte des Erzbistums Magdeburg bis in das 12. Jahrhundert* (Cologne and Vienna, 1972), 1:158ff.; on the support various imperial bishops gave to Henry, among them the archbishops of Trier, Cologne, and Magdeburg, see Erkens, *". . . more Grecorum conregnantem instituere vultis?"* 275–76.

29. Gerd Althoff, "Zur Frage nach der Organisation sächsischer *coniurationes* in der Ottonenzeit," FMSt 16 (1982): 129–42; idem, *Adels- und Königsfamilien*, 96ff.

30. See Thietmar, *Chronicon*, IV, 2, pp. 132ff., with the enumeration of the people named in the text.

31. Ibid., IV, 3, p. 134: "Quod dux comperiens suos magnis muneribus ditatos cum gratia dimisit; ipse autem cum valida manu ad perturbandam hanc coniurationem seu pacificandam ad Werlu properans, Popponem misit episcopum, ut adversantes sibi disiungere vel reconciliari temptaret. Qui cum cepto itinere persisteret, hostes congregatos iamque ducem petere paratos inveniens, vix pacem mutuam in loco, qui Seusun dicitur, ad condictum pepigit diem." On the peculiarities and characteristics of conflicts in this period, see Althoff, "Königsherrschaft," 268–73, and idem, "Konfliktverhalten und Rechtsbewußtsein: Die Welfen in der Mitte des 12. Jahrhunderts," FMSt 26 (1992): 336–37, each with additional references.

32. The behavior of the candidates for the crown in 1002 is comparable; see Giese, *Stamm der Sachsen*, 26–31.

33. Thietmar, *Chronicon*, IV, 3, p. 134: "hostilis immanitas urbem comitis Ekberti, quae Ala dicitur, possedit; destructisque protinus muris intrantes Ethelheidam inperatoris filiam, quae hic nutriebatur, cum pecunia ibi plurimum collecta rapiunt gaudentesque redeunt."

34. Ibid., IV, 4, pp. 134ff.: "Dux autem, conversis ad se omnibus Bawariorum episcopis comitibusque nonnullis, Francorum terminos his fretus sociis adiit et in pascuis ad Bisinstidi pertinentibus ad alloquendos regionis illius principes consedit. Magontinae tunc provisor aeclesiae Willigisus cum duce Conrado caeterisque optimatibus huc venit. Hos dux, quibuscumque valuit modis, sibi coniungere temptans eosque a promissa regi suo cum sacramentis fide numquam vita comite recessuros unanimi eorum responso percipiens, coactus est futuri timore duelli cum iuramentis affirmare, ut III. Kal. Iulii ad locum, qui Rara vocatur, veniret puerumque matri suae illisque redderet."

35. Ibid., IV, 7, p. 138: "Quid plura? quicquid exposcunt, crastino impetrant eumque ad Merseburg, ubi ductrix Gisla longo tristis sedebat abcessu, hii discedentes ire permittunt. Is vero cum fidelibus suis singula quaeque discutiens seque ob Dei timorem patriaeque salutem a proposito recessurum suo veraciter indicans, grates auxilii suimet ac bonae voluntatis condignas refert et, ut cum illo ad condictum pergerent diem, omnes caritative postulat."

36. *Annales Quedlinburgenses*, a. 984, p. 66: "Habitoque inibi consilio maximo, mirandum memorandumque posteris signum, stella videlicet perlucida in ipso partium conflictu, medio coeli axe, media ultra morem die, quasi divinum regi capto praebitura iuvamen, cunctis qui aderant cernentibus stupentibusque radiavit. Qua visa, perterrita moxque cedente parte iniusta, Heinricus praefatus, usurpato nomine et regno iure privatus, regem aviae, matri et amitae praesentare cogitur; interventuque regis Conradi soceri sui ac principum qualicunque gratia donatus, in patriam moestus abcessit." Thietmar also

mentions the star, *Chronicon*, iv, 8, p. 140: "Stella a Deo predestinati rectoris media die cernentibus universis clara refulsit." Thietmar had access to the Quedlinburg Annals.

37. Thietmar, *Chronicon*, IV, 8, p. 140: "Rex a suimet matre aviaque diligenter succeptus, Hoiconis magisterio comitis commissus est. Inter regem et ducem pax firmatur usque ad supramemorata Bisinstidi prata, utrisque sua petentibus. Convenientibus autem his malorum instinctu in malo discesserunt, sicque multum temporis stetit intervallum. Oritur autem inter hunc et prefatum Heinricum, qui minor dicebatur, magna sedicio, qua Herimanni comitis consilio postmodum finita, regis gratiam in Francanafordi et ducatum dedicius promeruit." On this, see Reindel, *Die bayerischen Luitpoldinger*, 249–50.

38. Kohlenberger, "Vorgänge des Thronstreits," 60; Reindel, *Die bayerischen Luitpoldinger*, 232–56, esp. 251–52.

39. Althoff, "Demonstration und Inszenierung," 43–50, esp. 49–50.

40. *Annales Quedlinburgenses*, a. 985, p. 67: "Veniente in Frankanafurd rege infante tertio Othone, ibidem et ipse adveniens humiliavit se iuste, quo poenam evaderet elationis iniustae, regique puerulo, quem orbatum captivaverat, cuius regnum tyrannice invaserat, praesentibus dominis imperialibus, quas regni cura penes, avia, matre et amita regis eiusdem infantis, humilis habitu, humilis et actu, totius in aspectu populi, ambabus in unum complicatis manibus, militem se et vera ulterius fide militaturum tradere non erubuit, nil paciscendo nisi vitam, nil orando nisi gratiam. At dominae, quarum, ut diximus, cura regnum regisque regebatur infantia, tanti viri summissa deditione admodum gratulabundae,—quia piorum moris est, non solum mala pro bonis non reddere, sed etiam pro malis bona rependere,—digno eum honore susceptum, gratia fideli donatum, ductoria itidem dignitate sublimatum, deinde non tantum inter amicos, sed etiam inter amicissimos, uti ius propinquitatis exigebat, debito dilectionis venerantur affectu."

41. François Louis Ganshof, *Feudalism* (New York, 1961), 72–75; Walther Kienast, *Die fränkische Vasallität* (Frankfurt am Main, 1990), 74–79.

42. Timothy Reuter, "Unruhestiftung, Fehde, Rebellion, Widerstand," in *Die Salier und das Reich*, ed. Stefan Weinfurter (Sigmaringen, 1991), 3:320–25; see also Gerd Althoff, "Das Privileg der *deditio*," in *Nobilitas*, ed. Otto Oexle and Werner Paravicini (Göttingen, 1997); on the "language" of requests for mercy and forgiveness, see more generally Geoffrey Koziol, *Begging Pardon and Favor* (Ithaca and London, 1992).

43. See this reproach in the account of the *Annales Quedlinburgenses*, a. 985, p. 67, cited in note 40 above.

44. Thietmar, *Chronicon*, IV, 9, p. 140: "Celebrata est proxima paschalis sollemnitas in Quidelingeburg a rege, ubi quattuor ministrabant duces, Heinricus ad mensam, Conrad ad cameram, Hecil ad cellarium, Bernhardus equis prefuit." After this follows the other news paraphrased in the text: "Huc etiam Bolizlavus et Miseco cum suis conveniunt omnibusque rite peractis muneribus locupletati discesserunt. In diebus illis Miseco semet ipsum regi dedit et cum muneribus aliis camelum ei presentavit et duas expediciones cum eo fecit."

45. On the court chapel, see Fleckenstein, *Hofkapelle der deutschen Könige*, 2:77–117; for the regency period, esp. 77–83; more recently, see idem, "Hofkapelle und Kanzlei unter der Kaiserin Theophanu," in *Kaiserin Theophanu*, ed. Euw and Schreiner, 305–8; on Theophanu's regency, see most recently Franz-Reiner Erkens, "Die Frau als Herrscherin in ottonisch-frühsalischer Zeit," in *Kaiserin Theophanu*, ed. Euw and Schreiner, 254–59; Laudage, "Das Problem der Vormundschaft über Otto III.," 268–71.

46. The nickname first appears in the modern era; see Kurt Reindel, "Heinrich II.," NDB 8 (1969): 341.

47. See the author's studies on this theme: "Königsherrschaft" and "Konfliktverhalten und Rechtsbewußtsein."

48. See especially the two-volume anniversary publication edited by Anton von Euw and Peter Schreiner, *Kaiserin Theophanu: Begegnung des Ostens und Westens um die Wende des ersten Jahrtausends*, 2 vols. (Cologne, 1991); the portrait in Odilo Engels, "Theophanu—die westliche Kaiserin aus dem Osten," in *Die Begegnung des Westens mit dem Osten*, ed. Odilo Engels and Peter Schreiner (Sigmaringen, 1993), 13–36; Gunther Wolf, ed., *Kaiserin Theophanu: Prinzessin aus der Fremde, des Westreichs große Kaiserin* (Cologne, Weimar, and Vienna, 1991); Rosamond McKitterick, "Ottonian Intellectual Culture in the Tenth Century and the Role of Theophanu," *Early Medieval Europe* 2 (1993): 53–74; Wendy Davies, ed., *Theophanu and Her Times* (Cambridge, 1994).

49. Thietmar, *Chronicon*, IV, 10, p. 142: "Haec, quamvis sexu fragilis, modestae tamen fiduciae et, quod in Graecia rarum est, egregiae conversationis fuit regnumque filii eius custodia servabat virili, demulcens in omnibus pios terrensque ac superans erectos."

50. Uhlirz, *Jahrbücher des Deutschen Reiches*, 2:139–40; newly emphasized by Johannes Fried, "Theophanu und die Slawen," in *Kaiserin Theophanu*, ed. Euw and Schreiner, esp. 362; for an opposing view, see Joachim Ehlers, "Otto II. und Kloster Memleben," SaAn 18 (1994): 79.

51. On this issue, see the comments in the introduction.

52. Fleckenstein, "Hofkapelle und Kanzlei," 307.

53. Paul Kehr, *Die Urkunden Otto III.* (Innsbruck, 1890), 39ff.; Fleckenstein, "Hofkapelle und Kanzlei," 307–8.

54. See Karl Uhlirz, "Die Interventionen in den Urkunden König Ottos III. bis zum Tode Theophanus," NA 21 (1896): 115–37.

55. On this controversy, see most recently Görich, *Otto III.*, 123–32; idem, "Der Gandersheimer Streit zur Zeit Ottos III.," ZRG KA 110 (1993): 56–94.

56. Thangmar, *Vita Bernwardi episcopi Hildesheimensis*, ed. Georg Pertz, in MGH SS 4 (Hannover, 1841), chap. 13, p. 764: "faventibus illi fere omnibus, quia archiepiscopi animositas, etsi metu illius dissimularent, cunctis displicebat."

57. Ibid.: "Destitutus itaque archiepiscopus multitudinis favore, qui prius suo iuri omnia promisit, vix domna Theuphanu et episcopis obtinentibus, ipso quoque ultra quam credi potest supplicante, obtinuit, ut ad principale altare misteria ipsa die ageret, ita videlicet, ut domnae Sophiae velationem simul agerent, caeterarum quoque domnus Osdagus solus prospiceret."

58. On Hatto, see Ernst Dümmler, *Geschichte des ostfränkischen Reiches* (Leipzig, 1882), 3:497ff.; on Anno and Adalbert, see Georg Jenal, *Erzbischof Anno II. von Köln (1056–75) und sein politisches Wirken* (Stuttgart, 1974–75), 407–14.

59. See Uhlirz, *Jahrbücher des Deutschen Reiches*, vol. 2, esp. 67ff., 78–87, 97–103; Kienast, *Deutschland und Frankreich in der Kaiserzeit*, 99–127; Brühl, *Deutschland—Frankreich*, 575–605. Interestingly, and—as is stressed in the remarks that follow in the text—justifiably, Bernd Schneidmüller devotes no space to discussion of the empress's western policy in "Ottonische Familienpolitik," 349–59.

60. See Uhlirz, *Jahrbücher des Deutschen Reiches*, 2:105–18.

61. This is especially true of Archbishop Adalbero of Rheims, but also of King Hugh; on this, see Riché, *Gerbert d'Aurillac*, 53–56 and 102–9.

62. See Gerbert, *Briefsammlung*, nos. 62 and 66: "Sed quae res institutum colloquium dominarum sic commutavit, ut solus veniat Henricus?" (no. 62, p. 93); "Metis colloquium dominarum habendum vos quam plurimum interesse optamus" (no. 66, p. 97); on these meetings, see also Heinrich Fichtenau, *Living in the Tenth Century* (Chicago, 1991), 179–80.

63. The quotation is from letter no. 63, p. 94; it is not certain to whom the congratulations were sent, although it is assumed in Uhlirz, *Jahrbücher des Deut-*

schen Reiches, 2:54. On this issue, see also the references supplied by the editor of the letter collection (94 n. 2). This example shows clearly the difficulties in connecting concrete historical events with the statements and declarations in the letters.

64. On this, see Uhlirz, *Jahrbücher des Deutschen Reiches,* 2:54; BU, no. 972b, pp. 453–54.

65. See Gerbert, *Briefsammlung,* no. 97, pp. 126–27.

66. On the specifics, see Uhlirz, *Jahrbücher des Deutschen Reiches,* 2:81–82.

67. See Gerbert, *Briefsammlung,* no. 101, pp. 131–32: "Sed quoniam per ignorantiam dominę Th. imperatricis semper augustę hoc fiebat, dolum subesse intelligentes, uti per se potius pax fieret, consuluimus, utque prius per vos, quę conditio pacis foret, experiretur. Quod laudatum est vestrique itineris sotii denominati. xv kl. iun. Francorum colloquio nobis occurrendum ibique, si pacem cum rege senior noster confecerit, pro pace regnorum plurimum elaborabit." See also BU, no. 991e, pp. 473–74.

68. Gerbert, *Briefsammlung,* no. 120, pp. 147–48.

69. Significantly, in and around Canossa noble ladies played a role as intermediaries between Pope Gregory VII and Henry IV; see Althoff, "Demonstration und Inszenierung," 37–38; also important is the occasion on which the Milanese threw their crosses into the bower of Empress Beatrice, the wife of Frederick Barbarossa, in order to obtain her mediation; on this, see Joachim Bumke, *Höfische Kultur* (Munich, 1986), 491–92; Thomas Zotz, "Präsenz und Repräsentation," in *Herrschaft als soziale Praxis,* ed. Alf Lüdtke (Göttingen, 1991), 181.

70. This shows again the problem in assuming that abstract concepts (here, political activities) cause events (here, residences of the court and the empress). The *Regesten* and *Jahrbücher* of Otto III are filled with this sort of conclusion.

71. See the extensive primary and secondary references in Lübke, *Regesten,* vol. 3, nos. 220–24, pp. 15–22.

72. Ibid., no. 236, pp. 36–37, and no. 239, pp. 40–41.

73. See note 26 above.

74. See Thietmar, *Chronicon,* IV, 9, p. 140; Lübke, *Regesten,* vol. 3, no. 239, pp. 40–41.

75. Lübke, *Regesten,* vol. 3, no. 261, pp. 76–77.

76. Thietmar, *Chronicon,* IV, 22, pp. 156ff. On Kizo, see also Lübke, *Regesten,* vol. 3, no. 226, pp. 23–24; no. 266, pp. 83–84; no. 272, pp. 92ff.; nos. 280ff., pp. 106–14; no. 289, pp. 116–17; no. 291, pp. 119–20; no. 294, pp. 123–24.

77. See the detailed description of his struggle with his uncle Hermann Billung and Otto the Great in Widukind, *Res gestae Saxonicae,* III, 50–70, pp. 129–48; see also Lübke, *Regesten,* vol. 2, no. 122, pp. 168ff.; no. 144, pp. 200ff., with references to the older literature.

78. Widukind, *Res gestae Saxonicae,* III, 69, pp. 143ff.

79. Thietmar, *Chronicon,* IV, 12/13, pp. 144–48.

80. See the suggestions for areas of further research in Lübke, *Regesten,* vol. 3, no. 255a, pp. 65–66.

81. Thus most recently Fried, "Theophanu und die Slawen," 369—"It [the gift] hardly was unlikely to have been made in opposition to Theophanu's policy, but much rather in agreement with her"—developing an idea of Herbert Ludat, *An Elbe und Oder um das Jahr 1000* (Cologne, 1971), 163–64 nn. 440–41. Walter Schlesinger interpreted this in a completely different fashion in Helmut Beumann and Walter Schlesinger, "Urkundenstudien zur deutschen Ostpolitik unter Otto III.," in Schlesinger, *Mitteldeutsche Beiträge zur deutschen Verfassungsgeschichte des Mittelalters* (Göttingen, 1961), 374ff., which many historians have followed.

82. See, in Chapter 4, the section titled "The Journey."

83. See Fried, "Theophanu und die Slawen," 366; for another view, see Ehlers, "Otto II. und Kloster Memleben," 79–80.

84. See MGH DO III, no. 75, pp. 482–83; on this, see Fried, "Theophanu und die Slawen," 365.

85. BU, no. 1017l, pp. 502–3; see the corresponding description in Bruno of Querfurt, *Vita sancti Adalberti*, ed. Jadwiga Karwasińska, MPH, n.s., 4.2 (Warsaw, 1969), chap. 12, pp. 13–15. Here Bruno directly links Otto II's death to a "sin against Saint Lawrence" and also asserts care for Theophanu's husband's *memoria* as the primary reason for her journey to Italy: "Ibi tunc pulchrum luctum Greca imperatrix augusta, que iam longos dies mortuum fleuit, sepulti coniugis memoriam reparat, dulcem ottonem elemosinis et orationibus cẹlo commendat. . . . Hec tunc ubi sanctum uirum adesse cognouit Adelbertum, nominatissimum episcopum, et Hierosolimam properare audiuit, clam ad se uocat oransque ut pro anima senioris oraret, massam argenteam obtulit ingentem. Ubi accepit uir Dei onus argenti, suo itineri aut necessitati parum prouidens omnia secutura nocte pauperibus expendit."

86. See most recently Erkens, "Die Frau als Herrscherin," 256, and 251 n. 95 for numerous references to the role of the female ruler in Byzantium.

87. See the Charter of Theophanu, no. 2, in MGH DO III, pp. 876–77; on the use of male titles for women, see Brühl, *Deutschland—Frankreich*, 582 with n. 222, also n. 220 for discussion of the possibility of a copyist's error, which Brühl considered unlikely but not completely impossible.

88. On Johannes, see a detailed discussion in Chapter 3, the section titled "The Fight Against Crescentius and the Antipope."

89. On this issue, see Brühl, *Fodrum, gistum, servitium regis*, 506–9, as well as the commentary in the edition of the *Honorantie civitatis Papie* by Carlrichard Brühl and Cinzio Violante (Cologne and Vienna, 1983), 72.

90. See BU, no. 1038a, p. 527; on this, see Roland Pauler, *Das Regnum Italiae in ottonischer Zeit* (Tübingen, 1982), 85.

91. See MGH DO III, no. 69, pp. 476–77; see also Johannes's striking self-praise in MGH DO II, no. 283, pp. 329–30.

92. See Brühl and Violante, *Honorantie civitatis Papie*, 73.

93. See BU, no. 972a, p. 453.

94. On Theophanu's death and burial, see BU, no. 1035b, pp. 524–25; on the choice of her burial place, see Gerd Althoff, "Vormundschaft, Erzieher, Lehrer: Einflüsse auf Otto III.," in *Kaiserin Theophanu*, ed. Euw and Schreiner, 284 with n. 43.

95. See Odilo of Cluny, *Epitaphium domine Adelheide auguste*, ed. Herbert Paulhart (Innsbruck, 1962), chap. 3 (IV), p. 32; on this, see Corbet, *Les saints ottoniens*, 59–64.

96. On this, see Claude, *Geschichte des Erzbistums Magdeburg*, 1:175.

97. See Karl Benz, *Untersuchungen zur politischen Bedeutung der Kirchweihe* (Kallmünz, 1975), 21–54; on the connection with the reestablishment of the bishopric of Merseburg, see Gerd Althoff, "Magdeburg—Halberstadt—Merseburg," in *Herrschaftsrepräsentation im ottonischen Sachsen*, ed. Althoff and Schubert.

98. *Gesta episcoporum Halberstadensium*, ed. Ludwig Weiland, in MGH SS 23 (Hannover, 1874), 87: "Interfuit etiam dedicationi huic serenissimus rex Otto III, corona ceterisque regalibus indumentis sollempniter insignitus, qui summa devotione et humilitate baculum suum aureum obtulit ad altare beati Stephani, qui usque hodie in Halberstadensi ecclesia est servatus."

99. See, in Chapter 2, the section titled "The First Italian Expedition."

CHAPTER 2: THE BEGINNING OF
INDEPENDENT RULE

1. Uhlirz, *Jahrbücher des Deutschen Reiches*, 2:174–75; BU, no. 1117a, pp. 579–80.

2. See Laudage, "Das Problem der Vormundschaft über Otto III.," 274.

3. MGH DO III, no. 146, p. 556: "quomodo nos divinae pietatis attactu commoniti nec non dominae matris nostrae

Theophanu imperatricis augustae in die hominem exeuntis interventu rogati . . ."

4. Ibid., no. 67, p. 474, on Sophia.

5. Thietmar, *Chronicon*, IV, 15, p. 150: "Quod cum inclita inperatrix Aethelheidis comperiret, tristis protinus effecta regem tunc VII annos regnantem visitando consolatur ac vice matris secum tamdiu habuit, quoad ipse, protervorum consilio iuvenum depravatus, tristem illam dimisit."

6. See Gerbert, *Briefsammlung*, no. 215, pp. 256–57.

7. MGH DO III, no. 148, pp. 558–59.

8. Ibid., no. 155, pp. 566–67.

9. Ibid., nos. 159 and 160, pp. 570–71; on this issue, see Joachim Wollasch, "Das Grabkloster der Kaiserin Adelheid in Selz am Rhein," FMSt 2 (1968): 135ff.

10. MGH DO III, no. 157, p. 569: "quomodo nos cuidam monasterio Uualdkiricha vocitato . . . quod per traditionem Burghardi strenuissimi ducis Alemannorum una cum consensu et comprobatione contectalis suę Hadeuuigę hereditario iure in nostrum decidit ius, talem donamus atque largimur libertatem qualem Augea, Corbeia aliaque monasteria habent nostri regni, in quibus monachi vel monachę sub regula sancti Benedicti digna deo prębent servitia."

11. BU, nos. 1150b ff., pp. 601ff.

12. Ibid., no. 1141c, pp. 595–96. An edition of the letter may be found in MGH Epp. Selectae III, no. 16, p. 16.

13. Uhlirz, *Jahrbücher des Deutschen Reiches*, vol. 2, app. X, 478ff.; Kienast, *Deutschland und Frankreich in der Kaiserzeit*, 128–29; Brühl, *Deutschland— Frankreich*, 600ff.

14. BU, no. 1133a, pp. 588–89, and no. 1135b, pp. 590–91.

15. Richer, *Histoire de France*, IV, 96, pp. 304ff. See also Gerbert of Aurillac, *Acta concilii Mosomensis*, ed. Georg Pertz, MGH SS 3 (Hannover, 1839), 690.

16. Hans Kortüm, *Richer von Saint-Remi* (Stuttgart, 1985), 8. For the characterization of Richer's history as a "cock-and-bull story" (*Räuberpistole*), see

Brühl, *Deutschland—Frankreich*, 602. By contrast, the French take Richer more seriously. See Michel Bur, "Adalbéron, archevêque de Reims, reconsidéré," in *Le roi de France et son royaume autour de l'an mil*, ed. Michel Parisse and Xavier Barral I Altet (Paris, 1992), 59.

17. See Kienast, *Deutschland und Frankreich in der Kaiserzeit*, 130 and 125 n. 297.

18. BU, no. 1117, pp. 578–79.

19. Bernward died on the island of Euboea; BU, no. 1146a, p. 599.

20. Fleckenstein, *Hofkapelle der deutschen Könige*, 2:84–85; Heribert Müller, *Heribert, Kanzler Ottos III. und Erzbischof von Köln* (Cologne, 1977), 88ff.

21. See Chapter 4, the section titled "Preconceptions and Preparations."

22. BU, no. 1143a, p. 597.

23. MGH DO III, no. 186, pp. 595–96; see Beumann and Schlesinger, "Urkundenstudien zur deutschen Ostpolitik unter Otto III.," 306ff.

24. Ibid., 306–7 and 317ff.

25. See Johannes Fried, *Otto III. und Boleslaw Chrobry* (Wiesbaden, 1989), 13ff. On the characteristics of the Meissen charter, see Karol Maleczynski, "Die Politik Ottos III. gegenüber Polen und Böhmen im Lichte der Meißener Bistumsurkunde vom Jahre 995," *Letopis*, ser. B, 10 (1963): 162–203. Maleczynski, unlike Gerard Labuda or Beumann and Schlesinger, regards the charter as authentic and analyzes it (on pp. 200–201) as Otto's reaction to the extermination of the Slavníks by the duke of Bohemia because the border expansion in Meissen's favor also encompassed the most important centers of the murdered Slavníks. Maleczynski argues (on p. 202) that this step was specifically aimed against Duke Boleslav of Bohemia.

26. BU, no. 1142a, p. 596.

27. Arnold, *Libri de s. Emmerammo*, ed. Georg Waitz, in MGH SS 4, II, 31, p. 566; see also John Bernhardt, *Itinerant Kingship and Royal Monasteries in Early Medieval Germany, c. 936–1076* (Cambridge, 1993), 101ff.

28. Arnold, *Libri de s. Emmerammo*, II, 31–33, pp. 566–67: with the words "Domine, quid tibi contigit, quod adeo perfusus es lacrimis et sudore?" the members of the entourage join the king.

29. Althoff, "Demonstration und Inszenierung," 33.

30. On this issue, see Gerd Althoff, "Der König weint," in *"Aufführung" und "Schrift" in Mittelalter und früher Neuzeit*, ed. Jan-Dirk Müller (Stuttgart, 1996).

31. So, for example, Uhlirz, *Jahrbücher des Deutschen Reiches*, 2:196.

32. BU, no. 1164b, p. 610.

33. Arnold Angenendt, *Kaiserherrschaft und Königstaufe* (Berlin, 1984), 123–24.

34. BU, no. 1165a, pp. 611–12.

35. BU, no. 1168b, pp. 615–16; Görich, *Otto III.*, 229.

36. On this point, see Althoff, "Königsherrschaft," 273.

37. Gerbert, *Briefsammlung*, no. 215, pp. 256–57.

38. Heinz Wolter, *Die Synoden im Reichsgebiet und in Reichsitalien von 916 bis 1056* (Paderborn, 1988), 144ff.; Görich, *Otto III.*, 222.

39. See Chapter 3.

40. Görich, *Otto III.*, 231.

41. BU, no. 1174a, pp. 621–22; no. 1195, pp. 631–32; Uhlirz, *Jahrbücher des Deutschen Reiches*, 2:216–17.

42. BU, no. 1195, pp. 631–32. Gerbert, *Briefsammlung*, no. 216, pp. 257–58.

43. On the charter MGH DO III, no 389, pp. 818ff., see Chapter 5; see the critique of scholarly hypotheses in Görich, *Otto III.*, 228ff., who rightly argued that there is no evidence of a break.

44. See Uhlirz, *Jahrbücher des Deutschen Reiches*, 2:204.

45. Görich already argued thus (*Otto III.*, 28ff.) against Mathilde Uhlirz's thesis, which hitherto researchers had accepted or even strengthened, as had, for example,

Teta Moehs, *Gregorius V* (Stuttgart, 1972), 41–42 or 66–67.

46. See BU, no. 1210/1b, p. 639; Uhlirz, *Jahrbücher des Deutschen Reiches*, vol. 2, app. XIV, 511ff.

47. On this, see the extensive discussion in Chapter 3.

48. On the synod, see BU, no. 1217i, p. 647; BZ, no. 786, pp. 314–15; Lübke, *Regesten*, vol. 3, no. 314a, p. 150; also vol. 2, no. 211, pp. 297ff., which includes primary and secondary sources concerning the restoration of the bishopric.

49. A letter from Gregory V to Willigis of Mainz contains this threat; see *Epistolae Maguntinae*, in *Monumenta Maguntina*, ed. Philipp Jaffé (Berlin, 1866), chap. 20, p. 352: "Placuit etiam omnibus, ut Gisilharius episcopus, qui contra canones sedem suam dimisit et aliam invasit, in natale Domini Romam vocatus ad satisfaciendum veniat; quod si renuerit, a sacerdotali officio suspendatur." On this, see Robert Holtzmann, "Die Aufhebung und Wiederherstellung des Bistums Merseburg," SaAn 2 (1926): 56; Claude, *Geschichte des Erzbistums Magdeburg*, 1:183 with n. 320.

50. See Beumann and Schlesinger, "Urkundenstudien zur deutschen Ostpolitik unter Otto III.," 377ff.; Holtzmann, *Geschichte der sächsischen Kaiserzeit*, 343; Claude, *Geschichte des Erzbistums Magdeburg*, 1:183–84. In contrast and more appropriately, Görich regarded Otto III's instigation probable; see Görich, *Otto III.*, 163–64. Concerning this problem with new arguments, see Althoff, "Magdeburg—Halberstadt—Merseburg."

51. Beumann and Schlesinger, "Urkundenstudien zur deutschen Ostpolitik unter Otto III.," 378; see also Chapter 1, notes 80–81.

52. Thietmar, *Chronicon*, IV, 10, p. 142.

53. Up to this time, only Görich, *Otto III.*, 167–68, has called attention to the connection; see the extended discussion in Althoff, "Magdeburg—Halberstadt—Merseburg."

54. See the account in the *Gesta episcoporum Halberstadensium*, 88. On Arnulf's background, see Fleckenstein, *Hofkapelle der deutschen Könige*, 2:86.

55. Thietmar, *Chronicon*, IV, 38, pp. 175–76; Claude, *Geschichte des Erzbistums Magdeburg*, 1:170, with justification calls Giselher's behavior "incomprehensible."

56. On this issue, see Althoff, "Magdeburg—Halberstadt—Merseburg," and Thietmar, *Chronicon*, IV, 44 and 46, pp. 182 and 184.

57. After his return he stayed in Mainz for a month without engaging in any kingly activities. On this, see BU, no. 1210/Ia, p. 638.

58. Concerning the course of Gerbert's life and his significance, see the articles in *Gerberto: Scienza, storia e mito* (Bobbio, 1985); see also Riché, *Gerbert d'Aurillac*.

59. On Adalbert, see Wenskus, *Studien zur historisch-politischen Gedankenwelt Bruns von Querfurt*; Peter Hilsch, "Der Bischof von Prag und das Reich in sächsischer Zeit," *DA* 28 (1972): 26 ff.; Görich, *Otto III.*, 125–26. For Otto III's journey to Gniezno, see Chapter 4.

60. On this issue, see Uhlirz, *Jahrbücher des Deutschen Reiches*, 2:209 ff.; Riché, *Gerbert d'Aurillac*, 164 ff.; Görich, *Otto III.*, 211 ff.

61. See Harald Zimmermann, "Gerbert als kaiserlicher Rat," in *Gerberto: Scienza, storia e mito*, 235 ff.; Riché, *Gerbert d'Aurillac*, 32 ff.

62. See Gerbert, *Briefsammlung*, no. 215, pp. 256–57.

63. See ibid., no. 181, p. 213: "Sola michi solatio est clari cesaris Ot. pietas, benivolentia, liberalitas, qui tanto amore vos vestraque diligit, ut dies noctesque mecum sermonem conferat, ubi et quando vos familiariter videre possit, coevum sibi et studiis consimilem, seniorem meum Rot. alloqui et complexari." Significantly, this statement indicates that such a close association with Gerbert did not come

about because of Gerbert's own desires, but rather because of the need to prepare a meeting with Robert of France and Robert's mother, Adelheid. Reports of the confidential companionship of the emperor and Bishop Adalbert in Mainz are found in the Roman *Vita s. Adalberti episcopi*, by Johannes Canaparius, ed. Jadwiga Karwasińska, MPH, n.s., 4.1 (Warsaw, 1962), chap. 23, pp. 34–35: "Cum quo uir Dei mansit bonum tempus, quia familiarissimus sibi erat; et nocte pariter ac die velut dulcissimus cubicularius imperiali camere adhęsit." This report was also adopted by the later *vitae*; on this point, see also Chapter 6, note 38. To establish the time of the stay in Mainz, see BU, no. 1210/Ia, p. 638.

64. See the text quoted in note 63.

65. See Gerbert, *Briefsammlung*, no. 186, pp. 220–23; on this much-discussed letter, see Ter Braak, *Kaiser Otto III.*, 103 ff.; Uhlirz, *Jahrbücher des Deutschen Reiches*, vol. 2, app. XI, 487 ff.; Percy Ernst Schramm, "Kaiser, Basileus und Papst in der Zeit der Ottonen," in *Kaiser, Könige und Päpste* (Stuttgart, 1969), 3:228 ff.; Uta Lindgren, *Gerbert von Aurillac und das Quadrivium* (Wiesbaden, 1976), 78–79.

66. See Gerbert, *Briefsammlung*, no. 187, p. 225: "cum homo genere Grecus, imperio Romanus quasi hereditario iure thesauros sibi Grecię ac Romanę repetit sapientię"; on this, see also Zimmermann, "Gerbert als kaiserlicher Rat," 246.

67. See Schramm, "Kaiser, Basileus und Papst," 229.

68. Thus Brackmann, "Der 'Römische Erneuerungsgedanke,' " 115 with n. 36.

69. Zimmermann, "Gerbert als kaiserlicher Rat," 243 ff., was already skeptical about the intensity of the relationship; on the collaboration of Gerbert and Otto III in this early phase of their relationship, see also Fleckenstein, *Hofkapelle der deutschen Könige*, 2:93 ff.

70. See Uhlirz, *Jahrbücher des Deutschen Reiches*, 2:492; Riché, *Gerbert d'Aurillac*, 182 ff.

71. On this, see Thietmar, *Chronicon*, VI, 100, pp. 392–93; BU, no. 1229a, p. 657;

Lindgren, *Gerbert von Aurillac und das Quadrivium*, 78.

72. On Sasbach, see Karl Schmid, "Sasbach und Limburg," ZGO 137 (1989): esp. 43 ff.; on the title *musicus*, see Fleckenstein, *Hofkapelle der deutschen Könige*, 2:94.

73. Concerning the sources, see Wilhelm Wattenbach and Robert Holtzmann, eds., *Deutschlands Geschichtsquellen im Mittelalter* (Darmstadt, 1967), 1:46 ff.; for the eulogy of Adalbert, see A. Kolberg, "Das Lobgedicht auf den heiligen Adalbert," *Zeitschrift für Geschichte und Altertumskunde Ermlands* 7 (1879–81): 373–598; for the specific details, see Uhlirz, *Jahrbücher des Deutschen Reiches*, 2:118–19, 211 ff.

74. See the extended discussion of this issue in Chapter 4.

75. For details, see, in Chapter 6, the section titled "'Friends' of Otto III and His Interaction with Them."

76. Canaparius, *Vita s. Adalberti episcopi*, chap. 23, p. 35: "Nam die siue nocte, cum turba locum dedit, sanctis alloquiis aggreditur illum, docens, ne magnum putaret se imperatorem esse, cogitaret, se hominem moriturum, cinerem ex pulcherrimo, putredinem et uermium escam esse futurum; viduis se exhibere maritum, pauperibus et pupillis monstrare se patrem; timere Deum et iustum ac districtum iudicem, amare ut pium uenię largitorem ac misericordię fontem; sollicite pensare, quam angusta uia, quę ducit ad uitam, et quam perpauci, qui intrant per eam; bene agentibus esset per humilitatem socius, contra delinquentium uicia per zelum Iustitię erectus . . . monet carum filium, presentis uitę bona despicere, ęternitatis electionem desiderare, mansura quęrere."

77. Bruno of Querfurt, *Vita sancti Adalberti*, chap. 2, p. 25: "Horis congruis semper de cęlestibus docuit regis pueros et circapositos proceres suauissime admonuit."

78. On this issue, see, in Chapter 6, the section titled "'Friends' of Otto III and His Interaction with Them."

CHAPTER 3: THE "REVENGE EXPEDITION" TO ROME AND THE BEGINNING OF THE "ROMAN RENEWAL"

1. For the chronology, see Uhlirz, *Jahrbücher des Deutschen Reiches*, vol. 2, app. XIV, 517; for the assessment, see Görich, *Otto III.*, 209 ff.

2. For the stopping places of this Roman expedition, see BU, nos. 1247a–1255a, pp. 669–72; Uhlirz, *Jahrbücher des Deutschen Reiches*, 2:253–57.

3. BU, no. 1250a, p. 671.

4. Leopold Auer, "Der Kriegsdienst des Klerus unter den sächsischen Kaisern," MIÖG 80 (1972): 68–69.

5. BU, no. 1259c, p. 676; the report of a *compositio*, a peaceful settlement, comes from the *Cronica Pontificum et Imperatorum S. Bartholomei in insula Romani*, ed. Oswald Holder-Egger, in MGH SS 31 (Hannover, 1903), p. 214: "audito imperatoris adventu timore concusi conposuerunt cum ipso . . ."

6. *Annales Quedlinburgenses*, a. 998, p. 74: "Quod audientes praefati Sathanae ministri, Iohannes quidem fugam iniit, Crescentius vero praesidio, quod veterem Romam et Leonianum coniungit castellum, se cum suis inclusit. Tunc quidam non tantum imperatoris quantum Christi amici insequentes Iohannem, comprehenderunt eum, et timentes, ne, si eum ad augustum destinarent, impunitus abiret, linguam ei et nares pariter absciderunt oculosque illi penitus eruerunt."

7. On this issue in general, see W. Brückner, "Devestierung," in *Handwörterbuch zur deutschen Rechtsgeschichte*, ed. Adalbert Erler and Ekkehard Kaufmann (Berlin, 1971), vol. 1, cols. 724–26, with further references. Klaus Schreiner, "Gregor VIII., nackt auf einem Esel," in *Ecclesia et regnum*, ed. Dieter Berg and Hans-Werner Goetz (Bocum, 1989), 155–202, shows how the significance of the dishonoring donkey ride changed through the centuries. For the specific case of Johannes Philagathos, see Harald Zimmermann, *Papstabset-*

zungen des Mittelalters (Graz, Vienna, and Cologne, 1968), 110–14; Moehs, *Gregorius V,* 64–65; August Nitschke, "Der mißhandelte Papst," in *Staat und Gesellschaft in Mittelalter und früher Neuzeit,* ed. Historische Seminar der Universität Hannover (Hannover, 1983).

8. *Vita s. Nili abbatis Cryptae Ferratae,* ed. Georg Pertz, in MGH SS 4, chap. 91, p. 617: "Estote igitur scientes fore, ut quemadmodum vos non doluistis vicem, nec miserti estis eius, quem Deus tradidit manibus vestris, ita vobis quoque pater coelestis peccata nequaquam dimissurus sit." On Nilus, see M.-A. Dell'Ono, "Neilos," in *Lexikon des Mittelalters* (Munich and Zurich, 1993), vol. 6, col. 1085.

9. *Vita s. Nili,* chap. 90, pp. 616–17: "Tunc imperator paulum collacrymatus— neque enim totum, quod successerat, erat revera de eius consilio—respondit beato viro: 'Parati sumus ad implenda omnia, quae tuae pietati placent. . . .' . . . Verum papa ille immitior non expletus malis, quibus Philagathum . . . affecerat, produxit illum, et sacerdotali habitu super ipsum disciso, circumduxit per totam urbem."

10. Ibid., chap. 91, p. 617: "Non multos post dies papa quidem numero vivorum vi exturbabatur quasi tyrannus, ut dicentes quosdam audivi, et effossis sibi oculis, quos pendentes ad genas ferebat, ea pompa sepulturae mandabatur."

11. See ibid. for the direct connection: "Imperator autem poenitentiae causa susceptum indicans laborem, ab Urbe ad Garganum pedibus iter fecit." From the context, one can only conclude that the treatment of Johannes Philagathos was the reason for the penitence; BU, no. 1304b, p. 709.

12. MGH DO III, no. 311, p. 738; see the discussion in Gerd Althoff, "Warum erhielt Graf Berthold im Jahre 999 ein Marktprivileg für Villingen?" in *Die Zähringer,* ed. Karl Schmid (Sigmaringen, 1990), 273.

13. The report appears in Thietmar, *Chronicon,* IV, 43, p. 181. On this issue in

general, see Hagen Keller, "Die Investitur," FMSt 27 (1993), esp. 61–66; on the significance of handing over the crosier, see also Althoff, "Magdeburg—Halberstadt—Merseburg."

14. See the text in note 6 above.

15. For examples, see Althoff, "Königsherrschaft," 272–76.

16. Uhlirz, *Jahrbücher des Deutschen Reiches,* vol. 2, app. XVI, 528.

17. Thietmar, *Chronicon,* IV, 30, pp. 167–68; Rudolfus Glaber, *Historia,* in *Opera,* ed. and trans. John France (Oxford, 1989), I, 12, pp. 24–25.

18. See Arnulf of Milan, *Liber gestorum recentium,* ed. Claudia Zey, MGH SSrG 67 (Hannover, 1994), I, 11, p. 133; Landulf, *Historia Mediolanensis,* ed. Ludwig Bethmann and Wilhelm Wattenbach, in MGH SS 8 (Hannover, 1848), II, 19, p. 56; Petrus Damiani, *Vita beati Romualdi,* ed. Giovanni Tabacco, FSI 94 (Rome, 1957), chap. 25, pp. 52–53; on this, see Uhlirz, *Jahrbücher des Deutschen Reiches,* vol. 2, app. XVI, 529.

19. Uhlirz, *Jahrbücher des Deutschen Reiches,* vol. 2, app. XVI, 530–31.

20. For an assessment of the value of the *Fundatio* as a source, see Hans Patze, "Adel und Stifterchronik," BDLG 100 (1964): 51–52; on the Ezzo clan, see most recently Helmuth Kluger, "*Propter claritatem generis*: Genealogisches zur Familie der Ezzonen," in *Köln: Stadt und Bistum in Kirche und Reich,* ed. Hanna Vollrath and Stefan Weinfurter (Cologne, Weimar, and Vienna, 1993), 223–58.

21. *Brunwilarensis monasterii fundatorum actus,* ed. Georg Waitz, in MGH SS 14 (Hannover, 1883), 131: "Interim Crescentio non sua, sicut opinabatur, munitio imperii gloriam, sed longam carceris efficiebat custodiam, et quem imperatoris longanimitas sua suorumque sibi induta impunitate flectere non potuit ad dedicionem, iustam suae Dei iudicio pertinaciae passus est ultionem. Tandem enim ad presentiam eius, fide interposita, evocatus, venit; monitus, ut sese cum omnibus suis imperatoris gratiae dederet, tumens abnuit; redire permissus, electis

militibus, qui fidem suam virtute probarent, eum perniciter insequentibus, revertitur et ad altioris aedis secretum ascendere hostiumque pessulo obfirmare nititur. Sed repente velociori persequentium impetu repulsus, clamore in altum elato, simulque e latere strictis quos absconderant gladiis, perterritis suis, ipse vecors impigre a cavea sua extrahitur, imperatori presentatus, ut reus maiestatis capite dampnatur."

22. Rudolfus Glaber, Historia, I, 12, p. 26: "Cernens quoque Crescentius nullam posse euadendi uiam reperire, licet tardius, penitudinis adinuenit consilium, non tamen ei prestitit miserendi aditum. Quadam igitur die, quibusdam de imperatoris exercitu consentientibus, egrediens latenter Crescentius de turre, scilicet birro indutus et operto capite, ueniensque inprouisus corruit ad imperatoris pedes, oransque se ab imperatoris pietate uitae seruari. Quem cum respexisset imperator conuersus ad suos, ut erat amaro animo, dixit: 'Cur' inquiens 'Romanorum principem, imperatorum decretorem datoremque legum atque ordinatorem pontificum, intrare siuistis magalia Saxonum? Nunc quoque reducite eum ad thronum suę sublimitatis, donec eius honori condignam uidelicet preparemus susceptionem.' Qui suscipientes illum, scilicet ut iussum fuerat, inlesum reduxerunt ad turris introitum. Ingressusque nuntiauit secum pariter reclusis quoniam solummodo tantum contingeret illis uiuere quandiu ipsa turris tueri ualeret ab hostium captione, nec ullam prorsus salutem ultra debere sperare. At imperatoris exercitus a foris urgendo impellens machinas, paulatimque euntes applicatę sunt turri. Sicque pugnę inito certamine, dumque alii desuper contendentes intrare, alii prorupere ad ostium turris illudque concidentes euellunt, sursumque certatim gradientes ad turris superiora peruenerunt. Respiciens quoque Crescentius, cernit se teneri ab his quos putabat pugnando longius arceri posse. Capto numque ipso ac grauiter uulnerato, ceterisque qui cum illo inuenti fuerant trucidatis, miserunt ad imperatorem quid de eo preciperet. Qui ait, 'Per superiora' inquit 'propugnacula illum deicite aperte,

ne dicant Romani suum principem uos furatos fuisse.'"

23. On this point, see Althoff, "Königsherrschaft," 272–76.

24. Gerbert, Briefsammlung, no. 220, p. 261: "et ille Joannes Graecus, quod nobis placuerit, se facturum pollicetur."

25. This, however, is a case of an act agreed upon by all parties, with all the specifics established beforehand. On this, see Althoff, "Demonstration und Inszenierung," 35–40; idem, "Huld," 270 with n. 45. For an overview of the rituals requesting forgiveness and pardon, see Koziol, Begging Pardon and Favor.

26. On this issue, see Thietmar, Chronicon, IV, 30, p. 169, and Uhlirz, Jahrbücher des Deutschen Reiches, vol. 2, app. XIV, 512 ff.

27. Görich, Otto III., 214–15, rightly emphasizes this point.

28. BU, no. 1272a, pp. 685–86.

29. See MGH DO III, no. 285, p. 710.

30. See the extensive evidence in Zimmermann, Papstabsetzungen des Mittelalters, 98–118.

31. Uhlirz, Jahrbücher des Deutschen Reiches, 2:204; on this issue, see the statement of the Annales Hildesheimenses, ed. Georg Waitz, MGH SSrG 8 (Hannover, 1878), a. 996, p. 27: "quendam Crescentium, quia priorem papam iniuriis sepe laceravit, exilio statuit deportari. Sed ad preces novi apostolici imperator omnia remisit. Sed non multo post imperatore Urbe excedente, idem Crescentius dominum apostolicum nudum omnium rerum Urbe expulit."

32. Most recently, see the discussion by Althoff, "Das Privileg der deditio."

33. Paul Hinschius, Das Kirchenrecht der Katholiken und Protestanten in Deutschland (Berlin, 1893), 5/1:488.

34. Thietmar, Chronicon, IV, 30, p. 167.

35. See Schramm, Kaiser, Rom und Renovatio, 4th ed., 116–35; see also the articles on related themes reprinted, with commentary, in Schramm, Kaiser,

Könige und Päpste (Stuttgart, 1969), 3:200–297.

36. Görich, *Otto III.*, 276–81.

37. See ibid., 187–94 and 267–81.

38. On the significance of the supposed Donation of Constantine in this period, see Horst Fuhrmann, *Einfluß und Verbreitung der pseudoisidorischen Fälschungen* (Stuttgart, 1972–75), 2:389 ff.; most recently Zeillinger, "Otto III. und die Konstantinische Schenkung."

39. The current assessment of Otto III is distinguished by this correction. See, for example, Helmut Beumann, *Die Ottonen*, 2d ed. (Stuttgart, 1991), 143 ff.; Hlawitschka, *Vom Frankenreich zur Formierung der europäischen Staaten- und Völkergemeinschaft*, 144 ff.; Johannes Fried, *Die Formierung Europas: 840–1046* (Munich, 1991), 82; idem, *Der Weg in die Geschichte* (Berlin, 1994), 588–91.

40. On this point, see Görich, *Otto III.*, 194–98.

41. See MGH DO III, no. 285, p. 710.

42. On this issue, see Görich, *Otto III.*, 267–74, with the certainly plausible argument that the *renovatio* was completed in essence with Crescentius's fall and the later reestablishment of order in Rome. Only then was the period of *aurea Roma* introduced.

43. Schramm, *Kaiser, Rom und Renovatio*, 4th ed., 101. On the *Libellus*, see also Riché, *Gerbert d'Aurillac*, 189–94; Carla Frova, "Gerberto Philosophus," in *Gerberto: Scienza, storia e mito*, 351 ff. See also Görich, *Otto III.*, 206–7.

44. See Schramm, *Kaiser, Rom und Renovatio*, 4th ed., 101; on Gerbert's letter, see also Carl Erdmann, "Das ottonische Reich als Imperium Romanum," DA 6 (1943): 424–26.

45. Leo of Vercelli, *Versus de Gregorio et Ottone augusto*, ed. Karl Strecker, MGH Poetae Latini 5.2 (Berlin, 1939), 477–80; on this work, see Schramm, *Kaiser, Rom und Renovatio*, 4th ed., 119 ff.; Görich, *Otto III.*, 198–99.

46. As Schramm argued in *Kaiser, Rom und Renovatio*, 4th ed., 124.

47. On this, see Percy Ernst Schramm and Florentine Mütherich, *Die deutschen Kaiser und Könige in Bildern ihrer Zeit 751–1190* (Munich, 1983), 84; Hartmut Hoffmann, *Buchkunst und Königtum im ottonischen und frühsalischen Reich* (Stuttgart, 1986), 39, nos. 12 and 14; Brühl, *Deutschland—Frankreich*, 615 ff., with color illustrations.

48. See Görich, *Otto III.*, 197 with n. 62; on the ruler portraits with *nationes* paying homage, see also Gerhart Ladner, *L'immagine dell'imperatore Ottone III* (Rome, 1988), 46–47 and 52–53, with ills. 10–12 and 22–24.

49. See the text in *Constitutum Constantini*, ed. Horst Fuhrmann, MGH Fontes iuris Germanici antiqui in usum scholarum 10 (Hannover, 1968), chap. 18, pp. 94–95: "quoniam, ubi principatus sacerdotum et christianae religionis caput ab imperatore caelesti constitutum est, iustum non est, ut illic imperator terrenus habeat potestatem."

50. See Bruno of Querfurt, *Vita quinque fratrum eremitarum*, ed. Jadwiga Karwasińska, in MPH, n.s., 4.3 (Warsaw, 1973), chap. 7, p. 43, with the famous statement: "Num cum sola Roma ei placeret, et ante omnes Romanum populum pecunia et honore dilexisset, ibi semper stare, hanc renouare ad decorem secundum pristinam dignitatem ioco puerili in cassum cogitauit." On this statement, see Görich, *Otto III.*, 264–65.

51. For this, see Schramm, *Kaiser, Rom und Renovatio*, 4th ed., 112, and especially, in the 1929 edition, app. II: "Der 'byzantinische Hofstaat' Ottos III., sein historischer Kern und dessen Bedeutung," 2:17–33; see there also (p. 24) the critique of the older research on "sea prefects."

52. See the appendix cited in note 51 and, in the same 1929 volume, pp. 68–104, the edition of the "Graphia Aureae Urbis Romae." There is a commentary on both in Schramm, *Kaiser, Könige und Päpste*, 3:280 ff. and 313 ff.

53. See Chapter 4, p. 95.

54. MGH DO III, no. 339, pp. 767 ff., a copy transmitted in the *Registrum Far-*

fense from the end of the eleventh century. On this document, see Schramm, *Kaiser, Rom und Renovatio,* 2:23. Significantly, the puzzling title *archiepiscopus S. Adalberti* for Gaudentius, the later archbishop of Gniezno, also appears in this document. On this, see Chapter 4, p. 96.

55. See Görich, *Otto III.,* 237–50.

56. For this issue, see Schramm, *Kaiser, Rom und Renovatio,* 4th ed., 103 ff.; Uhlirz, *Jahrbücher des Deutschen Reiches,* 2:263 ff.; Görich, *Otto III.,* 203.

57. See BU, no. 1279a, p. 689; the source (Hugo of Farfa, *Exceptio relationum de monasterii Farfensis diminutione,* ed. Ugo Balzani, in FSI 33 [Rome, 1903], 64–65) interestingly takes no offense at this behavior: "quo viso imperator ac papa nimis irati post eum properarunt, et papa secum me ire precepit, dicens mihi: 'Veni mecum ad Cere, eo pacto, ut si comes Benedictus reddiderit mihi ipsam civitatem, recipiat filium, et stet finis inter vos: sin autem, filium eius suspendi faciam ipso vidente, et tibi restituam Tribucum'. et tunc cum ad furcam duceretur ligatis post tergum manibus oculisque panniculo strictis, videns talia pater, reddidit civitatem et liberavit filium. eo die Romam reversi sumus."

58. See BU, no. 1291, pp. 696–97, with a discussion of the research sparked by this so-called *Capitulare Ticinense.*

59. See BU, no. 1279b, p. 689, and no. 1299c, pp. 702–3.

60. See *Ottonis III. et Gregorii V. concilium Romanum,* ed. Ludwig Weiland, in MGH Const. 1 (Hannover, 1893), c. 4, pp. 51–52: "Si Gislarius sanctae Magdeburgensis ecclesiae archiepiscopus potuerit canonice comprobare, quod per ambitionem de minori sede Merseburgensi ad maiorem Magdeburgensem non migraverit, ut non deponatur iudicatum est. Sed si cleri et populi invitatione et electione migravit, in eadem permaneat metropoli. Quodsi absque invitatione, non tamen per ambitionem et avaritiam, factum esse constiterit, ad priorem redeat sedem. At si ambitionem et avaritiam negare non potuerit, definitum est, ut amittat utram-

que." On this issue, see Claude, *Geschichte des Erzbistums Magdeburg,* 1:186 ff. On the continuation of the controversy, see Chapter 4.

61. See the discussion of this issue in Christian Pfister, *Études sur le règne de Robert le Pieux* (Paris, 1885), 47–60.

62. See BU, no. 1279c, p. 690.

63. BU, no. 1279b, p. 689; for an argument against this, see Görich, *Otto III.,* 228–32.

64. See the summary in Görich, *Otto III.,* 269 and 277.

CHAPTER 4: THE JOURNEY
TO GNIEZNO

1. Of the extensive literature on this topic, see especially Schramm, *Kaiser, Rom und Renovatio,* 4th ed., 135–46; Albert Brackmann, "Kaiser Otto III. und die staatliche Umgestaltung Polens und Ungarns," in *Gesammelte Aufsätze* (Weimar, 1941), 242–53; Uhlirz, *Jahrbücher des Deutschen Reiches,* 2:310–14; Beumann and Schlesinger, "Urkundenstudien zur deutschen Ostpolitik unter Otto III.," 386 ff.; Ludat, *An Elbe und Oder,* 69–73; Fried, *Otto III. und Boleslaw Chrobry,* esp. 65–68; Brühl, *Deutschland—Frankreich,* 621 ff.; Görich, *Otto III.,* 45–50, 59 ff., 80–84, 91 ff.; each with further references.

2. See the overview of the German and Polish views on the subject of Gniezno in Ludat, *An Elbe und Oder,* 69–76 with nn. 408–18 (pp. 157 ff.). Fundamental to the problem of German research on eastern Europe are Wolfgang Wippermann, *Der "deutsche Drang nach Osten"* (Darmstadt, 1981); Michael Burleigh, *Germany Turns Eastwards* (Cambridge, 1988); Gerd Althoff, "Die Beurteilung der mittelalterlichen Ostpolitik als Paradigma für zeitgebundene Geschichtsbewertung," in *Die Deutschen und ihr Mittelalter,* 147–64.

3. Albert Brackmann has opposed this view in several works. See, for example, Albert Brackmann, "Die Anfänge des polnischen Staates," in *Gesammelte Aufsätze,* 186; idem, "Reichspolitik und

Ostpolitik im frühen Mittelalter," in ibid., 204.

4. See BU, no. 1225a, p. 654, and no. 1238a, p. 664.

5. Uhlirz, *Jahrbücher des Deutschen Reiches*, 2:244.

6. On this point, see Beumann and Schlesinger, "Urkundenstudien zur deutschen Ostpolitik unter Otto III.," 370 ff.; Claude, *Geschichte des Erzbistums Magdeburg*, 1:165 ff.; with another interpretation, Ludat, *An Elbe und Oder*, 74 ff.; most recently Fried, "Theophanu und die Slawen," 369.

7. On this, see Robert Holtzmann, "Die Aufhebung und Wiederherstellung des Bistums Merseburg," 56–57; Beumann and Schlesinger, "Urkundenstudien zur deutschen Ostpolitik unter Otto III.," 378–79; Claude, *Geschichte des Erzbistums Magdeburg*, 1:184–85.

8. On this issue, see the works listed in note 2 above.

9. See Chapter 2, notes 48 ff.

10. Thietmar emphasizes this aspect. See Thietmar, *Chronicon*, III, 16, p. 118: "Sed quae res destruccionem hanc subsequerentur, lector attende." This is followed by a description of the Liutizi rebellion (III, 17, p. 118). Bruno of Querfurt comments in even more detail. See Bruno of Querfurt, *Vita sancti Adalberti*, chaps. 10 and 12, pp. 598–600. Claude attempts to reconcile these accounts (*Geschichte des Erzbistums Magdeburg*, 1:143).

11. Uhlirz, *Jahrbücher des Deutschen Reiches*, 2:292 and 534–37. On Romuald, see Giovanni Tabacco, "Romuald v. Camaldoli," in *Lexikon des Mittelalters* 7, cols. 1019–20.

12. See BU, no. 1304a, p. 709. The *Vita s. Nili*, chap. 91, p. 617, speaks of murder: "et effossis sibi oculis, quos pendentes ad genas ferebat." See Chapter 3, note 10.

13. See Thietmar, *Chronicon*, IV, 44, p. 182.

14. On Leo, see H. Bloch, "Beiträge zur Geschichte des Bischofs Leo von Vercelli und seiner Zeit," NA 22 (1897):

11–136; on the situation in the bishopric of Vercelli, see most recently Pauler, *Das Regnum Italiae in ottonischer Zeit*, 31–45.

15. See Lantbert, *Vita Heriberti archiepiscopi Coloniensis*, ed. Georg Pertz, in MGH SS 4, chap. 5, p. 743. On this issue, see Schramm, *Kaiser, Rom und Renovatio*, 4th ed., 134; Müller, *Heribert, Kanzler Ottos III. und Erzbischof von Köln*, 195 ff. On these and similar personal remarks, see, in Chapter 6, the section titled "'Friends' of Otto III and His Interaction with Them."

16. Lantbert, *Vita Heriberti*, chap. 6, p. 744; Müller, *Heribert, Kanzler Ottos III. und Erzbischof von Köln*, 199–200.

17. See *Vita Burchardi episcopi Wormatiensis*, ed. Georg Waitz, in MGH SS 4, chap. 3, p. 833: "Eodem tempore imperator et praedictus episcopus, induti ciliciis, pedibus penitus denudatis, quandam speluncam iuxta sancti Clementis ecclesiam clam cunctis intraverunt, ibique in orationibus et ieiuniis necnon in vigiliis quattuordecim dies latuerunt." See the summary evaluation of this and similar behaviors in Chapter 6, the section titled "Demonstrative Ritual Behaviors."

18. See Uhlirz, *Jahrbücher des Deutschen Reiches*, 2:301, and BU, nos. 1321b, c, and d, p. 724. Leo, abbot of the monastery of SS. Bonifacio e Alessio on the Aventine, became archbishop of Ravenna. Concerning his career and the significance of this monastery for papal and imperial mission policies during this period, see Görich, *Otto III.*, 216–23.

19. Görich summarizes the discussion in *Otto III.*, 254–55 with n. 404.

20. Uhlirz, *Jahrbücher des Deutschen Reiches*, 2:313–14.

21. Concerning the inscription "Otto Imperator Nepos eius Italiam aditurus invice sui Saxonie praeposuit Matriciam," see Edmund Stengel, "Die Grabinschrift der ersten Äbtissin von Quedlinburg," DA 3 (1939): 361 ff.; Carl Erdmann, "Das Grab Heinrichs I.," DA 4 (1940): 80 with n. 3; idem, *Forschungen zur politischen Ideenwelt des Frühmittelalters*, ed. Friedrich

Baethgen (Berlin, 1951), 97; on the controversy over interpretation of the inscription, see most recently Görich, *Otto III.*, 55.

22. See Thietmar, *Chronicon*, IV, 43, p. 180; on the context of this commission and Count Birichtilo/Bezelin/Berthold, see Chapter 3, pp. 74–75.

23. For this, see *Vita Burchardi*, chap. 3, p. 833; BU, no. 1305d, p. 711.

24. On this issue, see Kölzer, "Das Königtum Minderjähriger," 315 ff.

25. See BU, no. 1329c, p. 733, with the discussion of the charter transmitted in the *Codex Laureshamensis*, ed. Karl Glockner (Darmstadt, 1929), vol. 1, no. 73, p. 356, about which there is disagreement regarding its authenticity as one of Otto III's royal documents.

26. BU, no. 1329a, p. 733. An account of the proceedings is found in MGH DO III, no. 339, pp. 767 ff.

27. See MGH DO III, no. 339, p. 769. On how to understand this title, which remains controversial to the present, see Fried, *Otto III. und Boleslaw Chrobry*, 84 ff.; for an opposing view, see Knut Görich, "Ein Erzbistum in Prag oder in Gnesen?" ZOF 40 (1991): 24.

28. Concerning the case of Bruno, which has some parallels, see H. G. Voigt, *Brun von Querfurt* (Stuttgart, 1907), esp. 73.

29. See Fried, *Otto III. und Boleslaw Chrobry*, 87–93; for a contrasting view, see Görich, "Ein Erzbistum," 24.

30. See Uhlirz, *Jahrbücher des Deutschen Reiches*, 2:541–45, with detailed assessment of the individual sources.

31. See Thietmar, *Chronicon*, IV, 44, p. 182: "Postea cesar auditis mirabilibus, quae per dilectum sibi martyrem Deus fecit Aethelbertum, orationis gratia eo pergere festinavit." The *Annales Quedlinburgenses*, a. 1000, p. 77, also speaks of *causa orationis*.

32. See *Translatio s. Adalberti*, ed. Georg Waitz, in MGH SS 15.2 (Hannover, 1888), 708: "Et cum vellet augustus totum corpus secum deferre, cives Gneznenses

sed eque Polonie cuncti provincie habitatores audacter obstabant atque constantissime reclamabant. . . . Tandem atque instancia hominum devictus cessit. Partem tamen non minimam reliquiarum sibi retinuit atque postea quam plures in honore martiris construxit ecclesias, quas nimirum eius reliquiis decoravit."

33. Compare the account that follows in the text to Uhlirz, *Jahrbücher des Deutschen Reiches*, 2:316–20, as well as BU, no. 1340a ff., pp. 740 ff.

34. See Thietmar, *Chronicon*, IV, 44, p. 182: "Huic Gisillerus obviam pergens gratiam eius quamvis non firmam promeruit et comitatur." The fact that Giselher came to meet Otto III at Staffelsee comes from MGH DO III, no. 344, pp. 774–75.

35. See MGH DO III, no. 344, pp. 774–75; on the title, see Schramm, *Kaiser, Rom und Renovatio*, 4th ed., 141–46.

36. This new form first appeared in January 1001. During this month different new entitulatures, similar in programmatic intent, appear in the documents. MGH DO III, nos. 388–90, pp. 818–22: "Otto tercius secundum voluntatem Iesu Christi Romanorum imperator augustus sanctarumque ecclesiarum devotissimus et fidelissimius dilatator" (no. 388, p. 818, 18 January 1001, composed by Leo of Vercelli); "Otto servus apostolorum et secundum voluntatem dei salvatoris Romanorum imperator augustus" (no. 389, p. 819, without a date but put in the series here; on the document, see Schramm, *Kaiser, Rom und Renovatio*, 4th ed., 168–69; Görich, *Otto III.*, 196); "Otto tercius Romanus Saxonicus et Italicus, apostolorum servus, dono dei Romani orbis imperator augustus" (no. 390, p. 821, 23 January 1001, composed by Thangmar of Hildesheim or Otto III; see Hartmut Hoffmann, "Eigendiktat in den Urkunden Ottos III. und Heinrichs II.," DA 44 (1988): 394–98); concerning the titles, see Schramm, *Kaiser, Rom und Renovatio*, 4th ed., 147–60.

37. See Thietmar, *Chronicon*, IV, 44, p. 182: "Nullus imperator maiori umquam gloria a Roma egreditur neque revertitur."

38. See *Annales Quedlinburgenses*, a. 1000, p. 77: "Transscensa vero Alpium difficultate . . . tota ei Gallia, Francia, Suevia, equestri et pedestri agmine turmatim obviam ruit. Dominae etiam imperiales, germanae suae sorores, Sophia et Adelheida, cum Saxoniae et Thuringiae utriusque sexus primis occurrendo, velut unicum unice dilectum ac merito diligendum, ipso, ut ita dicam, corridente mundo, unanimi gratulatione suscipiunt, ac cum eo pariter, quamdiu destinati itineris acceleratio patiebatur, debita caritate morantur."

39. See Thietmar, *Chronicon*, IV, 45, p. 182.

40. Ibid.: "Qualiter autem cesar ab eodem tunc susciperetur et per sua usque ad Gnesin deduceretur, dictu incredibile ac ineffabile est." A whole series of further sources confirm this assessment, see BU, no. 1349d, pp. 745 ff.

41. *Miracula s. Adalberti martiris*, ed. Georg Pertz, in MGH SS 4:615: "exceptus est in magnificencia et gloria magna a prefato duce Polonie Boleslao."

42. See Thietmar, *Chronicon*, IV, 45, p. 182: "Videns a longe urbem desideratam nudis pedibus suppliciter advenit et ab episcopo eiusdem Ungero venerabiliter succeptus aecclesiam introducitur, et ad Christi gratiam sibi inpetrandam martyris Christi intercessio profusis lacrimis invitatur." For a description of proceedings in other sources, see BU, no. 1349d–e, pp. 745 ff.

43. Thietmar, *Chronicon*, IV, 45, p. 184: "fecit ibi archiepiscopatum, ut spero legitime, sine consensu tamen prefati presulis, cuius diocesi omnis haec regio subiecta est." On the role of Unger, see Fried, *Otto III. und Boleslaw Chrobry*, 101–16 and 144–47.

44. By withholding their consent, William of Mainz and Bernhard of Halberstadt evidently delayed Otto I in his intention to create the Archdiocese of Magdeburg; in the following decades they always threw up obstructions when an episcopal vacancy opened new possibilities for change. See the discussion in Althoff, "Magdeburg—Halberstadt—Merseburg."

45. Thietmar, *Chronicon*, IV, 46, p. 184: "Perfectis tunc omnibus imperator a prefato duce magnis muneribus decoratur et, quod maxime sibi placuit, trecentis militibus loricatis. Hunc abeuntem Bolizlavus comitatu usque ad Magadaburg deducit egreio."

46. *Annales Quedlinburgenses*, a. 1000, p. 77: "Ibi summo conanime a duce Sclavonico Bolizlavone susceptus, xeniis omnigeni census ubique terrarum studiosissime quaesiti obsequialiter donatur; licet nihil tunc temporis ex his acceperit, quippe qui non rapiendi nec sumendi, sed dandi et orandi causa eo loci adventasset."

47. Concerning this source's value and drawbacks for research, see Wenskus, "Forschungsbericht," 524–25; Ludat, *An Elbe und Oder*, 71 ff. with nn. 412 ff.; Oskar Kossmann, "Deutschland und Polen um das Jahr 1000—Gedanken zu einem Buch von Herbert Ludat," ZOF 21 (1972): 409 ff.; Fried, *Otto III. und Boleslaw Chrobry*, 69–70, with further references.

48. Gallus Anonymus, *Chronicae et gesta ducum sive principum Polonorum*, ed. Karol Maleczynski, MPH, n.s., 2 (Cracow, 1952), 1, 6, pp. 18 ff.: "Illud quoque memorie commendandum estimamus, quod tempore ipsius Otto Rufus imperator ad sanctum Adalbertum orationis ac reconciliationis gratia simulque gloriosi Bolezlavi cognoscendi famam introivit, sicut in libro de passione martiris potest propensius inveniri. Quem Bolezlauus sic honorifice et magnifice suscepit, ut regem, imperatorem Romanum ac tantum hospitem suscipere decens fuit. Nam miracula mirifica Boleslaus in imperatoris adventu preostendit, acies inprimis militum multimodas, deinde principum in planitie spaciosa quasi choros ordinavit, singulasque seperatim acies diversitas indumentorum discolor variavit. Et non quelibet erat ibi vilis varietas ornamenti, sed quicquid potest usquam gencium preciosus reperiri. Quippe Bolezlavi tempore quique milites et queque femine curiales palliis pro lineis vestibus vel laneis utebantur, nec pelles quantumlibet

preciose, licet nove fuerint, in eius curia sine pallio et aurifrisio portabantur. Aurum enim eius tempore commune quasi argentum ab omnibus habebatur, argentum vero vile quasi pro stramine tenebatur. Cuius gloriam et potentiam et divitias imperator Romanus considerans, admirando dixit: Per coronam imperii mei, maiora sunt que video, quam fama percepi. Suorumque consultu magnatum coram omnibus adiecit: Non est dignum tantum ac virem talem sicut unum de principibus ducem aut comitem nominari, sed in regale solium gloranter redimitum diademate sublimari. Et accipiens imperiale diadem capitis sui, capiti Bolezlaui in amicicie fedus inposuit et pro vexillo triumphali clavum ei de cruce Domini cum lanceo sancti Maritij dono dedit, pro quibus illi Bolezlauus sancti Adalberti brachium redonavit. Et tanta sunt illa die dileccione couniti, quod imperator eum fratrem et cooperatorem imperii constituit, et populi Romani amicum et socium appelavit. Insuper etiam in ecclesiasticis honoribus quicquid ad imperium pertinebat in regno Polonorum, vel in aliis superatis ab eo vel superandis regionibus barbarorum, sue suorumque sucessorum potestati concessit, cuius paccionis decretum papa Silvester sancte Romane ecclesie privilegio confirmavit. Igitur Bolezlauus in regem ab imperatore tam gloriose sublimatus inditam sibi liberalitatem exercuit, cum tribus sue consecracionis diebus convivium regaliter et imperialiter celebravit, singulisque diebus vasa omnia et supellectilia transmutavit, aliaque diversa multoque preciosiora presentavit. Finito namque convivio pincernas et dapiferos vasa aurea et argentea, nulla enim lignea ibi habebantur, cyphos videlicet et cuppas, lances et scutellas et cornua de mensis omnibus trium dierum congregare precepit et imperatori pro honore, non pro principali munere presentavit. A camerariis vero pallia extensa et cortinas, tapetia, strata, mantilia, manuteria et quecumque servicio presentata fuerunt, iussit similiter congregrare et in cameram imperatoris comportare. Insuper etiam alia plura dedit vasa, scilicet aurea et argentea diversi operis, pallia vero diversi

coloris, ornamenta generis ignoti, lapides preciosos et huiusmodi tot et tanta presentavit, quod imperator tanta munera pro miraculo reputavit. Singulos vero principes eius ita magnifice muneravit, quod eos ex amicis amicissimos acquisivit. Sed quis dinumerare poterit qualia et quanta maioribus dona dedit, cum nec unus quidem inquilinus de tanta multitudine sine munere recessit. Imperator autem letus magnis cum muneribus ad propria remeavit, Bolezlauus vero regnans in hostes iram veterem renovavit."

49. This judgment retains its validity despite the efforts of Fried (in *Otto III. und Boleslaw Chrobry*, 76–80) to find in Bruno's works an echo of Boleslav's elevation to kingship at Gniezno, which Fried once again postulates. In the end Fried is only able to assert the following: "But however little . . . Bruno's works demonstrate the opposite, the missionary's mode of expression betrays a fluctuation, a certain uncertany in titulature, which could be the result of a contested raising to kingship in Gniezno."

50. See the overview of the relevant sources and literature in Lübke, *Regesten*, vol. 4, no. 575, p. 127. See also Fried, *Otto III. und Boleslaw Chrobry*, 118 with n. 7. The remarks of the *Annales Quedlinburgenses*, a. 1025, p. 90, especially suggest indignation: "Bolizlawo Dux Poloniae, obitu Heinrici imperatoris augusti comperto, elatus animo viscere tenus superbiae veneno perfunditur, adeo ut uncto etiam sibi imponi coronam temere sit usurpatus. Quam animi sui praesumptionis audaciam divina mox subsecuta est ultio. In brevi namque tristem mortis sententiam compulsus subit."

51. This was already convincingly argued by Ludat, *An Elbe und Oder*, 72 with n. 429, which includes a reference to a parallel in the Byzantine tradition, pointed out by T. Wasilewski, "Bizantyńska symbolika zjazdu gnieźnieńskiego i jej prawnopolityczna wymowa," *Przeglad historyczny* 57 (1966): 1–14. When Emperor Heraclius received a Turkish ruler into the "family of kings," he placed his crown upon the Turk's head;

see the reference by Herbert Ludat in *Jahrbücher für die Geschichte Osteuropas* 14 (1966): 632. For a western parallel—Frederick Barbarossa used his own crown at the coronation of Vladislav of Bohemia—see Jiří Kejř, "Böhmen und das Reich unter Friedrich I.," in *Friedrich Barbarossa* (Sigmaringen, 1992), 252 with n. 61. Even though the following transaction had a different significance, it is nonetheless noteworthy that Otto III, after his meeting with Nilus, left his crown behind with the abbot—according to the *Vita s. Nili*, chap. 93, p. 618: "Quae [Nilus's admonition] imperator audiens, lacrymarum guttas fundebat ex oculis; deinde corona demissa in manus beati viri, et benedictione percepta, cum toto suo comitatu commisit se viae." In this case and at Gniezno the emperor used his crown in a similar fashion to make a specific point.

52. See Fried, *Otto III. und Boleslaw Chrobry*, 117–22.

53. See Ludat, *An Elbe und Oder*, 72, with the extensive evaluation of the matter in n. 429. The decisive sentence in the Gallus Anonymus, *Chronicae et gesta ducum sive principum Polonorum*, I, 6, p. 19, is: "Et accipiens imperiale diadem capitis sui, capiti Bolezlavi in amicicie fedus imposuit . . ."; on this issue, see also Kossmann, "Deutschland und Polen um das Jahr 1000," 421–28.

54. On the significance of *foedera amicitiae* in Polish life in the tenth century, see Althoff, *Verwandte, Freunde und Getreue*, 88 ff.; idem, *Amicitiae und Pacta* (Hannover, 1992), 16 ff.

55. See the works listed in note 53 above and also Althoff, "Demonstration und Inszenierung," 40–41, analyzing a ceremony sealing a friendship treaty between a *rex* and a *dux* that has many similiarities to the Gniezno meeting. Also comparable is the meeting of the "great" and "little" kings that is described in *Ruodlieb*. See *Ruodlieb*, in *Lateinische Epik des Mittelalters in Versen*, ed. Karl Langosch (Darmstadt, 1956), v, 202 ff., pp. 126–27.

56. See Thietmar, *Chronicon*, v, 10, p. 232: "Deus indulgeat imperatori, quod tributarium faciens dominum."

57. See the Latin text in note 48 above: "et imperatori pro honore, non pro principali munere presentavit."

58. On this point, see Ludat, *An Elbe und Oder*, 72; on the bride, Richeza, see Eduard Hlawitschka, "Königin Richeza von Polen—Enkelin Herzog Konrads von Schwaben, nicht Kaiser Ottos II.?" in *Institutionen, Kultur und Gesellschaft im Mittelalter*, ed. Fenske Lutz et al. (Sigmaringen, 1984), 221 ff.; Glocker, *Die Verwandten der Ottonen*, 216. Boleslav's son born that year was also probably named Otto, which is best explained with the assumption that the emperor was his godfather; see Angenendt, *Kaiserherrschaft und Königstaufe*, 302–5.

59. For this, see Althoff, *Verwandte, Freunde und Getreue*, 102 ff., with numerous examples.

60. See here Fried, *Otto III. und Boleslaw Chrobry*, 128–29 and 137–41.

61. See the summary of older views in Claude, *Geschichte des Erzbistums Magdeburg*, 1:188–94.

62. This belief is based a document of Pope John XII from 12 February 962 (*Papsturkunden 896–1046*, ed. Harald Zimmermann [Vienna, 1984–89], no. 154, pp. 282 ff.). It decreed that "censum et decimationem omnium gentium, quas predictus piisimus imperator baptizavit vel per eum suumque filium . . . baptizandae sunt" be divided among the newly founded bishoprics. Scholars have inferred from this that "the eastern boundary of the Magdeburg mission diocese was open." See Claude, *Geschichte des Erzbistums Magdeburg*, 1:80.

63. See Keller, "Reichsstruktur und Herrschaftsauffassung," 85–86 and 126–27.

64. Several Roman officials accompanied Otto, including the *patricius* Ziazo. See Uhlirz, *Jahrbücher des Deutschen Reiches*, 2:313–14.

65. See note 45 above.

66. Claude, *Geschichte des Erzbistums Magdeburg*, 1:190ff.

67. See the discussion in Althoff, "Magdeburg—Halberstadt—Merseburg."

68. Thietmar, *Chronicon*, IV, 44 and 46, pp. 182 and 184.

69. Ademar of Chabannes, *Chronicon*, ed. Jules Chavanon (Paris, 1897), I, III, p. 154; see also Knut Görich, "Otto III. öffnet das Karlsgrab in Aachen," in *Herrschaftsrepräsentation im ottonischen Sachsen*, ed. Althoff and Schubert. For the aftermath of Boleslav's visit in Aachen, see the overview by Roman Michalowski, "Aix-la-Chapelle et Cracovie au XIe siècle," *Bullettino dell'Istituto Storico Italiano per il Medioevo e Archivio Muratoriano* 95 (1989): 45–69.

70. *Annales Hildesheimenses*, a. 1000, p. 28; see also Görich, "Otto III. öffnet das Karlsgrab."

71. For a discussion of earlier research, see Görich, "Otto III. öffnet das Karlsgrab," esp. nn. 27 and 28.

72. *Chronicon Novaliciense*, ed. Ludwig Bethmann, in MGH SS 7 (Hannover, 1846), III, 32, p. 106: "Intravimus ergo ad Karolum. Non enim iacebat, ut mos est aliorum defunctorum corpora, sed in quandam cathedram ceu vivus residebat. Coronam auream erat coronatus, sceptrum cum mantonibus indutis tenens in manibus, a quibus iam ipse ungule perforando processerant. Erat autem supra se tugurium ex calce et marmoribus valde compositum. Quod ubi ad eum venimus, protinus in eum foramen frangendo fecimus. At ubi ad eum ingressi sumus, odorem permaximum sentivimus. Adoravimus ergo eum statim poplitibus flexis ac ienua; statimque Otto imperator albis eum vestimentis induit, ungulasque incidit, et omnia deficientia circa eum reparavit. Nil vero ex artibus suis putrescendo adhuc defecerat, sed de sumitate nasui sui parum minus erat; quam ex auro ilico fecit restitui, abstraensque ab illius hore dentem unum, reaedificato tuguriolo abiit."

73. BU, no. 1370b, pp. 760–61.

74. Görich, "Otto III. öffnet das Karlsgrab."

75. For an overview, see Arnold Angenendt, "Der ganze und der unverweste Leib," in *Aus Archiven und Bibliotheken*, ed. Hubert Mordek (Frankfurt am Main, Bern, New York, and Paris, 1992), 33–50.

76. BU, no. 1370b, pp. 760–61.

77. In this period, charters went to the following (MGH DO III, nos. 362–73, pp. 791–80): the monastery of Saint Felix at Metz, the nunnery of Oedingen, Abbot Oftrad of Saint Maximin, the steward Esciko, the cathedral of Würzburg (on this, see Chapter 5, note 2), the monastery of Oesen (2), the Church of Saint Peter in Worms (2), Count Adalbero, and the monastery of Lorsch (2).

78. See *Annales Quedlinburgenses*, a. 1000, p. 77.

CHAPTER 5: THE LAST
EXPEDITION TO ROME

1. Aachen, mid-May of 1001. The document itself has not survived. On this matter, see Uhlirz, *Jahrbücher des Deutschen Reiches*, 2:336, 381 n. 87; BU, no. 1366a, p. 758. See Thangmar, *Vita Bernwardi*, chap. 31, p. 772: "episcopus Bernwardus . . . abbatiam Hildewardensis aecclesiae, sibi ab imperatore traditam, et sollempni ab ipso dedicatione devotissime consecratam, et divino servitio excultam, pluribus beneficiis ac donis ab eo ditatam, ubi etiam sua matertera matris regimen agebat . . ."; see also Heinrich Böhmer, *Willigis von Mainz* (Leipzig, 1895), 86.

2. See Fleckenstein, *Die Hofkapelle der deutschen Könige*, 2:87, 113. On Henry of Würzburg as recipient and intervener in royal documents in the period under discussion here, see MGH DO III, no. 351, pp. 780–81; no. 352, pp. 781–82; no. 354, pp. 783–84; no. 358, pp. 787–88; no. 361, pp. 790–91; no. 365, p. 794; no. 366, p. 795; no. 393, p. 824.

3. See BU, no. 1370b, pp. 760–61.

4. On the meeting, see BU, nos. 1376a and b, p. 764; on the burial monastery of Selz, see Wollasch, "Das Grabkloster der Kaiserin Adelheid in Selz am Rhein," 135 ff.

5. See the details in Fried, *Otto III. und Boleslaw Chrobry*, 21 ff.

6. See BU, nos. 1380a and 1381a, pp. 766 ff.; for an overview of Ottonian policy regarding Venice, see Wolfgang Giese, "Venedig-Politik und Imperiums-Idee bei den Ottonen," in *Festschrift für Friedrich Prinz zu seinem 65. Geburtstag*, ed. Georg Jenal (Stuttgart, 1993), 219–43.

7. See Althoff, "Colloquium familiare," esp. 160 ff.

8. BU, no. 1407d, pp. 797–98; Giovanni Diacono, *Cronaca veneziana*, ed. Giovanni Monticolo, in FSI 9 (Rome, 1890), chap. 33B, pp. 161–62; see also Ursula Swinarski, *Herrschen mit den Heiligen* (Bern and Berlin, 1991), 210 ff.

9. BU, no. 1407e, pp. 798–99; on the events in Venice, see Giovanni Diacono, *Cronaca veneziana*, chaps. 33B and 34A, pp. 162 ff.

10. BU, no. 1408a, p. 799; Giovanni Diacono, *Cronaca veneziana*, chap. 34B, p. 164.

11. See Manfred Hellmann, *Grundzüge der Geschichte Venedigs* (Darmstadt, 1976), 29–30; Gerhard Rösch, *Venedig und das Reich* (Tübingen, 1982), 14 ff.

12. On this, see Arnold Angenendt, *Kaiserherrschaft und Königstaufe*, although he does not handle this particular case; see also Chapter 4, note 48.

13. See the similar-sounding formulation in Thietmar, *Chronicon*, IV, 58, pp. 196 and 198, and the discussion of it in Angenendt, *Kaiserherrschaft und Königstaufe*, 302 n. 55.

14. See Althoff, "Colloquium familiare," 160.

15. On this, see Chapter 4, notes 45 and 55, and Chapter 6, note 17.

16. See Pauler, *Das Regnum Italiae in ottonischer Zeit*, 19–45, esp. 19–20, 23 ff.,

31–32, 37–38; Adelheid Krah, *Absetzungsverfahren als Spiegelbild von Königsmacht* (Aalen, 1987), 316 ff.

17. See BU, nos. 1380b, 1381, 1384, 1392, and 1393, pp. 767, 769, 774 ff.; MGH DO III, no. 374, pp. 800–801; no. 376, pp. 803–4; no. 383, pp. 811–12; no. 384, pp. 812 ff.

18. MGH DO III, no. 383, p. 811: "Ardicinus filius Ardoini marchionis, quia vocatus ad palacium Papiense ut legem faceret, noctu aufugit et imperatoris presenciam nullius reverencie habuit."

19. See Chapter 1, note 57. See also Hans Goetting, *Das Bistum Hildesheim*, vol. 1, *Das reichsunmittelbare Kanonissenstift Gandersheim* (Berlin and New York, 1973), 89–93; idem, *Das Bistum Hildesheim*, vol. 3, *Die Hildesheimer Bischöfe von 815 bis 1221 (1227)* (Berlin and New York, 1984), 159 ff., 180–93, 197 ff., 239–47; most recently Görich, "Der Gandersheimer Streit."

20. See Görich and Kortüm, "Otto III., Thangmar und die Vita Bernwardi"; Hans Schuffels, "Bernward, Bischof von Hildesheim," in *Bernward von Hildesheim und das Zeitalter der Ottonen*, ed. Michael Brandt and Arne Eggebrecht (Hildesheim and Mainz, 1993), 1:29–43. See also the reproduction of the "memorandum" itself in the catalogue portion of Brandt and Eggebrecht, *Bernward von Hildesheim*, 2:489 ff. In place of polemic against other interpretations, Schuffels would be well advised to publish his own findings.

21. Thangmar, *Vita Bernwardi*, chap. 22, p. 769: "quam si ipse papa procedat."

22. See Fichtenau, *Living in the Tenth Century*, 228–29; Gunther Wolf, "Prinzessin Sophie (978–1039)," NdsJb 61 (1989): 105–23; Gerd Althoff, "Gandersheim und Quedlinburg," FMSt 25 (1991): 131–32.

23. Thangmar, *Vita Bernwardi*, chap. 17, p. 766: "Verum cum ad oblationem ventum est, oblatas indignatione et incredibili furore proiciunt, saeva maledicta episcopo ingerunt. Quo insolito tumultu perculsus, lacrimis perfusus antistes, non

suam iniuriam, quam parvi ducebat, pensans, sed veri pastoris pro persecutoribus orantis exemplo, ignorantiam seu potius malivolentiam furentium feminarum deplorans, ad altare rediit, missam suo ordine magna animi contritione peragit."

24. Ibid., chap. 19, p. 767: "Quod humillimus ac piisimus imperator audiens, miro affectu dilectum magistrum videndi flagrans, ad suam praesentiam tamen eum fatigare nolebat, sed festinus a palatio fere duo miliaria ad Sanctum Petrum illi occurrit, benignissimeque susceptum, inter amplexus familiarissime deosculatum, ad hospitium deduxit, diuque cum illo confabulans, sequenti die ad palatium illum venire rogavit, nec permisit ut quantulumcumque de suo proprio in ministerium suum impenderet, sed per sex septimanas, quibus apud illum morabatur, sufficienter in usum sui suorumque cuncta indigua largiter ministrari praecepit. Mane vero domnum apostolicum convocavit in occursum carissimi hospitis, venientem quoque foris in atrium obviam procedentes libentissime susceperunt, nec permissus est ad suum domicilium reverti, sed iuxta ubi ipse domnus imperator habitabat, splendidissimum illi habitaculum exhibebat. Vicissim quoque nunc imperatoris cubiculo, interdum episcopi considentes, et forenses causas et rei publicae necessaria conferebant. Nam de archiepiscopo et tumultu Gandenesheim oborto ante accessum domni episcopi fama praecurrens cuncta divulgaverat; unde non opus habebat singula evolvere, sed breviter strictimque, imperatore interrogante, pauca contexuit." Mentioned in the older Dresden Codex (which appears in the MGH edition only in variant h) is an interesting detail: that Otto III had meals prepared for Bernward as they were in his Saxon homeland.

25. Ibid., chap. 20, p. 767.

26. On Henry II's education in Hildesheim, see Siegfried Hirsch et al., *Jahrbücher des Deutschen Reiches unter Heinrich II* (Leipzig, 1862), 1:90–91; on relations with Gandersheim, see Goetting, *Das Bistum Hildesheim*, 1:28 and 294–95.

27. Thangmar, *Vita Bernwardi*, chap. 22, p. 768: "si synodus habenda vel vocanda esset, quam archiepiscopus cum suis quos adduxerat collegisset, in aecclesia ab Hildenesheimensibus episcopis semper possessa, praecipue cum episcopus defuerit et ad Romanam sedem pro eisdem causis confugerit; vel quo nomine tale conventiculum vocitandum sit."

28. Ibid., chap. 22, p. 769: "iuvenis aetate sed senior morum probitate."

29. Ibid., chap. 28, p. 771: "omnibus insigniis apostolicis acsi papa procedat infulatus, equis apostolica sella Romano more ostro instratus. Scripta quoque a papa et imperatore episcopis et caeteris principibus mittuntur, ut Romanum legatum digno honore suscipiant, eiusque legationi indubitanter omnes, quasi apostolicus praesens cernatur, oboediant."

30. Ibid., chap. 28, p. 771: "archiepiscopus vero et qui ei favebant mira indignatione et execratione illum spernebant. Episcopus vero Bernwardus, et Lievezo Hammenburgensis archipraesul aliique conplures, reverenter eum tractabant praecipuoque honore colebant. Sed postquam ad concilium ventum est, vix dici poterit, quanta seditione et tumultu agitaretur. Nam nec locus sessionis vicario apostolici idoneus conceditur, horribilis strepitus ingeminatur, ius fasque contempnitur, canonica disciplina annullatur. Vicarius inter episcopos Lievizonem et Bernwardum sedens, apostolici scripta et legationem ad episcopos se habere; facultatem exequendi quae ferat, sibi exhiberi orabat. Impetrato denique silentio, primo dulci affamine episcopos de pace et caritate et concordia commonet, deinde epistolam papae archiepiscopo specialiter directam profert, publiceque in auribus omnium recitari precatur. Quam cum archiepiscopus tangere vel videre dedignaretur, episcoporum iudicio palam est recitata."

31. See ibid., chap. 36, p. 774; for analysis, see Görich, *Otto III.*, 123–32, especially 127–32.

32. On this point, see Görich, "Der Gandersheimer Streit," 90.

33. On Otto III's relationship with Willigis, see Fleckenstein, *Die Hofkapelle der deutschen Könige*, 2:204–5; most recently Althoff, "Vormundschaft, Erzieher, Lehrer," 282 ff.

34. As, for example, in Frederick Barbarossa's conflict with the Italian cities; on this case, see Knut Görich, "Der Herrscher als parteiischer Richter: Barbarossa in der Lombardei," FMSt 29 (1995): 273–88.

35. See BU, no. 1397a, p. 782.

36. Thangmar, *Vita Bernwardi*, chap. 23, pp. 769–70: "Aliquot diebus exactis, domnus Bernwardus et apostolicus praefatam urbem adeunt. Cives laeti adventantes servos Dei honorifice excipiunt, urbi intromittunt; nec prius desistunt, quam omnes pacatos imperatoris ditioni Dei gratia adiuti subdunt. Postera namque die, nobili triumpho subsequente, episcopi imperatorem adeunt. Nam cuncti primarii cives praescriptae civitatis assunt nudi, femoralibus tantum tecti, dextra gladios, laeva scopas ad palatium praetendentes; imperiali iuri se suaque subactos; nil pacisci, nec ipsam quidem vitam; quos dignos iudicaverit, ense feriat, vel pro misericordia ad palam scopis examinari iubeat. Si muros urbis solo complanari votis eius suppetat, promptos libenti animo cuncta exequi, nec iussis eius maiestatis dum vivant contradicturos. Imperator pacis conciliatores, papam et domnum Bernwardum episcopum, magnifice gratando extollit, atque ad illorum nutum reis veniam tribuit; placitoque habito, urbem non destrui in commune deliberant. Urbani gratia imperatoris donantur, et ut se pacifice agant, nec ab imperatore deficiant, commonentur." For interpretation, see Althoff, "Demonstration und Inszenierung," 34–35. Interestingly, Petrus Damiani (*Vita beati Romualdi*, chap. 23, p. 49) names Romuald as the sole negotiator of the peace with Tivoli.

37. See Chapter 1, note 40; Chapter 3, note 22.

38. MGH DO III, no. 389, pp. 818 ff.; on this, see recently Zeillinger, "Otto III.

und die Konstantinische Schenkung," 512 ff.; Görich, *Otto III.*, 241.

39. This goes back to the investigations by H. Bloch, "Beiträge zur Geschichte des Bischofs Leo von Vercelli und seiner Zeit," 61 ff.; on this, see Zeillinger, "Otto III. und die Konstantinische Schenkung," 512 n. 11.

40. MGH DO III, no. 388, p. 818.

41. Ibid., no. 390, pp. 820–21; on this, see Hoffmann, "Eigendiktat in den Urkunden Ottos III. und Heinrichs II.," 394–98.

42. See Schramm, *Kaiser, Rom und Renovatio*, 4th ed., 157–58; Görich, *Otto III.*, 106 ff.

43. MGH DO III, no. 389, pp. 818 ff.; Schramm, *Kaiser, Rom und Renovatio*, 4th ed., 168–69; Görich, *Otto III.*, 196.

44. See Görich, *Otto III.*, 241, who cites this striking formulation by Heinrich Fichtenau.

45. MGH DO III, no. 389, p. 820: "Hec sunt enim commenta ab illis ipsis inventa quibus Iohannes diaconus cognomento Digitorum mutilus preceptum aureis litteris scripsit et sub titulo magni Constantini longi mendacii tempora finxit. Hec sunt etiam commenta quibus dicunt quendam Karolum sancto Petro nostra publica tribuisse. Sed ad hec respondemus, ipsum Karolum nichil dare iure potuisse, utpote iam a Karolo meliore fugatum, iam imperio privatum, iam destitutum et adnullatum; ergo quod non habuit dedit, sic dedit, sicut nimirum dare potuit, utpote qui male adquisivit et diu se possessurum non speravit." On this passage, see Schramm, *Kaiser, Rom und Renovatio*, 4th ed., 163 ff.; most recently Zeillinger, "Otto III. und die Konstantinische Schenkung," 515 ff.

46. MGH DO III, no. 389, p. 820: "ex nostra liberalitate sancto Petro donamus que nostra sunt, non sibi que sua sunt, veluti nostra conferimus." On this point, see Schramm, *Kaiser, Rom und Renovatio*, 4th ed., 164 ff.

47. Schramm, *Kaiser, Rom und Renovatio*, 4th ed., 174–75.

48. MGH DO III, no. 89, p. 820: "offerimus et donamus, ut ad honorem dei et sancti Petri cum sua et nostra salute habeat teneat et ad incrementa sui apostolatus nostrique imperii ordinet."

49. See Chapter 3, note 51.

50. Bruno of Querfurt, *Vita quinque fratrum eremitarum*, chap. 7, pp. 44–45; on this, see Uhlirz, *Jahrbücher des Deutschen Reiches*, 2:586–87.

51. Uhlirz, *Jahrbücher des Deutschen Reiches*, 2:362. Only the *Gesta episcoporum Cameracensium*, ed. Ludwig Bethmann, in MGH SS 7 (Hannover, 1846), I, 114, p. 451, reports a most dangerous situation and a dramatic flight from the city. But this should not be accorded too much importance in light of the assessments by Thangmar and Thietmar discussed below.

52. Thangmar, *Vita Bernwardi*, chap. 24, p. 770: "Romani denique indigne ferentes, Tyberinos cum imperatore pacatos, urbis quoque suae portas seris muniunt, vias obstruunt; libere intrandi vel exeundi Romam facultas negatur, vendendi et emendi mercimonium interdicitur; nonnulli quoque regis amicorum iniuste perimuntur. Palatini autem a domno Bernwardo episcopo salutaribus monitis instructi, confessione nichilominus purgati, sacro quoque viatico inter missarum sollempnia muniti, econtra egredi et hostes fortiter impetere parant. Bernwardus episcopus dominicam hastam subiit; se quoque atque omnes vivificae crucis munimine signat, benedictione publice data, ac vitalibus monitis consolans et corroborans, signifer ipse cum sancta hasta in prima fronte aciei egredi parat. Sequenti autem mane imperator cum suis post missarum sollempnia a venerabili Bernwardo episcopo sacramentis caelestibus ac divinis exhortationibus consolati, adversus hostes certamen instruunt, ipso antistite cum sancta hasta in principio terribiliter fulminante, cordis vero instantia pacem ab auctore pacis suppliciter flagitante. Unde contigit, devoti militis sui precibus exoratam pacifici regis Christi mox adesse praesentiam, cuius et in nativitatis ortu primum pacis gaudia nunciantur, et postmodum eiusdem pacis amatores euangelica veritate filiorum Dei appellatione censentur. Ipsius itaque pietate totius discordiae rebellione sopita, hostes pacem exposcunt, arma proiciunt, in crastinum se ad palatium venturos promittunt. Mane Dei clementia assunt, pacem petunt, sacramenta innovant, fidem se imperatori perpetuo servaturos promittunt."

53. Thietmar, *Chronicon*, IV, 48, p. 186: "Post haec Gregorius, qui cesari valde carus erat, dolo eum capere nisus occultas tendebat insidias. Quibus collectis et ex inproviso adversus eum iam insurgentibus, inperator de porta cum paucis evasit, maxima suorum caterva sociorum inclusa; et vulgus numquam suis contentum dominis malus huic pro ineffabili pietate restituit. Deinc nuntio suimet omnes cesar sibi familiares convenire illuc rogat et precipit, demandas singulis quibusque, si umquam de honore sui vel incolumitate curarent, ad ulciscendum eum ac amplius tuendum armato ad se milite properarent. Romani autem, manifestati tunc sceleris culpa se erubescentes seque invicem supra modum redarguentes, omnes inclusos emisere securos, gratiam imperatoris et pacem modis omnibus suppliciter expetentes. Quos ubicumque vel in ipsis vel in rebus suis cesar ledere potuit, verbis eorundem mendacibus diffidens, nocere non tardavit. Omnes regiones, quae Romanos et Longobardos respiciebant, suae dominacioni fideliter subditas, Roma solum, quam pre caeteris diligebat ac semper excolebat, excepta, habebat."

54. See Gerd Tellenbach, "Kaiser, Rom und Renovatio," in *Tradition als historische Kraft*, ed. Norbert Kamp and Joachim Wollasch (Berlin, 1982), 231ff.; idem, "Zur Geschichte der Päpste im 10. und früheren 11. Jahrhundert," in *Institutionen, Kultur und Gesellschaft im Mittelalter*, ed. Lutz et al., 171.

55. Görich and Kortüm, "Otto III., Thangmar und die Vita Bernwardi."

56. Thangmar, *Vita Bernwardi*, chap. 25, p. 770: "Interim piissimus ac mitissimus imperator cum paucis turrim quandam ascendens, ad illos concionabatur

dicens: 'Auscultate verba patris vestri et attendite, et ea mente diligenter reponite. Vosne estis mei Romani? Propter vos quidem meam patriam propinquos quoque reliqui. Amore vestro meos Saxones et cunctos Theotiscos, sanguinem meum, proieci; vos in remotas partes nostri imperii adduxi, quo patres vestri, cum Orbem ditione premerent, numquam pedem posuerunt; scilicet ut nomen vestrum et gloriam ad fines usque dilatarem; vos filios adoptavi, vos cunctis praetuli. Causa vestra, dum vos omnibus proposui, universorum in me invidiam et odium commovi. Et nunc pro omnibus his patrem vestrum abiecistis, familiares meos crudeli morte interemistis, me exclusistis, cum tamen excludere non potestis; quia quos paterno animo complector, numquam ab affectu meo exulari patior. Scio equidem et nutu oculorum seditionis principes assigno; nec verentur, dum publice omnium oculis notantur; nichilominus etiam fidissimos meos, de quorum innocentia triumpho, sceleratorum admixtione commaculari, nec posse distingui, monstro simile arbitror.' Hac ratione imperatoris ad fletus usque compuncti, satisfactionem promittunt, duos corripiunt, Benilonem et alium quendam, quos crudeliter caesos, nudos pedibus per gradus tractos, semivivos in praefata turri ante imperatorem proiciunt."

57. Thangmar, *Vita Bernwardi*, chap. 26, p. 770: "Hac autem seditione sedata, venerabilis pater Bernwardus ad Sanctum Paulum orationis causa accessit."

58. Althoff, "Demonstration und Inszenierung," 48–49, with an initial remark on this theme, which is certainly worth a more intensive investigation.

59. See Uhlirz, *Jahrbücher des Deutschen Reiches*, 2:588, and BU, no. 1402b, p. 789. The critical statements of Bruno of Querfurt point in roughly the same direction; see note 77 below; see also Josef Benzinger, *Invectiva in Romam* (Lübeck and Hamburg, 1968), 36ff.

60. See BU, nos. 1402b and c, p. 789.

61. Compare the assessment in Schramm, *Kaiser, Rom und Renovatio*, 4th ed., 179; similarly Josef Fleckenstein,

Grundlagen und Beginn der deutschen Geschichte (Göttingen, 1974), 200: "a blow that struck him to the depths." Even more dramatic is Fried, *Der Weg in die Geschichte*, 601: "Wildly he swore revenge, that he would not rest until he saw the rebels humbled. However, it was not Rome that fell, but he. Fever seized him and ended the Roman catastrophe of the Roman emperor!"

62. Thangmar, *Vita Bernwardi*, chap. 27, pp. 770–71.

63. Petrus Damiani, *Vita beati Romualdi*, chap. 25, pp. 52–54; Bruno of Querfurt, *Vita quinque fratrum*, chap. 2, pp. 34–35; see also BU, no. 1404b, pp. 792–93.

64. Petrus Damiani, *Vita beati Romualdi*, chap. 25, p. 54: "Promisit itaque beato Romualdo quod imperium relinquens, monachicum susciperet habitum; et cui innumeri mortales erat obnoxii, iam ipse pauperculo Christo subiectus cępit esse debitor sui"; Bruno of Querfurt, *Vita quinque fratrum*, chap. 2, p. 34: "Ex hac hora promitto deo et sanctis eius post tres annos intra quo imperii mei errata corrigam, meliori meo regnum dimittam, et expensa pecunia, quam mihi mater pro hereditate reliquit, tota anima nudus sequar Christum."

65. See Uhlirz, *Jahrbücher des Deutschen Reiches*, 2:368–69 n. 80 and 413.

66. See Chapter 6, notes 10ff.

67. See Petrus Damiani, *Vita beati Romualdi*, chap. 25, pp. 53–54: "ubi ieiunio et psalmodię, prout valebat, intentus, cilitio ad carnem indutus, aurata desuper purpura tegebatur . . ."

68. See BU, no. 1406a, p. 794; on the consecration of the church of Saint Adalbert in Pereum, see also Benz, *Untersuchungen zur politischen Bedeutung der Kirchweihe*, 75ff.

69. See BU, no. 1406b, p. 794.

70. MGH DO III, no. 396, pp. 827ff., esp. p. 828; see also BU, no. 1407, pp. 794ff.

71. See Thietmar, *Chronicon*, IV, 59, p. 198: "Inperatoris autem predicti gratia

et hortatu gener Heinrici, ducis Bawariorum, Waic in regno suimet episcopales
cathedras faciens, coronam et benedic-
cionem accepit." See also BU, no. 1407c,
pp. 796–97.

72. See Uhlirz, *Jahrbücher des
Deutschen Reiches*, 2:575 ff.; Fried, *Otto
III. und Boleslaw Chrobry*, 132–33.

73. See Chapter 4.

74. See notes 53 ff. above.

75. Bruno of Querfurt, *Vita quinque
fratrum*, chap. 7, pp. 43–44: "Eadem tem-
pestate superuenientis hiemis, cum cesar
in uiribus regni et electo exercitu uirorum
fortium contra Romuleam urbem non
dextro omine seculare iter ageret, moritur
sine filiis, eheu, Otto pius; mortuus est
dum minus putatur, magnus imperator, in
angusto castello. Cum plura bona fecisset,
hac in parte errauit ut homo, quia oblitus
est Dominum dicentem: Mihi uindicta et
ego retribuam, non dedit honorem Deo, et
qui clauem gerit alti cęli eius precioso
apostolo Petro, secundum illud: Honora
Dominum tuum sanctum Israel. Num
cum sola Roma ei placeret, et ante omnes
Romanum populum pecunia et honore
dilexisset, ibi semper stare, hanc renouare
ad decorem secundum pristinam dignitatem ioco puerili in cassum cogitauit.
Nec longe queras exemplum, sed in
psalmista inuenies: Cogitationes
hominum uanę sunt. Peccatum regis hoc
fuit. Terram suę natiuitatis, delectabilem
Germaniam, iam nec uidere uoluit; tan-
tus sibi amor habitare Italiam fuit, ubi
mille languoribus, mille mortibus seua
clades armata currit. Cadunt circa latus
eius capellanus, episcopus, comes,
seruiens quam plurimus moritur, miles
non unus, et populus optimus; furit glad-
ius sanguine nobilium, multa sudans
morte karorum, cor cesaris atrocissime
uulnerans. Non iuuat inperium nec egrę
diuicię nec exercitus ille quem ingentem
frustra congregauit; hasta et acutus glad-
ius non eruerunt eum de manu mortis,
que sola nescit honorare reges. Erat autem
bonus cesar in non recto itinere, cogitans
destruere ingentes muros maximę Romę,
cuius ciues quamuis sibi pro bonis mala
fecissent, ipsa Roma tamen a Deo datum

apostolorum domicilium erat. Nec sic
natiua terra et desiderabilis Germania ad
amorem ei uenit, uerum Romulea tellus,
morte suorum karorum pasta, adultera
pulchritudine adhuc melius placet.
Enimuero more regum antiquorum et
pagnorum, qui suam uoluntatem difficile
relinquit, inueteratae Romę mortuum
decorem renouare superuacuo labore
insistit." See also Uhlirz, *Jahrbücher des
Deutschen Reiches*, 2:581–86.

76. But see Uhlirz, *Jahrbücher des
Deutschen Reiches*, 2:391–92.

77. See BU, no. 1450/IVa, pp. 827–28;
more accurately Uhlirz, *Jahrbücher des
Deutschen Reiches*, 2:589 ff. There are
detailed reports in Thangmar, *Vita Bernwardi*, chap. 37, p. 775; Bruno, *Vita
quinque fratrum*, chap. 7, pp. 43 ff.; Thietmar, *Chronicon*, IV, 49, p. 188.

78. See BU, no. 1450/IVa, p. 828.

79. BU, no. 1450/IVb, p. 829.

80. BU, no. 1450/IVg, p. 831; on this,
see most recently Karl Brunner, *Herzogtümer und Marken* (Vienna, 1994), 176.

81. BU, no. 1450/IVf, pp. 830–31.

82. BU, no. 1450/IVk, 1, p. 832.

CHAPTER 6: BUILDING BLOCKS FOR
AN ASSESSMENT OF OTTO III

1. On the ruler as barefooted penitent
or pilgrim, see notes 10 ff. below; on the
public tears, see Chapter 2, note 28.

2. See Chapter 5, notes 8 ff.

3. On this issue, see, in Chapter 6, the
section titled " 'Friends' of Otto III and
His Interaction with Them."

4. See Chapter 5, note 56.

5. On this point, see Althoff, "Demonstration und Inszenierung," esp. 31–50; see
also idem, *Spielregeln der Politik im Mittelalter*, with an introductory overview of
the relevant research.

6. See Kohlenberger, "Vorgänge des
Thronstreits," 60 ff.; for the context and
classification of proceedings, see Althoff,
"Das Privileg der *deditio*."

7. See Chapter 3, notes 22 ff.

8. Wolfherius, *Vita Godehardi episcopi Hildenesheimensis*, ed. Georg Pertz, in MGH SS 11 (Hannover, 1854), chap. 27, pp. 187–88.

9. For the background, see Thietmar, *Chronicon*, VI, 31/32, pp. 310ff.; for the specifics, see also BG, no. 1645a, pp. 937–38; no. 1646, p. 938.

10. See the evidence in Chapter 4, notes 11, 17, 42, and Chapter 5, note 64. Note the contemporary portrayal of the holy nobleman Gerald of Aurillac by Odo of Cluny, who reports that Gerald wore a monk's habit under his secular clothing. See Friedrich Lotter, "Das Idealbild adliger Laienfrömmigkeit in den Anfängen Clunys," in *Benedictine Culture, 750–1050*, ed. W. Lourdaux and D. Verhelst (Louvain, 1983), 83–84.

11. On the voluntary and involuntary penance of Louis the Pious, see Rudolf Schieffer, "Von Mailand nach Canossa: Ein Beitrag zur Geschichte der christlichen Herrscherbuße von Theodosius dem Großen bis zu Heinrich IV.," DA 28 (1972): 354ff.; for Henry II's barefoot entry into Magdeburg, see David A. Warner, "Henry II at Magdeburg: Kingship, Ritual, and the Cult of Saints," *Early Medieval Europe* 3 (1994): 141–45; on Henry III and his public penitential acts, see Stefan Weinfurter, *Herrschaft und Reich der Salier* (Sigmaringen, 1991), 86–87.

12. On Heribert, see Müller, *Heribert, Kanzler Ottos III. und Erzbischof von Köln*, 199–200; on Halberstadt, see Gerd Althoff, "Widukind von Corvey," FMSt 27 (1993): 264ff.; idem, "Magdeburg—Halberstadt—Merseburg."

13. See Schieffer, "Von Mailand nach Canossa," for many further examples.

14. See Chapter 2, note 28.

15. See a similar description in Wipo, *Gesta Chuonradi II. imperatoris*, ed. Harry Bresslau, in MGH SSrG 61 (Hannover and Leipzig, 1915), chap. 3, p. 23, of spectators' reaction to the experienced *pietas* of Conrad II. On this and comparable cases, see Althoff, "Der König weint."

16. Sources treating Otto III's "friends" report similar behavior. See later in Chap

ter 6 the section titled "'Friends' of Otto III and His Interaction with Them."

17. See, for example, Percy Ernst Schramm, *Herrschaftszeichen* (Göttingen, 1957), 162ff.; Percy Ernst Schramm and Florentine Mütherich, *Denkmale der deutschen Könige und Kaiser* (Munich, 1962), 1:51ff., 77ff., 84ff.; Jürgen Hannig, "*Ars donandi:* Zur Ökonomie des Schenkens im früheren Mittelalter," in *Armut, Liebe, Ehre*, ed. Richard van Dülmen (Frankfurt am Main, 1988), 15–18, with further references.

18. See Thangmar, *Vita Bernwardi*, chap. 27, pp. 770–71, and chap. 36, pp. 774–75.

19. On this issue, see most recently Michael Borgolte, "Die Stiftungsurkunden Heinrichs II.: Eine Studie zum Handlungsspielraum des letzten Liudolfingers," in *Festschrift für Eduard Hlawitschka*, ed. Karl Schnith and Roland Pauler (Kallmünz, 1993), 231–50.

20. See note 33 below.

21. See note 38 below.

22. On this, see Althoff, "Huld," 275ff., with examples.

23. See Gerhard, *Vita s. Oudalrici episcopi Augustani*, ed. Georg Waitz, in MGH SS 4, chap. 21, p. 407; Ruotger, *Vita Brunonis archiepiscopi Coloniensis*, ed. Irene Ott, MGH SSrG, n.s., 10 (Cologne and Graz, 1951), chap. 17, pp. 15–16; chap. 20, pp. 19ff.; chap. 41, pp. 43–44.

24. See Chapter 4, note 45; note 17 above.

25. See Chapter 4, note 55.

26. See Thietmar, *Chronicon*, IV, 47, pp. 184ff.; see also the discussion in Schramm, *Kaiser, Rom und Renovatio*, 4th ed., 111–12.

27. See Ingrid Voss, *Herrschertreffen im frühen und hohen Mittelalter* (Cologne and Vienna, 1987), esp. 123ff.; more generally on this theme, see also Werner Kolb, *Herrscherbegegnungen im Mittelalter* (Bern, Frankfurt, New York, and Paris, 1988).

28. See Chapter 4, note 50.

29. Schramm, *Kaiser, Rom und Renovatio,* 4th ed., 135.

30. Fleckenstein, *Die Hofkapelle der deutschen Könige,* 2:96.

31. For a general discussion of the "institute" of medieval friendship, see Bruno Paradisi, *L'"amicitia" internazionale nell'alto medioevo* (Milan, 1947), 178–225; Wolfgang H. Fritze, "Die fränkische Schwurfreundschaft in der Merowingerzeit," ZRG GA 71 (1954): 74–125; Margaret Wielers, *Zwischenstaatliche Beziehungsformen im frühen Mittelalter* (Münster, 1959); Althoff, *Verwandte, Freunde und Getreue,* 85 ff.

32. See Althoff, *Verwandte, Freunde und Getreue,* 88–89.

33. Josef Fleckenstein first used the term "genius for friendship" in *Grundlagen und Beginn der deutschen Geschichte,* 98. It has since been widely adopted.

34. See Thangmar, *Vita Bernwardi,* chap. 3, p. 759; chap. 19, p. 767; chap. 23, pp. 769–70; chap. 27, pp. 770–71.

35. See *Vita Burchardi episcopi Wormatiensis,* chap. 3, p. 833.

36. See Lantbert, *Vita Heriberti archiepiscopi Coloniensis,* chap. 4, p. 742.

37. Ibid., chap. 5, p. 743.

38. Bruno of Querfurt, *Vita sancti Adalberti,* chap. 20, p. 25: "Cum quo aliquos dies commoratus, nec nocte nisi ante conspectum imperatoris iacere permissus est."

39. Thangmar, *Vita Bernwardi,* chap. 19, p. 767.

40. See *Vita Heinrici IV. imperatoris,* ed. Wilhelm Eberhard, MGH SSrG 58 (Hannover, 1899), chap. 1, pp. 10–11; on this passage, see Lothar Bornscheuer, *Miseriae regum* (Berlin, 1968), 156–64.

41. See Bruno of Querfurt, *Vita sancti Adalberti,* chap. 20, p. 25: "Noctibus quoque calceos dormientium clam raptos aqua abluit, discipulus humilitatis manibus suis lutum tulit, lotos restituit. Ibi nocte sopora parum molli lecto requiescens, vitę suę desiderabilem terminum aspexit."

42. See, for example, the characterization of Bernward's reception in Rome in Thangmar, *Vita Bernwardi,* chap. 19, p. 767; see also, in Chapter 5, the section titled "The Gandersheim Conflict."

43. Petrus Damiani, *Vita beati Romualdi,* chap. 25, p. 52: "qui sicut dicitur in tantum regi familiaris et carus extiterat, ut utriusque vestes utrumque contegerent et amborum manus una parobsis communi sepe convivio sotiaret." On this passage, see C. Stephen Jaeger, "L'amour des rois: Structure sociale d'une forme de sensibilité aristocratique," *Annales ESC* 46, no. 3 (1991): 549.

44. On this issue, see Karl Hauck, "Rituelle Speisegemeinschaft im 10. und 11. Jahrhundert," *Studium Generale* 3 (1950): 611–21; Franz Felten, *Äbte und Laienäbte im Frankenreich* (Stuttgart, 1980), 22 ff.; Gerd Althoff, "Der frieden-, bündnis- und gemeinschaftstiftende Charakter des Mahles im früheren Mittelalter," in *Essen und Trinken im Mittelalter und Neuzeit,* ed. Irmgard Bitsch et al. (Sigmaringen, 1987), 13–25.

45. Petrus Damiani, *Vita beati Romualdi,* chap. 27, p. 56: "Hic denique regis fuerat consanguineus et ita carus, ut rex illum non alio vocaret nomine nisi anima mea."

46. See Lantbert, *Vita Heriberti archiepiscopi Coloniensis,* chap. 5, p. 743.

47. Schramm, *Kaiser, Rom und Renovatio,* 4th ed., 134.

48. Ibid., 135.

49. See the Latin text in MGH DO III, no. 241, p. 659: "Versus numquam conposui / Nec in studio habui; / Dum in usu habueio, / Et in eis viguero / Quot habet viros Gallia, / Tot vobis mittam carmina."

50. See Bruno of Querfurt, *Vita quinque fratrum eremitarum,* chap. 7, p. 44: "qui suam uoluntatem difficile relinquit."

51. Petrus Damiani, *Vita beati Romualdi,* chap. 22, pp. 47–48.

52. See most recently Boshof, *Königtum und Königsherrschaft im 10. und 11.*

Jahrhundert, 23–28 and 97; Fried, *Der Weg in die Geschichte*, 602–32, esp. 610.

53. The formulation cited here is from Carlrichard Brühl, *Die Anfänge der deutschen Geschichte* (Wiesbaden, 1972), 177; for an assessment of Henry II as a realist politician, see the essential work by Stefan Weinfurter, "Die Zentralisierung der Herrschaftsgewalt im Reich unter Kaiser Heinrich II.," HJb 106 (1986): 241–97.

54. See the earlier work of Theodor Schieffer, "Heinrich II. und Konrad II.: Die Umprägung des Geschichtsbildes durch die Kirchenreform des 11. Jahrhunderts," DA 8 (1950): 385–86; for another view, see Hartmut Hoffmann, *Mönchskönig und "rex idiota": Studien zur Kirchenpolitik Heinrichs II. und Konrads II.* (Hannover, 1993).

55. See the Introduction, notes 38 ff.

56. See Lübke, *Regesten*, vol. 3, nos. 350 ff., pp. 190 ff.; Althoff, *Adels- und Königsfamilien*, 108 ff.

57. See Thietmar, *Chronicon*, v, 18, pp. 241 ff.; Lübke, *Regesten*, vol. 3, no. 356, pp. 200 ff.

58. See the contemporary assessments of Thietmar, *Chronicon*, v, 31, pp. 255–56 (for other sources, see Lübke, *Regesten*, vol. 3, no. 366, pp. 211 ff.), and the letter of Bruno of Querfurt to Henry II. On the latter, see Lübke, *Regesten*, vol. 3, no. 415, p. 267.

59. See Walter Schlesinger, "Die sogenannte Nachwahl Heinrichs II. in Merseburg," in *Geschichte in der Gesellschaft*, ed. Friedrich Prinz et al. (Stuttgart, 1974), 350 ff.; Lübke, *Regesten*, vol. 3, no. 354, pp. 197 ff.

60. See Wipo, *Gesta Chuonradi II. imperatoris*, chap. 7, p. 30; Harry Bresslau, *Jahrbücher des deutschen Reiches unter Konrad II.* (Leipzig, 1879), 1:65–68.

61. See, in Chapter 3, the section titled "Otto III's 'Idea of Roman Renewal' in Older and Newer Scholarship."

62. See Weinfurter, "Die Zentralisierung der Herrschaftsgewalt," 243–50, 286–87; Hagen Keller, "Reichsorganisation, Herrschaftsformen und Gesellschaftsstrukturen im Regnum Teutonicum," in *Settimane di studio del Centro italiano di studi sull'alto medioevo*, vol. 38, *Il secolo di ferro* (Spoleto, 1990), 180–86.

63. Thietmar, *Chronicon*, iv, 49, 188–89; on the probably personal nature of this opposition, see Görich, *Otto III.*, 146 ff.

64. Borgolte, "Die Stiftungsurkunden Heinrichs II.," 242 with n. 52; for the characteristic ways Henry II referred to Otto III, see, for example, MGH DH II, no. 59, p. 73: "nobisque dilectissimi senioris tercii videlicet Ottonis augusti . . ."; no. 83, p. 105: "karissimi senioris et antecessoris."

65. This is the remark by Thietmar already mentioned several times. See Thietmar, *Chronicon*, iv, 47, pp. 184 ff.

Bibliography ‡ ‡ ‡

Primary Sources

Ademar of Chabannes. *Chronicon.* Edited by Jules Chavanon. Collection de textes pour servir à l'étude et à l'enseignement de l'histoire 20. Paris, 1897.

Annales Hildesheimenses. Edited by Georg Waitz. MGH SSrG 8. Hannover, 1878.

Annales Quedlinburgenses. Edited by Georg Heinrich Pertz. In MGH SS 3:22–90. Hannover, 1839.

Arnold. *Libri de s. Emmerammo.* Edited by Georg Waitz. In MGH SS 4:543–74. Hannover, 1841.

Arnulf of Milan. *Liber gestorum recentium.* Edited by Claudia Zey. MGH SSrG 67. Hannover, 1994.

Böhmer, Johann Friedrich, and Theodor Graff, eds. *Regesta Imperii* ii, 4: *Die Regesten des Kaiserreiches unter Heinrich II.* Cologne, 1971.

Böhmer, Johann Friedrich, and Hanns Leo Mikoletzky, eds. *Regesta Imperii* ii, 2: *Die Regesten des Kaiserreiches unter Otto II.* Cologne, 1950.

Böhmer, Johann Friedrich, and Mathilde Uhlirz, eds. *Regesta Imperii* ii, 3: *Die Regesten des Kaiserreiches unter Otto III.* Cologne, 1956.

Böhmer, Johann Friedrich, and Harald Zimmermann, eds. *Regesta Imperii* ii, 5: *Papstregesten, 911–1024.* Cologne, 1969.

Bruno of Querfurt. *Vita quinque fratrum eremitarum.* Edited by Jadwiga Karwasińska. In MPH, n.s., 4.3:1–41. Warsaw, 1973.

———. *Vita sancti Adalberti.* Redactio longior. Edited by Jadwiga Karwasińska. In MPH, n.s., 4.2:3–41. Warsaw, 1969.

———. *Vita sancti Adalberti episcopi secunda.* Edited by Georg Heinrich Pertz. In MGH SS 4:596–612. Hannover, 1941.

Brunwilarensis monasterii fundatorum actus. Edited by Georg Waitz. In MGH SS 14:121–41. Hannover, 1883.

Chronicon Novaliciense usque a. 1048. Edited by Ludwig Carl Bethmann. In MGH SS 7:73–133. Hannover, 1846.

Codex Laureshamensis. Edited by Karl Glockner. Vol. 1, *Einleitung, Regesten, Chronik.* Arbeiten der historischen Kommission für den Volkstaat Hessen. Darmstadt, 1929.

Constitutum Constantini. Edited by Horst Fuhrmann. MGH Fontes iuris Germanici antiqui in usum scholarum 10. Hannover, 1968.

Cronica Pontificum et Imperatorum S. Bartholomei in insula Romani. Edited by Oswald Holder-Egger. In MGH SS 31:189–225. Hannover, 1903.

Epistolae Maguntinae. In *Monumenta Maguntina,* edited by Philipp Jaffé, Bibliotheca rerum Germanicarum 3:316–421. Berlin, 1866.

Gallus Anonymus. *Chronicae et gesta ducum sive principum Polonorum.* Edited by Karol Maleczynski. MPH, n.s., 2. Cracow, 1952.

Gerbert of Aurillac. *Acta concilii Mosomensis.* Edited by Georg Heinrich Pertz. In MGH SS 3:690–91. Hannover, 1839.

———. *Briefsammlung.* Edited by Fritz Weigle. MGH Epp. DK 2. Berlin, 1966.

———. *The Letters of Gerbert, with His Papal Privileges as Sylvester II.* Translated by Harriet Lattin. New York, 1961.

———. *Lettres (983–997).* Translated by Julien Havet. Paris, 1889.

Gerhard. *Leben des hl. Ulrich, Bischofs von Augsburg.* In *Lebensbeschreibungen einiger Bischöfe des 10.–12. Jahrhunderts,* translated by Hatto Kallfelz, FSGA 22:35–167. Darmstadt, 1973.

———. *Vita s. Oudalrici episcopi Augustani.* Edited by Georg Waitz. In MGH SS 4:377–419. Hannover, 1841.

Geschichte in Quellen. Edited by Wolfgang Lautemann and Manfred Schlenke. Vol. 2, *Mittelalter.* Munich, 1970.

Gesta episcoporum Cameracensium. Edited by Ludwig Carl Bethmann. In MGH SS 7:402–525. Hannover, 1846.

Gesta episcoporum Halberstadensium. Edited by Ludwig Weiland. In MGH SS 23:73–123. Hannover, 1874.

Giovanni Diacono. *Cronaca veneziana.* Edited by Giovanni Monticolo. In FSI 9:57–171. Rome, 1890.

Hugo of Farfa. *Destructio monasterii Farfensis.* Edited by Ugo Balzani. In FSI 33:25–51. Rome, 1903.

———. *Exceptio relationum de monasterii Farfensis diminuatione.* Edited by Ugo Balzani. In FSI 33:59–70. Rome, 1903.

———. *Relatio constitutionis.* Edited by Ugo Balzani. In FSI 33:53–58. Rome, 1903.

Die Jahrbücher von Quedlinburg. Translated by Eduard Winkelmann. Geschichtsschreiber der deutschen Vorzeit 36. Leipzig, 1891.

Johannes Canaparius. *Vita s. Adalberti episcopi.* Edited by Jadwiga Karwasińska. MPH, n.s., 4.1. Warsaw, 1962.

Landulf. *Historia Mediolanensis.* Edited by Ludwig Carl Bethmann and Wilhelm Wattenbach. In MGH SS 8:32–100. Hannover, 1848.

Lantbert. *Vita Heriberti archiepiscopi Coloniensis.* Edited by Georg Heinrich Pertz. In MGH SS 4:739–53. Hannover, 1841.

Leo of Vercelli. *Versus de Gregorio et Ottone augusto.* Edited by Karl Strecker. In MGH Poetae Latini 5.2:477–80. Berlin, 1939.

———. *Versus de Ottone et Heinrico.* Edited by Karl Strecker. In MGH Poetae Latini 5.2:480–83. Berlin, 1939.

Lübke, Christian. *Regesten zur Geschichte der Slaven an Elbe und Oder (vom Jahr 900 an).* 5 vols. Gießener Abhandlungen zur Agrar- und Wirtschaftsforschung des europäischen Ostens 131, 133, 134, 152, and 157. Berlin, 1984–88.

Miracula s. Adalberti martiris. Edited by Georg Heinrich Pertz. In MGH SS 4:613–16. Hannover, 1841.

Die Necrologien von Merseburg, Magdeburg und Lüneburg. Edited by Gerd Althoff and Joachim Wollasch. MGH Libri memoriales et Necrologia, n.s., 2. Hannover, 1983.

Odilo of Cluny. *Epitaphium domine Adelheide auguste.* Edited by Herbert Paulhart. MIÖG, suppl. vol. 20.2. Innsbruck, 1962.

Ottonis III. et Gregorii V. concilium Romanum. Edited by Ludwig Weiland. In MGH Const. 1:51–52. Hannover, 1893.

Papsturkunden 896–1046. 3 vols. Edited by Harald Zimmermann. Denkschriften der philosophisch-historischen Klasse der österreichischen Akademie der Wissenschaften 174. Vienna, 1984–89.

Petrus Damiani. *Vita beati Romualdi.* Edited by Giovanni Tabacco. FSI 94. Rome, 1957.

Platen, August von. *Werke.* Critically edited and expanded edition. 2 vols. Edited by Georg Arnold Wolff and Viktor Schweizer. Meyers Klassiker-Ausgaben. Leipzig, 1895.

Richer of Rheims. *Histoire de France (888–995).* Edited and translated by Robert Latouche. Vol. 2. Les classiques de l'histoire de France au Moyen Âge 17. Paris, 1937.

———. *Historiarum Libri* IIII. Edited by Georg Waitz. MGH SSrG 51. Hannover, 1877.

Rudolfus Glaber. *Historia.* In *Opera,* edited and translated by John France, 2–253. Oxford, 1989.

———. *Vita Domni Willelmi Abbatis.* In *Opera,* edited and translated by John France, 254–99. Oxford, 1989.

Ruodlieb. In *Lateinische Epik des Mittelalters in Versen,* edited by Karl Langosch, 87–215. Darmstadt, 1956.

Ruotger. *Leben des hl. Bruno, Erzbischofs von Köln.* In *Lebensbeschreibungen einiger Bischöfe des 10.–12. Jahrhunderts,* translated by Hatto Kallfelz, FSGA 22:169–261. Darmstadt, 1973.

———. *Vita Brunonis archiepiscopi Coloniensis.* Edited by Irene Ott. MGH SSrG, n.s., 10. Cologne and Graz, 1951.

Die Tegernseer Briefsammlung (Froumund). Edited by Karl Strecker. MGH Epp. Selectae III. Berlin, 1925.

Thangmar. *Leben des hl. Bernward, Bischofs von Hildesheim.* In *Lebensbeschreibungen einiger Bischöfe des 10.–12. Jahrhunderts,* translated by Hatto Kallfelz, FSGA 22:263–361. Darmstadt, 1973.

———. *Vita Bernwardi episcopi Hildesheimensis.* Edited by Georg Heinrich Pertz. In MGH SS 4:754–82. Hannover, 1841.

Thietmar of Merseburg. *Chronicon.* Edited by Robert Holtzmann. 2d ed. MGH SSrG, n.s., 9. Berlin, 1955.

———. *Chronik.* Translated by Werner Trillmich. FSGA 9. Darmstadt, 1957.

Translatio s. Adalberti. Edited by Georg Waitz. In MGH SS 15.2:708. Hannover, 1888.

Die Urkunden Ottos II. Edited by Theodor Sickel. MGH DD 2.1. Hannover, 1888.

Die Urkunden Ottos III. Edited by Theodor Sickel. MGH DD 2.2. Hannover, 1893.

Vita Burchardi episcopi Wormatiensis. Edited by Georg Waitz. In MGH SS 4:829–46. Hannover, 1841.

Vita Heinrici IV. imperatoris. Edited by Wilhelm Eberhard. 3d ed. MGH SSrG 58. Hannover, 1899.

Vita s. Nili abbatis Cryptae Ferratae. Edited by Georg Heinrich Pertz. In MGH SS 4:616–18. Hannover, 1841.

Widukind of Corvey. *Res gestae Saxonicae.* Edited by Paul Hirsch and Hans Eberhard Lohmann. MGH SSrG 60. Hannover, 1935.

Wipo. *Gesta Chuonradi II. imperatoris.* Edited by Harry Bresslau. 3d ed. In MGH SSrG 61:1–62. Hannover and Leipzig, 1915.

———. *Gesta Chuonradi II. imperatoris.* In *Quellen des 9. und 11. Jahrhunderts zur Geschichte der Hamburgischen Kirche und des Reiches,* translated by Werner Trillmich, FSGA 11:507–613. Darmstadt, 1961.

Wolfherius. *Vita Godehardi episcopi Hildenesheimensis.* Edited by Georg Heinrich Pertz. In MGH SS 11:162–221. Hannover, 1854.

Secondary Sources

Althoff, Gerd. *Adels- und Königsfamilien im Spiegel ihrer Memorialüberlieferung: Studien zum Totengedenken der Billunger und Ottonen.* Münstersche Mittelalterschriften 47. Munich, 1984.

———. *Amicitiae und Pacta: Bündnis, Einung, Politik und Gebetsgedenken im beginnenden 10. Jahrhundert.* Schriften der MGH 37. Hannover, 1992.

———. "Die Beurteilung der mittelalterlichen Ostpolitik als Paradigma für zeitgebundene Geschichtsbewertung." In *Die Deutschen und ihr Mittelalter,* edited by Althoff, 147–64.

———. "Colloquium familiare—colloquium secretum—colloquium publicum: Beratung im politischen Leben des früheren Mittelalters." FMSt 24 (1990): 145–67.

———. "Demonstration und Inszenierung: Spielregeln der Kommunikation in mittelalterlicher Öffentlichkeit." FMSt 27 (1993): 27–50.

———. "Der frieden-, bündnis- und gemeinschaftstiftende Charakter des Mahles im früheren Mittelalter." In *Essen und Trinken im Mittelalter und Neuzeit,* edited by Irmgard Bitsch et al., 13–25. Sigmaringen, 1987.

———. "Gandersheim und Quedlinburg: Ottonische Frauenklöster als Herrschafts- und Überlieferungszentren." FMSt 25 (1991): 123–44.

———. "Genugtuung *(satisfactio)*: Zur Eigenart gütlicher Konfliktbeilegung im Mittelalter." In *Modernes Mittelalter,* edited by Joachim Heinzel, 247–65. Frankfurt am Main, 1994.

———. "Huld: Überlegungen zu einen Zentralbegriff der mittelalterlichen Herrschaftsordnung." FMSt 25 (1991): 259–82.

———. "Konfliktverhalten und Rechtsbewußtsein: Die Welfen in der Mitte des 12. Jahrhunderts." FMSt 26 (1992): 331–52.

———. "Königsherrschaft und Konfliktbewältigung im 10. und 11. Jahrhundert." FMSt 23 (1989): 265–90.

———. "Der König weint." In *"Aufführung" und "Schrift" in Mittelalter und früher Neuzeit,* edited by Jan-Dirk Müller. Stuttgart, 1996.

———. "Magdeburg—Halberstadt—Merseburg: Bischöfliche Repräsentation und Interessenvertretung im ottonischen Sachsen." In *Herrschaftsrepräsentation im ottonischen Sachsen,* edited by Gerd Althoff and Ernst Schubert. Frankfurt am Main, 1998.

————. "Das Privileg der *deditio:* Formen gütlicher Konfliktbeendigung in der mittelalterlichen Adelsgesellschaft." In *Nobilitas: Funktion und Repräsentation des Adels in Alteuropa,* edited by Otto Gerhard Oexle and Werner Paravicini. Göttingen, 1997.

————. "Der schwierige Weg zum Ohr des Herrschers." In *Spielregeln der Politik im Mittelalter.*

————. *Spielregeln der Politik im Mittelalter: Kommunikation in Frieden und Fehde.* Darmstadt, 1997.

————. "Ungeschriebene Gesetze: Wie funktioniert Herrschaft ohne schriftlich fixierte Normen?" In *Spielregeln der Politik im Mittelalter.*

————. *Verwandte, Freunde und Getreue: Zum politischen Stellenwert der Gruppenbindungen im früheren Mittelalter.* Darmstadt, 1990.

————. "Vormundschaft, Erzieher, Lehrer: Einflüsse auf Otto III." In *Kaiserin Theophanu,* edited by Euw and Schreiner, 277–89.

————. "Warum erhielt Graf Berthold im Jahre 999 ein Marktprivileg für Villingen?" In *Die Zähringer,* edited by Karl Schmid, 269–74. Sigmaringen, 1990.

————. "Widukind von Corvey: Kronzeuge und Herausforderung." FMSt 27 (1993): 253–72.

————. "Zur Frage nach der Organisation sächsischer *coniurationes* in der Ottonenzeit." FMSt 16 (1982): 129–42.

————, ed. *Die Deutschen und ihr Mittelalter: Themen und Funktionen moderner Geschichtsbilder vom Mittelalter.* Darmstadt, 1992.

Althoff, Gerd, and Ernst Schubert, eds. *Herrschaftsrepräsentation im ottonischen Sachsen.* Frankfurt am Main, 1998.

Angenendt, Arnold. "Der ganze und der unverweste Leib—eine Leitidee der Reliquienverehrung bei Gregor von Tours und Beda Venerabilis." In *Aus Archiven und Bibliotheken: Festschrift für Raymund Kottje,* edited by Hubert Mordek, Freiburger Beiträge zur mittelalterlichen Geschichte: Studien und Texte 3:33–50. Frankfurt am Main, Bern, New York, and Paris, 1992.

————. *Kaiserherrschaft und Königstaufe: Kaiser, Könige und Päpste als geistliche Patrone in der abendländischen Missionsgeschichte.* Berlin, 1984.

Appelt, Heinrich. "Die angebliche Verleihung der Patriciuswürde an Boleslaw Chrobry." In *Geschichtliche Landeskunde und Universalgeschichte: Festgabe für Hermann Aubin,* 65–81. Hamburg, 1950.

Auer, Leopold. "Der Kriegsdienst des Klerus unter den sächsischen Kaisern: Zweiter Teil: Verfassungsgeschichtliche Probleme." MIÖG 80 (1972): 48–70.

Bäumer, Gertrud. *Der Jüngling im Sternenmantel: Größe und Tragik Ottos III.* Munich, 1949.

Benrath, Henry. *Der Kaiser Otto III.* Stuttgart, 1951.

Benz, Karl Josef. *Untersuchungen zur politischen Bedeutung der Kirchweihe unter Teilnahme deutscher Herrscher im hohen Mittelalter.* Kallmünz, 1975.

Benzinger, Josef. *Invectiva in Romam: Romkritik im Mittelalter vom 9. bis zum 12. Jahrhundert.* Historische Studien vol. 404. Lübeck and Hamburg, 1968.

Bernhardt, John W. *Itinerant Kingship and Royal Monasteries in Early Medieval Germany, c. 936–1076.* Cambridge, 1993.

Beumann, Helmut. "Entschädigungen von Halberstadt und Mainz bei Gründung des Erzbistums Magdeburg." In *Ex ipsis rerum documentis: Festschrift für Harald Zimmermann zum 65. Geburtstag,* edited by Klaus Herbers et al., 383–98. Sigmaringen, 1991.

———. "Grab und Thron Karls des Großen zu Aachen." In *Karl der Große: Lebenswerk und Nachleben,* edited by Wolfgang Braunfels and Percy Ernst Schramm, vol. 4, *Das Nachleben,* 9–38. Düsseldorf, 1967. Reprinted in Beumann, *Wissenschaft vom Mittelalter,* 347–76.

———. "Otto III." In *Kaisergestalten des Mittelalters,* edited by Helmut Beumann, 73–97. Munich, 1984.

———. *Die Ottonen.* 2d ed. Stuttgart, 1991.

———. *Wissenschaft vom Mittelalter: Ausgewählte Aufsätze.* Cologne and Vienna, 1972.

———. "Zur Entwicklung transpersonaler Staatsvorstellungen." In *Wissenschaft vom Mittelalter,* 135–74. First appeared in *Das Königtum und seine geistigen und rechtlichen Grundlagen,* Vorträge und Forschungen 3:185–224. Constance, 1956.

Beumann, Helmut, and Walter Schlesinger. "Urkundenstudien zur deutschen Ostpolitik unter Otto III." Expanded reprint. In Walter Schlesinger, *Mitteldeutsche Beiträge zur deutschen Verfassungsgeschichte des Mittelalters,* 306–412 and 479–87. Göttingen, 1961. Shorter original first appeared in ADipl. 1 (1955): 132–256.

Bezzola, Gian Andri. *Das ottonische Kaisertum in der französischen Geschichtsschreibung des 10. und beginnenden 11. Jahrhunderts.* Graz and Cologne, 1956.

Bloch, H. "Beiträge zur Geschichte des Bischofs Leo von Vercelli und seiner Zeit." NA 22 (1897): 11–136.

Böhmer, Heinrich. *Willigis von Mainz.* Leipziger Stud. a. d. Geb. d. Gesch. 1/3. Leipzig, 1895.

Borgolte, Michael. "Die Stiftungsurkunden Heinrichs II.: Eine Studie zum Handlungsspielraum des letzten Liudolfingers." In *Festschrift für Eduard Hlawitschka,* edited by Karl Rudolf Schnith and Roland Pauler, 231–50. Kallmünz, 1993.

Bornscheuer, Lothar. *Miseriae regum: Untersuchungen zum Krisen- und Todesgedanken in den herrschaftstheologischen Vorstellungen der ottonisch-salischen Zeit.* Arbeiten zur Frühmittelalterforschung 4. Berlin, 1968.

Boshof, Egon. "Köln, Mainz, Trier—Die Auseinandersetzung um die Spitzenstellung im deutschen Episkopat in ottonisch-salischer Zeit." JbKGV 49 (1978): 19–48.

———. *Königtum und Königsherrschaft im 10. und 11. Jahrhundert.* Enzyklopädie deutscher Geschichte 27. Munich, 1993.

Brackmann, Albert. "Die Anfänge des polnischen Staates." In *Gesammelte Aufsätze,* 154–87. Weimar, 1941.

———. "Kaiser Otto III. und die staatliche Umgestaltung Polens und Ungarns." In *Gesammelte Aufsätze,* 242–58.

———. "Reichspolitik und Ostpolitik im frühen Mittelalter." In *Gesammelte Aufsätze,* 188–210.

———. "Der 'Römische Erneuerungsgedanke' und seine Bedeutung für die Reichspolitik der deutschen Kaiserzeit." In *Gesammelte Aufsätze,* 108–39.

Brandt, Michael, and Arne Eggebrecht, eds. *Bernward von Hildesheim und das Zeitalter der Ottonen: Katalog der Ausstellung Hildesheim 1993.* 2 vols. Hildesheim and Mainz, 1993.

Bresslau, Harry. *Jahrbücher des deutschen Reiches unter Konrad II.* 2 vols. Leipzig, 1879–84.

Brückner, W. "Devestierung." In *Handwörterbuch zur deutschen Rechtsgeschichte,* edited by Adalbert Erler and Ekkehard Kaufmann, vol. 1, cols. 724–26. Berlin, 1971

Brühl, Carlrichard. *Die Anfänge der deutschen Geschichte.* Sb. d. wiss. Gesellschaft an der Johann Wolfgang Goethe–Universität Frankfurt a. M., vol. 10, no. 5, 1972. Wiesbaden, 1972.

———. *Deutschland—Frankreich: Die Geburt zweier Völker.* Cologne, 1990.

———. *Fodrum, gistum, servitium regis: Studien zu den wirtschaftlichen Grundlagen des Königtums im Frankenreich und in den fränkischen Nachfolgestaaten Deutschland, Frankreich und Italien vom 6. bis zur Mitte des 14. Jahrhunderts.* 2 vols. Kölner historische Abhandlungen 14. Cologne and Graz, 1968.

Brühl, Carlrichard, and Cinzio Violante. *Die "Honorantie civitatis Papie."* Cologne and Vienna, 1983.

Brunner, Karl. *Herzogtümer und Marken: Vom Ungarnsturm bis ins 12. Jahrhundert.* Österreichische Geschichte 907–1156. Vienna, 1994.

Brüske, Wolfgang. *Untersuchungen zur Geschichte des Liutizenbundes: Deutsch-wendische Beziehungen des 10.–12. Jahrhunderts.* Mitteldeutsche Forschungen 3. Münster and Cologne, 1955.

Bumke, Joachim. *Höfische Kultur: Literatur und Gesellschaft im hohen Mittelalter.* 2 vols. Munich, 1986.

Bur, Michel. "Adalbéron, archevêque de Reims, reconsidéré." In *Le roi de France et son royaume autour de l'an mil: Actes du colloque Hughes Capet 987–1987: La France de l'an mil,* edited by Michel Parisse and Xavier Barral I Altet, 55–63. Paris, 1992.

Burleigh, Michael. *Germany Turns Eastwards: A Study of "Ostforschung" in the Third Reich.* Cambridge, 1988.

Cartellieri, Alexander. "Otto III.: Kaiser der Römer." In *Festschrift Walther Judeich,* 173–205. Weimar, 1929.

———. *Weltgeschichte als Machtgeschichte.* 5 vols. Munich, 1927–.

Classen, Peter. "Corona Imperii: Die Krone als Inbegriff des römischdeutschen Reiches im 12. Jahrhundert." In *Festschrift für Percy Ernst Schramm zu seinem 70. Geburtstag,* 1:90–101. Wiesbaden, 1964.

———. "Das Wormser Konkordat in der deutschen Verfassungsgeschichte." In *Investiturstreit und Reichsverfassung,* edited by Josef Fleckenstein, Vorträge und Forschungen 17:411–60. Sigmaringen, 1973.

Claude, Dietrich. *Geschichte des Erzbistums Magdeburg bis in das 12. Jahrhundert.* 2 vols. Mitteldeutsche Forschungen 67. Cologne and Vienna, 1972–75.

Corbet, Patrick. *Les saints ottoniens: Sainteté dynastique, sainteté royale et sainteté féminine autour de l'an mil.* Beihefte der Francia 15. Sigmaringen, 1986.

Davies, Wendy, ed. *Theophanu and Her Times.* Cambridge, 1994.

Dell'Ono, M.-A. "Neilos." In *Lexikon des Mittelalters,* vol. 6, col. 1085. Munich and Zurich, 1993.

Domeier, Victor. *Die Päpste als Richter über die deutschen Könige von der Mitte des 11. bis zum Ausgang des 13. Jahrhunderts: Ein Beitrag zur Geschichte des päpstlichen Einflusses in Deutschland.* Untersuchungen zur Deutschen Staats- und Rechtsgeschichte 53. Breslau, 1897.

Drabek, Anna Maria. *Die Verträge der fränkischen und deutschen Herrscher mit dem Papsttum von 754 bis 1020.* Veröffentlichungen des Instituts für österreichische Geschichtsforschung 22. Vienna, Cologne, and Graz, 1976.

Dümmler, Ernst. *Geschichte des ostfränkischen Reiches.* Vol. 3, *Die letzten Karolinger: Konrad I.* Leipzig, 1882.

Eggert, Wolfgang, and Barbara Pätzold. *Wir-Gefühl und Regnum Saxonum bei frühmittelalterlichen Geschichtsschreibern.* Forschungen zur mittelalterlichen Geschichte 31. Weimar, 1984.

Ehlers, Joachim. "Otto II. und Kloster Memleben." SaAn 18 (1994): 51–82.

Engels, Odilo. "Der Reichsbischof in ottonischer und frühsalischer Zeit." In *Beiträge zur Geschichte und Struktur der mittelalterlichen Germania Sacra,* edited by Irene Crusius, Studien zur Germania Sacra 17:135–75. Göttingen, 1989.

———. "Theophanu—die westliche Kaiserin aus dem Osten." In *Die Begegnung des Westens mit dem Osten,* edited by Odilo Engels and Peter Schreiner, 13–36. Sigmaringen, 1993.

Erdmann, Carl. *Forschungen zur politischen Ideenwelt des Frühmittelalters.* Edited by Friedrich Baethgen. Berlin, 1951.

———. "Das Grab Heinrichs I." DA 4 (1940): 76–97.

———. "Das ottonische Reich als Imperium Romanum." DA 6 (1943): 412–41.

Erkens, Franz-Reiner. "Die Frau als Herrscherin in ottonisch-frühsalischer Zeit." In *Kaiserin Theophanu,* edited by Euw and Schreiner, 245–59.

———. "In tota cunctis gratissimus aula? Egbert von Trier als Reichsbischof." In *Egbert, Erzbischof von Trier 977–993: Gedenkschrift der Diözese Trier zum 1000. Todestag,* edited by Franz J. Ronig, vol. 2,

Aufsätze, Trierer Zeitschrift für Geschichte und Kunst des Trierer Landes und seiner Nachbargebiete, Beiheft 18, 37–52. Trier, 1993.

———. *". . . more Grecorum conregnantem instituere vultis?* Zur Legitimation der Regentschaft Heinrichs des Zänkers im Thronstreit von 984." FMSt 27 (1993): 273–89.

Euw, Anton von, and Peter Schreiner, eds. *Kaiserin Theophanu: Begegnung des Ostens und Westens um die Wende des ersten Jahrtausends.* 2 vols. Cologne, 1991.

Felten, Franz J. *Äbte und Laienäbte im Frankenreich: Studie zum Verhältnis von Staat und Kirche im frühen Mittelalter.* Monographien zur Geschichte des Mittelalters 20. Stuttgart, 1980.

Fichtenau, Heinrich. *Lebensordnungen des 10. Jahrhunderts: Studien über Denkart und Existenz im einstigen Karolingerreich.* 2 vols. Monographien zur Geschichte des Mittelalters 30, 1 and 2. Stuttgart, 1984. [English: *Living in the Tenth Century.* Translated by Patrick Geary. Chicago, 1991.]

Fleckenstein, Josef. *Grundlagen und Beginn der deutschen Geschichte.* Göttingen, 1974.

———. *Die Hofkapelle der deutschen Könige.* Pt. 2, *Die Hofkapelle im Rahmen der ottonisch-salischen Reichskirche.* Schriften der MGH 16, 2. Stuttgart, 1966.

———. "Hofkapelle und Kanzlei unter der Kaiserin Theophanu." In *Kaiserin Theophanu,* edited by Euw and Schreiner, 305–10.

———. "Problematik und Gestalt der ottonisch-salischen Reichskirche." In *Ordnungen und formende Kräfte des Mittelalters: Ausgewählte Beiträge,* 222–42. Göttingen, 1989. First appeared in *Reich und Kirche vor dem Investiturstreit,* edited by Schmid, 83–98.

———. "Das Reich der Ottonen im 10. Jahrhundert." In *Gebhart: Handbuch der deutschen Geschichte,* edited by Herbert Grundmann, vol. 1. 9th ed. Stuttgart, 1970.

———. "Zum Begriff der ottonisch-salischen Reichskirche." In *Ordnungen und formende Kräfte des Mittelalters: Ausgewählte Beiträge,* 211–21. Göttingen, 1989. First appeared in *Geschichte, Wirtschaft, Gesellschaft: Festschrift für Clemens Bauer,* 61–71. Berlin, 1974.

Fornasari, Giuseppe. "*Pater rationabilium eremitarum:* Tradizione agiografica e attualizzezione eremitica nella Vita beati Romualdi." In *Fonte Avellana nel suo millenario,* vol. 2, *Idee, figure, luoghi,* 25–103. Urbino, 1983.

Frenzel, Elisabeth. "Otto III." In *Stoffe der Weltliteratur: Ein Lexikon dichtungsgeschichtlicher Längsschnitte,* 8th rev. and exp. ed., 608–10. Stuttgart, 1992.

Fried, Johannes. "Endzeiterwartung um die Jahrtausendwende." DA 45 (1989): 381–473.

———. *Die Formierung Europas: 840–1046.* Oldenbourg-Grundriß der Geschichte 6. Munich, 1991.

———. *Otto III. und Boleslaw Chrobry: Das Widmungsbild des Aachener Evangeliars, der "Akt von Gnesen" und das frühe polnische und ungarische Königtum: Eine Bildanalyse und ihre historischen Folgen.* Wiesbaden, 1989.

———. *Der päpstliche Schutz für Laienfürsten: Die politische Geschichte des päpstlichen Schutzprivilegs für Laien (11.–13. Jahrhundert).* Heidelberg, 1980.

———. "Theophanu und die Slawen: Bemerkungen zur Ostpolitik der Kaiserin." In *Kaiserin Theophanu,* edited by Euw and Schreiner, 361–70.

———. *Der Weg in die Geschichte: Die Ursprünge Deutschlands bis 1024.* Propyläen Geschichte Deutschlands 1. Berlin, 1994.

Fritze, Wolfgang H. "Die fränkische Schwurfreundschaft in der Merowingerzeit: Ihr Wesen und ihre politische Funktion." ZRG GA 71 (1954): 74–125.

———. "Der slawische Aufstand von 983—eine Schicksalswende in der Geschichte Mitteleuropas." In *Festschrift der landesgeschichtlichen Vereinigung für die Mark Brandenburg zu ihrem hundertjährigen Bestehen 1884–1984,* edited by Eckart Henning and Werner Vogel, 9–55. Berlin, 1984.

Frova, Carla. "Gerberto Philosophus: Il 'De rationali et ratione uti.'" In *Gerberto: Scienza, storia e mito,* 351–77.

Fuhrmann, Horst. "Konstantinische Schenkung und abendländisches Kaisertum: Ein Beitrag zur Überlieferungsgeschichte des Constitutum Constantini." DA 22 (1966): 63–178.

———. *Einfluß und Verbreitung der pseudoisidorischen Fälschungen: Von ihrem Auftauchen bis in die neuere Zeit.* 3 vols. Schriften der MGH 24. Stuttgart, 1972–75.

Ganshof, François Louis. *Was ist das Lehnswesen?* 6th ed. Darmstadt, 1983. [English: *Feudalism.* Translated by Philip Grierson. 2d English ed. New York, 1961.]

Gattermann, Günther. "Die deutschen Fürsten auf der Reichsheerfahrt: Studien zur Reichskriegverfassung in der Stauferzeit." Ph.D. diss., Frankfurt am Main, 1956.

Gerberto: Scienza, storia e mito. Atti del Gerberti Symposium. Archivum Bobiense, Studia 2. Bobbio, 1985.

Giese, Wolfgang. *Der Stamm der Sachsen und das Reich in ottonischer und salischer Zeit: Studien zum Einfluß des Sachsenstammes auf die politische Geschichte des deutschen Reichs im 10. und 11. Jahrhundert und zu ihrer Stellung im Reichsgefüge mit einem Ausblick auf das 12. und 13. Jahrhundert.* Wiesbaden, 1979.

———. "Venedig-Politik und Imperiums-Idee bei den Ottonen." In *Festschrift für Friedrich Prinz zu seinem 65. Geburtstag,* edited by Georg Jenal, Monographien zur Geschichte des Mittelalters 37:219–43. Stuttgart, 1993.

Giesebrecht, Wilhelm von. *Geschichte der deutschen Kaiserzeit.* 5 vols. 5th ed. Braunschweig, 1881.

Glocker, Winfrid. *Die Verwandten der Ottonen und ihre Bedeutung in der Politik: Studien zur Familienpolitik und zur Genealogie des sächsischen Kaiserhauses.* Dissertationen zur mittelalterlichen Geschichte 5. Cologne and Vienna, 1989.

Goetting, Hans. *Das Bistum Hildesheim.* Vol. 1, *Das reichsunmittelbare Kanonissenstift Gandersheim.* Germania sacra, n.s., 7. Berlin and New York, 1973.

———. *Das Bistum Hildesheim.* Vol. 3, *Die Hildesheimer Bischöfe von 815 bis 1221 (1227).* Germania sacra, n.s., 20. Berlin and New York, 1984.

Görich, Knut. "Ein Erzbistum in Prag oder in Gnesen?" ZOF 40 (1991): 10–27.

———. "Der Gandersheimer Streit zur Zeit Ottos III.: Ein Konflikt um die Metropolitanrechte des Erzbischofs Willigis von Mainz." ZRG KA 110 (1993): 56–94.

———. "Der Herrscher als parteiischer Richter: Barbarossa in der Lombardei." FMSt 29 (1995): 273–88.

———. "Kaiser Otto III." In *Gebetbuch Ottos III.: Clm 30111,* edited by Kulturstiftung der Länder and Bayerische Staatsbibliothek, 11–25. Munich, 1995.

———. "Otto III. öffnet das Karlsgrab in Aachen: Überlegungen zu Heiligenverehrung, Heiligsprechung und Traditionsbildung." In *Herrschaftsrepräsentation im ottonischen Sachsen,* edited by Althoff and Schubert.

———. *Otto III., Romanus Saxonicus et Italicus: Kaiserliche Rompolitik und sächsische Historiographie*. Sigmaringen, 1993.

Görich, Knut, and Hans Henning Kortüm. "Otto III., Thangmar und die *Vita Bernwardi*." MIÖG 98 (1990): 1–57.

Gradmann, Christoph. *"Historische Belletristik": Populäre historische Biographien in der Weimarer Republik*. Historische Studien 10. Frankfurt am Main, 1993.

Graus, František. "Der Heilige als Schlachtenhelfer: Zur Nationalisierung einer Wundererzählung in der mittelalterlichen Chronistik." In *Festschrift für Helmut Beumann zum 65. Geburtstag*, edited by Kurt-Ulrich Jäschke and Reinhard Wenskus, 330–48. Sigmaringen, 1977.

Gregorovius, Ferdinand. *Geschichte der Stadt Rom im Mittelalter vom 5. bis zum 16. Jahrhundert*. 3 vols. New ed. Edited by Waldemar Kampf. Tübingen, 1953–57.

Hampe, Karl. *Das Hochmittelalter: Geschichte des Abendlandes von 900 bis 1250*. Berlin, 1932.

———. "Kaiser Otto III. und Rom." HZ 140 (1929): 513–33.

Hannig, Jürgen. "*Ars donandi*: Zur Ökonomie des Schenkens im früheren Mittelalter." In *Armut, Liebe, Ehre: Studien zur historischen Kulturforschung*, edited by Richard van Dülmen, 11–37. Frankfurt am Main, 1988.

Hauck, Albert. *Kirchengeschichte Deutschlands*. 5 vols. 8th ed. Berlin and Leipzig, 1954.

Hauck, Karl. "Rituelle Speisegemeinschaft im 10. und 11. Jahrhundert." *Studium Generale* 3 (1950): 611–21.

Hellmann, Manfred. *Grundzüge der Geschichte Venedigs*. Darmstadt, 1976.

Hilsch, Peter. "Der Bischof von Prag und das Reich in sächsischer Zeit." DA 28 (1972): 1–41.

———. "Zur Rolle von Herrscherinnen: Emma Regina in Frankreich und Böhmen." In *Westmitteleuropa—Ostmitteleuropa: Festschrift für Ferdinand Seibt*, edited by Winfried Eberhard et al., 81–89. Munich, 1992.

Hinschius, Paul. *Das Kirchenrecht der Katholiken und Protestanten in Deutschland*. Vol. 5/1. Berlin, 1893.

Hirsch, Siegfried, et al. *Jahrbücher des Deutschen Reiches unter Heinrich II.* 3 vols. Leipzig, 1862–75.

Hlawitschka, Eduard. "Kaiser Otto III. (983–1002)." In *Mittelalterliche Herrscher in Lebensbildern von den Karolingern zu den Staufern*, edited by Karl Rudolf Schnith, 155–65. Graz, 1990.

———. "Königin Richeza von Polen—Enkelin Herzog Konrads von Schwaben, nicht Kaiser Ottos II.?" In *Institutionen, Kultur und Gesellschaft im Mittelalter: Festschrift für Josef Fleckenstein zu seinem 65. Geburtstag*, edited by Lutz Fenske et al., 221–44. Sigmaringen, 1984.

———. *Vom Frankenreich zur Formierung der europäischen Staaten- und Völkergemeinschaft 840–1046*. Darmstadt, 1986.

Hoffmann, Hartmut. *Buchkunst und Königtum im ottonischen und frühsalischen Reich*. 2 vols. Schriften der MGH 30. Stuttgart, 1986.

———. "Eigendiktat in den Urkunden Ottos III. und Heinrichs II." DA 44 (1988): 390–423.

———. *Mönchskönig und "rex idiota": Studien zur Kirchenpolitik Heinrichs II. und Konrads II*. Hannover, 1993.

Holtzmann, Robert. "Die Aufhebung und Wiederherstellung des Bistums Merseburg." SaAn 2 (1926): 35–75.

———. *Geschichte der sächsischen Kaiserzeit (900–1024)*. Munich, 1941.

Huch, Ricarda. *Römisches Reich, deutscher Nation*. Berlin, 1934.

Hüpper, Dagmar. "Poesie und Recht aus einem Bette: Zu Verhaltensnormen und Umgangsformen in der mittelalterlichen Familie und Verwandtschaft." FMSt 27 (1993): 87–123.

Jaeger, C. Stephen. "L'amour des rois: Structure sociale d'une forme de sensibilité aristocratique." *Annales ESC* 46, no. 3 (1991): 547–71.

Jenal, Georg. *Erzbischof Anno II. von Köln (1056–75) und sein politisches Wirken: Ein Beitrag zur Geschichte der Reichs- und Territorialpolitik im 11. Jahrhundert*. Monographien zur Geschichte des Mittelalters 8. Stuttgart, 1974–75.

Karpf, Ernst. *Herrscherlegitimation und Reichsbegriff in der ottonischen Geschichtsschreibung des 10. Jahrhunderts*. Historische Forschungen 10. Wiesbaden and Stuttgart, 1985.

———. "Von Widukinds Sachsengeschichte zu Thietmars Chronicon: Zu den literarischen Folgen des politischen Aufschwungs im ottonischen Sachsen." In *Settimane di studio del Centro Italiano di studi sull'alto medioevo* 32/2:547–84. Spoleto, 1986.

Kehr, Paul. *Die Urkunden Otto III*. Innsbruck, 1890.

Kejř, Jiří. "Böhmen und das Reich unter Friedrich I." In *Friedrich Barbarossa: Handlungsspielräume und Wirkungsweisen des staufischen Kaisers*, Vorträge und Forschungen 40:241–89. Sigmaringen, 1992.

Keller, Hagen. "Grundlagen ottonischer Königsherrschaft." In *Reich und Kirche vor dem Investiturstreit*, edited by Schmid, 17–34.

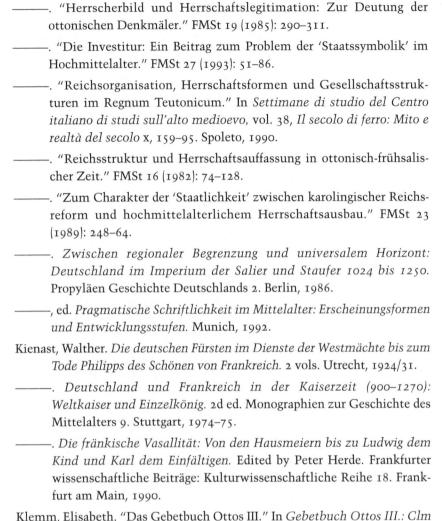

———. "Herrscherbild und Herrschaftslegitimation: Zur Deutung der ottonischen Denkmäler." FMSt 19 (1985): 290–311.

———. "Die Investitur: Ein Beitrag zum Problem der 'Staatssymbolik' im Hochmittelalter." FMSt 27 (1993): 51–86.

———. "Reichsorganisation, Herrschaftsformen und Gesellschaftsstrukturen im Regnum Teutonicum." In *Settimane di studio del Centro italiano di studi sull'alto medioevo*, vol. 38, *Il secolo di ferro: Mito e realtà del secolo* x, 159–95. Spoleto, 1990.

———. "Reichsstruktur und Herrschaftsauffassung in ottonisch-frühsalischer Zeit." FMSt 16 (1982): 74–128.

———. "Zum Charakter der 'Staatlichkeit' zwischen karolingischer Reichsreform und hochmittelalterlichem Herrschaftsausbau." FMSt 23 (1989): 248–64.

———. *Zwischen regionaler Begrenzung und universalem Horizont: Deutschland im Imperium der Salier und Staufer 1024 bis 1250.* Propyläen Geschichte Deutschlands 2. Berlin, 1986.

———, ed. *Pragmatische Schriftlichkeit im Mittelalter: Erscheinungsformen und Entwicklungsstufen.* Munich, 1992.

Kienast, Walther. *Die deutschen Fürsten im Dienste der Westmächte bis zum Tode Philipps des Schönen von Frankreich.* 2 vols. Utrecht, 1924/31.

———. *Deutschland und Frankreich in der Kaiserzeit (900–1270): Weltkaiser und Einzelkönig.* 2d ed. Monographien zur Geschichte des Mittelalters 9. Stuttgart, 1974–75.

———. *Die fränkische Vasallität: Von den Hausmeiern bis zu Ludwig dem Kind und Karl dem Einfältigen.* Edited by Peter Herde. Frankfurter wissenschaftliche Beiträge: Kulturwissenschaftliche Reihe 18. Frankfurt am Main, 1990.

Klemm, Elisabeth. "Das Gebetbuch Ottos III." In *Gebetbuch Ottos III.: Clm 30111*, edited by Kulturstiftung der Länder and Bayerische Staatsbibliothek, 39–87. Munich, 1995.

Kluger, Helmuth. "*Propter claritatem generis:* Genealogisches zur Familie der Ezzonen." In *Köln: Stadt und Bistum in Kirche und Reich: Festschrift für Odilo Engels*, edited by Hanna Vollrath and Stefan Weinfurter, 223–58. Cologne, Weimar, and Vienna, 1993.

Kohlenberger, Rudolf. "Die Vorgänge des Thronstreits während der Unmündigkeit Ottos III. 983–985." Ph.D. diss., Erlangen, 1931.

Kolb, Werner. *Herrscherbegegnungen im Mittelalter.* Bern, Frankfurt, New York, and Paris, 1988.

Kolberg, A. "Das Lobgedicht auf den heiligen Adalbert." *Zeitschrift für Geschichte und Altertumskunde Ermlands* 7 (1879–81): 373–598.

Kölzer, Theo. "Das Königtum Minderjähriger im fränkisch-deutschen Mittelalter: Eine Skizze." HZ 251 (1990): 291–324.

Kortüm, Hans Henning. *Richer von Saint-Remi: Studien zu einem Geschichtsschreiber des 10. Jahrhunderts.* Stuttgart, 1985.

Kossmann, Oskar. "Deutschland und Polen um das Jahr 1000—Gedanken zu einem Buch von Herbert Ludat." ZOF 21 (1972): 401–66.

Koziol, Geoffrey. *Begging Pardon and Favor: Ritual and Political Order in Early Medieval France.* Ithaca and London, 1992.

Krah, Adelheid. *Absetzungsverfahren als Spiegelbild von Königsmacht: Untersuchungen zum Kräfteverhältnis zwischen Königsmacht und Adel im Karolingerreich und seinen Nachfolgestaaten.* Untersuchungen zur deutschen Staats- und Rechtsgeschichte, n.s., 26. Aalen, 1987.

Ladner, Gerhart B. *L'immagine dell'imperatore Ottone III.* Rome, 1988.

Laqua, Hans Peter. *Tradition und Leitbilder bei dem Ravennater Reformer Petrus Damiani 1042–1052.* Münstersche Mittelalterschriften 30. Munich, 1976.

Laudage, Johannes. "Das Problem der Vormundschaft über Otto III." In *Kaiserin Theophanu,* edited by Euw and Schreiner, 261–75.

Leclerq, Jean. "Saint Romuald et le monachisme missionnaire." *Revue bénédictine* 72 (1962): 307–23.

Leyser, Karl J. "Ottonian Government." EHR 96 (1981): 721–53. Reprinted in Leyser, *Medieval Germany and Its Neighbours, 900–1250,* 69–101. London, 1982.

———. *Rule and Conflict in an Early Medieval Society: Ottonian Saxony.* London, 1979.

Lindgren, Uta. *Gerbert von Aurillac und das Quadrivium: Untersuchungen zur Bildung im Zeitalter der Ottonen.* Wiesbaden, 1976.

Lippelt, Helmut. *Thietmar von Merseburg: Reichsbischof und Chronist.* Mitteldeutsche Forschungen 72. Cologne and Vienna, 1973.

Lotter, Friedrich. "Das Idealbild adliger Laienfrömmigkeit in den Anfängen Clunys: Odos Vita des Grafen Gerald von Aurillac." In *Benedictine Culture, 750–1050,* edited by W. Lourdaux and D. Verhelst, Medievalia Lovaniensia, ser. 1, studia 11, 76–95. Louvain, 1983.

———. "Methodisches zur Gewinnung historischer Erkenntnisse aus hagiographischen Quellen." HZ 229 (1979): 298–356.

Ludat, Herbert. *An Elbe und Oder um das Jahr 1000: Skizzen zur Politik des Ottonenreiches und der slawischen Mächte in Mitteleuropa.* Cologne, 1971.

Maleczynski, Karol. "Die Politik Ottos III. gegenüber Polen und Böhmen im Lichte der Meißener Bistumsurkunde vom Jahre 995." *Letopis: Jahresschrift des Instituts für sorbische Volksforschung,* ser. B, 10 (1963): 162–203.

McKitterick, Rosamond. "Ottonian Intellectual Culture in the Tenth Century and the Role of Theophanu." *Early Medieval Europe* 2 (1993): 53–74.

Melville, Gert, ed. *Institutionen und Geschichte: Theoretische Aspekte und mittelalterliche Befunde.* Cologne, Weimar, and Vienna, 1992.

Michalowski, Roman. "Aix-la-Chapelle et Cracovie au xıe siècle." *Bullettino dell'Istituto Storico Italiano per il Medioevo e Archivio Muratoriano* 95 (1989): 45–69.

Moehs, Teta E. *Gregorius V (996–999): A Biographical Study.* Päpste und Papsttum 2. Stuttgart, 1972.

Morgenroth, Albert. "Kaiser Otto III. in der deutschen Dichtung." Ph.D. diss., Breslau, 1922.

Müller, Heribert. *Heribert, Kanzler Ottos III. und Erzbischof von Köln.* Cologne, 1977.

Müller, Jan-Dirk. "Ratgeber und Wissende in heroischer Epik." FMSt 27 (1993): 124–46.

Müller-Mertens, Eckhard. *Die Reichsstruktur im Spiegel der Herrschaftspraxis Ottos des Großen.* Forschungen zur mittelalterlichen Geschichte 25. Berlin, 1980.

Müller-Mertens, Eckhard, and Wolfgang Huschner. *Reichsintegration im Spiegel der Herrschaftspraxis Kaiser Konrads II.* Forschungen zur mittelalterlichen Geschichte 35. Weimar, 1992.

Nitschke, August. "Der mißhandelte Papst: Folgen ottonischer Italienpolitik." In *Staat und Gesellschaft in Mittelalter und früher Neuzeit: Gedenkschrift für Joachim Leuschner,* edited by Historische Seminar der Universität Hannover, 40–53. Hannover and Göttingen, 1983.

Paradisi, Bruno. *L'"amicitia" internazionale nell'alto medioevo.* Scritti in onore di Contardo Ferrini 2. Milan, 1947.

Patze, Hans. "Adel und Stifterchronik: Frühformen territorialer Geschichtsschreibung im hochmittelalterlichen Reich." BDLG 100 (1964): 8–81.

Pauler, Roland. *Das Regnum Italiae in ottonischer Zeit: Markgrafen, Grafen und Bischöfe als politische Kräfte.* Bibliothek des Deutschen Historischen Instituts in Rom 54. Tübingen, 1982.

Pfister, Christian. *Études sur le règne de Robert le Pieux (996–1031).* Paris, 1885.

Ragotzky, Hedda, and Horst Wenzel, eds. *Höfische Repräsentation: Das Zeremoniell und die Zeichen.* Tübingen, 1990.

Reindel, Kurt. *Die bayerischen Luitpoldinger 898–989: Sammlung und Erläuterung der Quellen.* Munich, 1953.

———. "Heinrich II." NDB 8 (1969): 341.

Reuter, Timothy. "The 'Imperial Church System' of the Ottonian and Salian Rulers: A Reconsideration." *Journal of Ecclesiastical History* 33 (1982): 347–74.

———. "Unruhestiftung, Fehde, Rebellion, Widerstand: Gewalt und Frieden in der Politik der Salierzeit." In *Die Salier und das Reich,* edited by Stefan Weinfurter, vol. 3, *Gesellschaftlicher und ideengeschichtlicher Wandel im Reich der Salier,* 297–325. Sigmaringen, 1991.

Riché, Pierre. *Gerbert d'Aurillac: Le pape de l'an mil.* Paris, 1987.

Roberts, Simon. *Order and Dispute: An Introduction to Legal Anthropology.* Oxford, 1979.

Rösch, Gerhard. *Venedig und das Reich: Handels- und verkehrspolitische Beziehungen in der deutschen Kaiserzeit.* Tübingen, 1982.

Sansterre, Jean-Marie. "Les coryphées des apôtres: Rome et la papauté dans les 'Vies' des Saints Nil et Barthélemy de Grottaferrata." *Byzantion* 55 (1985): 516–43.

———. "Otton III et les saints ascètes de son temps." *Rivista di storia della chiesa in Italia* 43 (1989): 377–412.

———. "Saint Nil de Rossano et le monachisme latin." *Bollettino della Badia Greca di Grottaferrata* 45 (1991): 339–86.

Santifaller, Leo. *Zur Geschichte des ottonisch-salischen Reichskirchensystems.* 2d ed. Sitzungsberichte der österreichischen Akademie der Wissenschaften: Philosophische Klasse 229/1. Vienna, 1964.

Scherff, Bruno. "Studien zum Heer der Ottonen und ersten Salier (1919–1056)." Ph.D. diss., Bonn, 1985.

Schieffer, Rudolf. "Der ottonische Reichsepiskopat zwischen Königtum und Adel." FMSt 23 (1989): 291–301.

———. "Von Mailand nach Canossa: Ein Beitrag zur Geschichte der christlichen Herrscherbuße von Theodosius dem Großen bis zu Heinrich IV." DA 28 (1972): 333–70.

Schieffer, Theodor. "Heinrich II. und Konrad II.: Die Umprägung des Geschichtsbildes durch die Kirchenreform des 11. Jahrhunderts." DA 8 (1950): 384–437.

Schlesinger, Walter. "Die sogenannte Nachwahl Heinrichs II. in Merseburg." In Geschichte in der Gesellschaft: Festschrift für Karl Bosl, edited by Friedrich Prinz et al., 350–69. Stuttgart, 1974.

Schmid, Karl. "Sasbach und Limburg: Zur Identifizierung zweier mittelalterlicher Plätze." ZGO 137 (1989): 33–63.

———, ed. Reich und Kirche vor dem Investiturstreit: Vorträge beim wissenschaftlichen Kolloquium aus Anlaß des 80. Geburtstags von Gerd Tellenbach. Sigmaringen, 1985.

Schneidmüller, Bernd. "Ottonische Familienpolitik und französische Nationsbildung im Zeitalter der Theophanu." In Kaiserin Theophanu, edited by Euw and Schreiner, 345–59.

Schramm, Percy Ernst. Herrschaftszeichen: Gestiftet, verschenkt, verkauft, verpfändet. Nachrichten der Akademie der Wissenschaften in Göttingen, phil.-hist. Klasse 5. Göttingen, 1957.

———. "Kaiser, Basileus und Papst in der Zeit der Ottonen." In Kaiser, Könige und Päpste: Gesammelte Aufsätze zur Geschichte des Mittelalters, vol. 3, Vom 10. bis zum 13. Jahrhundert, 200–245. Stuttgart, 1969.

———. Kaiser, Rom und Renovatio: Studien zur Geschichte des römischen Erneuerungsgedankens vom Ende des karolingischen Reiches bis zum Investiturstreit. 4th ed., including only pt. 1 of the original. Darmstadt, 1984. (Original: Leipzig and Berlin, 1929.)

———. Kaiser, Rom und Renovatio. Studien zur Geschichte des römischen Erneuerungsgedankens vom Ende des karolingischen Reiches bis zum Investiturstreit. Pt. 2, Exkurse und Texte. Leipzig and Berlin, 1929.

Schramm, Percy Ernst, and Florentine Mütherich. Denkmale der deutschen Könige und Kaiser. Vol. 1, Ein Beitrag zur Herrschergeschichte von Karl dem Großen bis Friedrich II. 768–1250. Veröffentlichungen des Zentralinstituts für Kunstgeschichte in München 2. Munich, 1962.

———. Die deutschen Kaiser und Könige in Bildern ihrer Zeit 751–1190. New ed. Edited by Peter Berghaus, Nikoaus Gussone, and Florentine Mütherich. Munich, 1983.

Schreiner, Klaus. "Gregor VIII., nackt auf einem Esel: Entehrende Entblößung und schandbares Reiten im Spiegel einer Miniatur der 'Sächsischen

Weltchronik.'" In *Ecclesia et regnum: Beiträge zur Geschichte von Kirche, Recht und Staat im Mittelalter: Festschrift für Franz-Josef Schmale zu seinem 65*. Geburtstag, edited by Dieter Berg and Hans-Werner Goetz, 155–202. Bocum, 1989.

Schuffels, Hans Jakob. "Bernward, Bischof von Hildesheim: Eine biographische Skizze." In *Bernward von Hildesheim*, edited by Brandt and Eggebrecht, 1:29–43.

Schulze, Hans K. *Hegemoniales Kaisertum: Ottonen und Salier*. Siedler Deutsche Geschichte: Das Reich und die Deutschen. Berlin, 1991.

Sigal, Pierre André. "Le travail des hagiographes aux xie et xiie siècles: Sources d'information et méthodes de rédaction." *Francia* 15 (1987): 149–82.

Steindorff, Ernst. *Jahrbücher des deutschen Reiches unter Heinrich III*. 2 vols. Berlin, 1874–81.

Stengel, Edmund E. "Die Grabinschrift der ersten Äbtissin von Quedlinburg." DA 3 (1939): 361–70.

Swinarski, Ursula. *Herrschen mit den Heiligen: Kirchenbesuche, Pilgerfahrten und Heiligenverehrung früh- und hochmittelalterlicher Herrscher (ca. 500–1200)*. Bern and Berlin, 1991.

Tabacco, Giovanni. "Romualdo di Ravenna e gli inizi dell'eremitismo camaldolese." In *L'eremitismo in Occidente nei secoli* xi e xii, Atti della seconda settimana internazionale di studio Mendola 1962, 73–119. Milan, 1965.

———. "Romuald v. Camaldoli." In *Lexikon des Mittelalters* 7:1019–20. Munich and Zurich, 1994.

Tellenbach, Gerd. "Kaiser, Rom und Renovatio: Ein Beitrag zu einem großen Thema." In *Tradition als historische Kraft: Interdisziplinäre Forschungen zur Geschichte des Mittelalters*, edited by Norbert Kamp and Joachim Wollasch, 231–53. Berlin and New York, 1982.

———. *Die westliche Kirche vom 10. bis zum frühen 12. Jahrhundert*. Die Kirche in ihrer Geschichte, vol. 2. Göttingen, 1988. [English: *The Church in Western Europe from the Tenth to the Early Twelfth Century*. Translated by Timothy Reuter. Cambridge, 1993.]

———. "Zur Geschichte der Päpste im 10. und früheren 11. Jahrhundert." In *Institutionen, Kultur und Gesellschaft im Mittelalter: Festschrift für Josef Fleckenstein zu seinem 65*. Geburtstag, edited by Fenske Lutz et al., 165–77. Sigmaringen, 1984.

Ter Braak, Menno. *Kaiser Otto III.: Ideal und Praxis im frühen Mittelalter*. Amsterdam, 1928.

Thomas, Heinz. *Kaiser Otto III.: Eine Skizze.* Gocher Schriften 2. Goch, 1980.

Trautz, Fritz. "Zur Geltungsdauer des Wormser Konkordats in der Geschichts-schreibung seit dem 16. Jahrhundert." In *Geschichtsschreibung und geistiges Leben im Mittelalter: Festschrift für Heinz Löwe*, edited by Karl Hauck and Hubert Mordek, 600–625. Cologne, 1978.

Uhlirz, Karl. "Die Interventionen in den Urkunden König Ottos III. bis zum Tode Theophanus." NA 21 (1896): 115–37.

———. *Die Jahrbücher des Deutschen Reiches unter Otto II. und Otto III.* Vol. 1, *Otto II. 973–983.* Leipzig, 1902.

Uhlirz, Mathilde. "Das deutsche Gefolge von Kaiser Otto III. in Italien." In *Gesamtdeutsche Vergangenheit: Festgabe für Heinrich Ritter von Srbik zum 60. Geburtstag*, 21–32. Munich, 1938.

———. "Der Fürstentag zu Mainz im Februar–März 983." MIÖG 58 (1950): 267–84.

———. *Die Jahrbücher des Deutschen Reiches unter Otto II. und Otto III.* Vol. 2, *Otto III. 983–1002.* Berlin, 1954.

———. "Kaiser Otto III. und das Papsttum." HZ 162 (1940): 258–68.

Voigt, H. G. *Brun von Querfurt: Mönch, Eremit, Erzbischof der Heiden und Märtyrer.* Stuttgart, 1907.

Voss, Ingrid. *Herrschertreffen im frühen und hohen Mittelalter.* Beiheft zum AK 26. Cologne and Vienna, 1987.

Wapnewski, Peter, ed. *Mittelalter-Rezeption: Ein Symposion.* Germanistische Symposien der Deutsche Forschungsgemeinschaft 6. Stuttgart, 1986.

Warner, David A. "Henry II at Magdeburg: Kingship, Ritual, and the Cult of Saints." *Early Medieval Europe* 3 (1994): 135–66.

Wasilewski, T. "Bizantyńska symbolika zjazdu gnieźnieńskiego i jej prawnopo-lityczna wymowa." *Przeglad historyczny* 57 (1966): 1–14.

Wattenbach, Wilhelm, and Robert Holtzmann, eds. *Deutschlands Geschichts-quellen im Mittelalter: Die Zeit der Sachsen und Salier.* Pt. 1, *Das Zeitalter des ottonischen Staates (900–1050).* 4th ed. Darmstadt, 1967.

Weinfurter, Stefan. *Herrschaft und Reich der Salier: Grundlinien einer Umbruchzeit.* Sigmaringen, 1991.

———. "Die Zentralisierung der Herrschaftsgewalt im Reich unter Kaiser Heinrich II." HJb 106 (1986): 241–97.

Wenskus, Reinhard. "Forschungsbericht: Brun von Querfurt und die Stiftung des Erzbistums Gnesen." ZOF 5 (1956): 524–37.

———. *Studien zur historisch-politischen Gedankenwelt Bruns von Querfurt.* Mitteldeutsche Forschungen 5. Münster, 1956.

Wielers, Margaret. *Zwischenstaatliche Beziehungsformen im frühen Mittelalter: Pax, Foedus, Amicitia, Fraternitas.* Münster, 1959.

Wippermann, Wolfgang. *Der "deutsche Drang nach Osten": Ideologie und Wirklichkeit eines politischen Schlagwortes.* Darmstadt, 1981.

Wolf, Gunther. "Prinzessin Sophie (978–1039): Äbtissin von Gandersheim und Essen, Enkelin, Tochter und Schwester von Kaisern." NdsJb 61 (1989): 105–23.

———, ed. *Kaiserin Theophanu: Prinzessin aus der Fremde, des Westreichs große Kaiserin.* Cologne, Weimar, and Vienna, 1991.

Wollasch, Joachim. "Das Grabkloster der Kaiserin Adelheid in Selz am Rhein." FMSt 2 (1968): 135–43.

Wolter, Heinz. *Die Synoden im Reichsgebiet und in Reichsitalien von 916 bis 1056.* Konziliengeschichte, ser. A: Darstellungen. Paderborn, 1988.

Zeillinger, Kurt. "Otto III. und die Konstantinische Schenkung: Ein Beitrag zur Interpretation des Diploms Kaiser Ottos III. für Papst Silvester II. (DO III. 389)." In *Fälschungen im Mittelalter* 2, Schriften der MGH 33/2:509–36. Hannover, 1988.

Zimmermann, Harald. "Gerbert als kaiserlicher Rat." In *Gerberto: Scienza, storia e mito,* 235–53.

———. *Papstabsetzungen des Mittelalters.* Graz, Vienna, and Cologne, 1968.

———. "Rechtstradition in Papsturkunden." In *Im Bann des Mittelalters: Ausgewählte Beiträge zur Kirchen- und Rechtsgeschichte: Festgabe zu seinem 60. Geburtstag,* edited by Immo Eberl and Hans-Henning Kortüm, 184–99. Sigmaringen, 1986. First appeared in *XII. Congrès international des sciences historiques, Vienne 1965: Rapports,* 4, *Methodologie et Histoire contemporaine,* 131–46. Louvain, 1966.

Zotz, Thomas. "Präsenz und Repräsentation: Beobachtungen zur königlichen Herrschaftspraxis im hohen und späten Mittelalter." In *Herrschaft als soziale Praxis,* edited by Alf Lüdtke, Veröffentlichungen des Max-Planck-Instituts für Geschichte 91:168–94. Göttingen, 1991.

Index